The
WITCH'S
Book of
POWER

About the Author

Devin Hunter (Antioch, CA) holds third-degree initiations in both the Northern Star Tradition of Wicca as well as the Dianic Tradition of Witchcraft (the Cult of Diana) and is the founder of his own tradition, Sacred Fires. His podcast, *The Modern Witch*, has helped thousands of people from all over the world discover and develop their magical abilities. Devin is currently teaching with the Black Rose School of Witchcraft and is the reigning Master of Ceremonies at the New Orleans Witches' Ball.

To Write the Author

If you wish to contact the author or would like more information about this book, please write to the author in care of Llewellyn Worldwide, and we will forward your request. Both the author and the publisher appreciate hearing from you and learning of your enjoyment of this book and how it has helped you. Llewellyn Worldwide cannot guarantee that every letter written to the author can be answered, but all will be forwarded. Please write to:

Devin Hunter
℅ Llewellyn Worldwide
2143 Wooddale Drive
Woodbury, MN 55125-2989

Please enclose a self-addressed stamped envelope for reply,
or $1.00 to cover costs. If outside the USA, enclose
an international postal reply coupon.

Many of Llewellyn's authors have websites with additional information and resources. For more information, please visit www.llewellyn.com.

DEVIN HUNTER

FOREWORD BY CHRISTOPHER PENCZAK

The WITCH'S *Book of* POWER

Llewellyn Publications
Woodbury, Minnesota

FIRST EDITION
Sixth Printing, 2021

Book design by Bob Gaul
Chapter brushstroke by Llewellyn art department
Cover images by iStockphoto.com/54980570/©GoodGnom
                    Shutterstock/151831208/©tgavrano
Cover design by Kevin R. Brown
Editing by Patti Frazee
Illustrations on pages 49, 64, 82, 94 by Storm Faerywolf
Illustrations on pages 50, 65, 83, 98, 206, 225–227,
   236, 258, 267, 273 by Llewellyn art department
Part page crown by iStockphoto.com/54980570/©GoodGnom

Llewellyn Publications is a registered trademark of Llewellyn Worldwide Ltd.

Library of Congress Cataloging-in-Publication Data
Names: Hunter, Devin– author.
Title: The witch's book of power / Devin Hunter.
Description: First Edition. | Woodbury : Llewellyn Worldwide, Ltd, 2016. |
   Includes bibliographical references and index.
Identifiers: LCCN 2016012770 (print) | LCCN 2016013866 (ebook) | ISBN
   9780738748191 | ISBN 9780738749150
Subjects: LCSH: Witchcraft. | Magic.
Classification: LCC BF1566 .H85 2016 (print) | LCC BF1566 (ebook) | DDC
   133.4/3—dc23
LC record available at http://lccn.loc.gov/2016012770

Llewellyn Worldwide Ltd. does not participate in, endorse, or have any authority or responsibility concerning private business transactions between our authors and the public.

All mail addressed to the author is forwarded, but the publisher cannot, unless specifically instructed by the author, give out an address or phone number.

Any Internet references contained in this work are current at publication time, but the publisher cannot guarantee that a specific location will continue to be maintained. Please refer to the publisher's website for links to authors' websites and other sources.

Llewellyn Publications
A Division of Llewellyn Worldwide Ltd.
2143 Wooddale Drive
Woodbury, MN 55125-2989
www.llewellyn.com

Printed in the United States of America

CONTENTS

PART TWO: COSMIC POWER

Chapter Seven: Star Power   129

PART THREE: ALLIES IN POWER

Chapter Nine: The Star Goddess and Ecstasy 235

Chapter Ten: Diana, Dianus, and Aradia 255

Chapter Eleven: The Allies of the Witch   283

DEDICATION &
ACKNOWLEDGMENTS

This book is dedicated first and foremost to my divine allies Diana, Dianus, and Aradia. Everywhere they go inspiration and power follows and without my continued relationship to them this project would have never happened.

To the ancestors of the craft. I stand on your shoulders, not in your footsteps. Your sacrifices and work shall never die, but will live forever in the teachings you shared. I honor you.

To the witches not yet born. This is the book I wish I'd had. May you find your power within the pages.

To Storm and Chas, my beloved partners. Your magic and support has changed the way I look at the world and what I believe I am capable of. This book was planted in the rich soil of our love and grown by your encouragement.

To my beloved Sacred Fires community. I have learned so much about power by watching and emulating you. You are my tribe, my heart, my community, and my hope for the future.

To Heather Killen, the biggest supporter of my work as a teacher and priest. You are truly an irrepressible force of nature and many years ago you showed me how to become one myself. You are the essence of beauty and power.

To Lisa Dawn, who has become one of my best friends and closest confidants. You have been the mirror and sounding board for so many tests in my life, especially those related to power. I wouldn't have made it here without you. Thank you for years of unconditional love and support.

To my father, Frank, who helped me understand that I was weird and that it was okay. You introduced me to the craft and because of that I have been able to create the life I wanted to live. I will always love and cherish you.

To Christopher Penczak, who has always fanned the flames of my work. Be it as a teacher, friend, or brother, you have encouraged me to become the witch I am capable of being. Without your support over the years I never would have had the guts to finally do this. I am forever in your debt. Finally, this book has made it to the world.

Lastly, to the amazing Eddy Gutiérrez. Although you are no longer with us in the physical I feel your spirit with me daily. You predicted accurately how this book would end up just before your death so I think that earns you a spot up front! I miss you, babe. You were the wickedest one of us all. You are my invisible light.

Joy and woe are woven fine,
A clothing for the soul divine,
Under every grief and pine,
Runs a joy with silken twine.
It is right it should be so,
We were made for joy and woe,
And when this we rightly know,
Through the world we safely go.
—*William Blake*—

FOREWORD

BY CHRISTOPHER PENCZAK

Power is a word we don't hear too often these days in the witchcraft world. Many consider it a dirty word, something we like to sweep under the rug. "Witchcraft has nothing to do with power," we tell others and sometimes tell ourselves. Witchcraft is about peace. Witchcraft is about love. Witchcraft is about nature. Yes, to all of those things, but witchcraft is also about power, and to lose sight of that important fact undermines all missions about peace, love, and nature. Power denotes a sense of control, and often erroneously conjures the images of "power over" others, rather than "power with" and the deeper meanings of self-control and self-discipline. But power is the fuel for the engine to make change. Without power, there is no magic. Without power, there is no healing. Without power, there is no life. Life feeds life, and vital power is the fuel that makes the wheels within wheels turn. Many people really do come to the craft, or at least magic, seeking power, but as a remedy for their own sense of powerlessness. They are seeking power over others and their life. Some learn that first you must have power within yourself. Others don't. And it's the behavior of those others that have caused us to shy away from the word *power*.

Many in the current generation of the craft have spent so much time and energy, so much personal power, in convincing everyone else and themselves that we are just like everyone else, harmless and normal, that we have begun to believe it. Spells are easily explained to the uninterested or fearful neighbor as another form of prayer. Visions are explained through the lens of hypnosis, dream therapy, and Jungian psychology. Potions and incense can be related to aromatherapy and holistic health. All potentially true, yet all very safe and sterile. Potions go beyond herbal chemistry and tap into a deep primal magic of our green allies. Visions are really contact with transdimensional realities beyond the bounds of our ordinary perceptions that are just as real as the world we see here. And spells are not just prayers. They might have a component of devotion, but the fuel of the spell is power—be it personal life force, the power of nature, the power of a deity, or the flowing power of the starry heavens. But to say this can look crazy to our well-meaning family, friends, and neighbors.

So we see why the witch has been so secretive, and why this current crossroads of being public and open runs the risk of us losing the power of the very mysteries we keep.

Yes, the impetus for such a campaign is to emphasize that we are all human. We are. We all deserve respect and equal rights. We all want to be respected and feel normal, loved, and supported by others. But if we are called to be a witch, we are not considered normal. We are "other," on some level. And our otherness should be accepted and even celebrated. It does not makes us better, but it calls us to serve in different ways and forces us to look at the world through different lenses.

We do have a voice to contribute to the growing global religious conversation. In fact, some would say that many of the messes we are in are due to a direct result of more Pagan and occult points of view squeezed from mainstream. When religions do not emphasize the sacredness of matter and nature, we get societies that create programs and paradigms that systemically desecrate the world, making it hard for those who do seek to honor nature to also work in and contribute to mainstream society. In our desire to be a part of the growing social change movements, many contribute solely on that level—politics, protests, and media outreach, among other avenues—but forget the foundation stone of the witch: magic. All because many have given up their esoteric power in favor of acceptance and normalcy. Witchcraft and Paganism become a religious philosophy, rather than an operative esoteric art.

Thankfully, there are those in this growing generation who have that public voice, yet have not forgotten that cornerstone of the Art. They couple magical action with social action. They tend to the altars and to those in the streets. They speak the old languages and symbols, and those of the new. And Devin Hunter is among them.

My own introduction to witchcraft hit me in the face with the concept of power. My teacher, Laurie Cabot, titled her first book *Power of the Witch*. Power was right there in the title! She taught on the reclaiming of lost power through self-awareness and self-esteem. It utterly changed my life. Those of the earlier generations recognized the significance of both personal power and occult power, and encouraged the generation and gathering of both.

People did not talk of energy or vibration in the older times. They talked about focusing your power. You see the same thing, under different symbols and language, in the seemingly more peaceful and benign Eastern traditions. We are clearing paths of power, and gathering energy for our transformation towards enlightenment. The realized yogi embodying the siddhi powers is as much a magician as the witch, if not more so, despite the claims to shun the siddhi talents as a distraction from enlightenment. Witches today look at operative magical skill as a test of gathered power, to prevent delusion and illusions from consuming us, as that is a danger for many drawn to our path.

Devin is a link in the chain of wisdom and power for the craft. He bridges the gap between the modern movement of the occult and New Age, with terminology familiar to more mainstream, non-witchcraft practitioners. He has the optimistic attitude of a coach, obviously from his many years as one who guides and coaches others through Tarot, mediumship, healing, and teaching witchcraft at various stores, centers, and festivals.

Devin has a deeper connection to the old traditions and darker lore that is not put into mainstream guides on magic. His very choice to tackle the hard issue of power head-on is proof of that. He's not afraid of those old myths of the Nephilim and the darker associations with Aradia and Diana from ages past. I'm sure his way will equally delight and disgruntle segments of our witchcraft community. That is always what happens when you bridge worlds.

There will be those who will see his use of the term *vibration* and correspondences with the musical scale, yogic breath, psychology, and modern Huna as too "light" for a book on real witchcraft power. Yet it's the language that builds the bridge to the modern world. Others will see his totem workings of spiders and serpents, magic with owl pellets, speaking to the dead, and references to Lucifer and the fall in the Garden of Eden as too "dark" for a book of personal empowerment. While Devin does not fear the myths of old, he is also free of the sin of "dark fluff," or including terminology that is dark and scary to the average reader just to give the impression of what a dark and scary badass he can be. He doesn't need to. He lets the work speak for itself. Those intimate with the true dark are the light bearers, and are often the most kind, jovial, optimistic, and clear without being overly sentimental or soporific.

He's also on the edge of modern media, producing podcasts and magazines and blogging about the current issues of our community. He speaks with the voice of the new and the voice of the old. He does this all while holding the center of his work through the establishment of his own Sacred Fires tradition, and offering his services with his partners in the form of a public metaphysical shop offering products, services, and classes, thus fulfilling the role of the modern-day cunning man.

If you are looking for a spell book to give you power over your boss, lover, or enemy with a list of strange ingredients but little effort or awareness, then put this book down now and look elsewhere. If the power you seek is the power that starts from within, that comes from the old Delphic wisdom of "know thyself," then this book is an excellent start in learning, loving, and empowering all parts of yourself through the modern traditions of witchcraft. It is rooted in the old, but blazes fully towards the new. Walk the path in love. Walk the path in wisdom. And walk the path in power.

"Ultimately, the only power to which man should aspire is that which he exercises over himself."
—*Elie Weisel*—

"With great power there must also come great responsibility!"
—*Stan Lee*—

"Mastering others is strength. Mastering yourself is true power."
—*Tao Te Ching*—

"Being powerful is like being a lady. If you have to tell people you are, you aren't."
—*Margaret Thatcher*—

"Power is given only to those who dare to lower themselves and pick it up. Only one thing matters, one thing: to be able to dare!"
—*Fyodor Dostoevsky*—

"It is for us to pray not for tasks equal to our powers, but for powers equal to our tasks, to go forward with a great desire forever beating at the door of our hearts as we travel toward our distant goal."
—*Helen Keller*—

"The most powerful weapon on earth is the human soul on fire."
—*Ferdinand Foch*—

INTRODUCTION

Knowing others is intelligence; knowing yourself is true wisdom.
Mastering others is strength; mastering yourself is true power.

—Lao-Tzu—

A few years ago I was interviewed on a podcast about my own Internet AV Club–favorited radio show and magazine, *Modern Witch*. The host asked me how I got involved in witchcraft and I found myself feeling a bit put on the spot. No one had asked me that in years and I wanted to give a genuine answer. Struggling for words, I retold the story of how I met a witch for the first time, a story I had long forgotten, which ultimately became the inspiration for this book.

When I was twelve I was given a wishing spell by a friend whom I had met at a school dance the week prior. She handed me an Altoids tin and gave me specific instructions not to open it until I was ready to make my wish. She was the only other person I knew at the time who called themselves a witch and was much more knowledgeable than I was, being a year older. I held the tin in my hand all day and took it from class to class, staring at it and trying to figure out what my wish was going to be.

At the end of the school day, as we all made our Monday mass exodus to the buses, I ran behind a tree and made my wish. "I wish to be the most powerful witch in the world!" I opened the tin and was wholeheartedly disappointed. Instead of the flash of lightning and sudden jolt of energy that I had anticipated, there was a half-burnt blade of bent grass, some dried flower petals, and a tiny piece of paper written in some strange language. I closed the tin, put it in my backpack, and got on the bus.

As I sat alone in my seat I reached into my bag and opened the tin once more. This time I inspected every last piece contained therein. The burnt blade of grass smelled sweet, the flower petals were slightly scented with rose oil, the paper had drops of wax on it, and the interior of the tin was made to look like a collage of magical symbols. I realized what I was holding in my hands was not some dumb Altoids tin but the single most magical thing on earth, made just for me, and I knew that spell was going to work.

When I came to the craft, I wanted to learn to cast ancient spells and to influence people. I was the weird kid in the middle of No-Where, Ohio, and being a powerful witch sounded much more appealing than being a hillbilly. Being a witch also felt like *who* I was. You see, long before I was a professional psychic-medium and witch, I was a scared, lonely little boy with psychic abilities and no explanations. I came to witchcraft because I was looking for answers to questions that I'd had about who I was. I wanted to understand my gifts and I wanted to use them someday to get out of my small hometown.

After the first few years I began to think witchcraft was actually quite boring. At some point all the books started to sound the same and I began looking for formal training. I found a teacher, and then another, and then another, and eventually I realized even after all that training I still hadn't found what I was looking for—even if I didn't know what that was. What I did find during that period were all the tools that I needed to make my dreams a reality, but I didn't know it just yet. I loved witchcraft and I loved the people I met because of it, but I knew there had to be more.

I began to study every magical system and its history that I could and discovered that there were actually quite a few people in history who were not only powerful witches and magicians but who came from seemingly insignificant backgrounds like me. The history of witchcraft was full of people who were all looking for the same thing I was looking for—power.

As I finished the interview I was first brought to the realization that what I thought power was had changed since I was that little boy. Power is one of those hot-button words in the witchcraft community. It is a word that makes a lot of people uncomfortable because it's something we aren't really supposed to have too much of. The phrase, "Absolute power corrupts, absolutely," is used a lot to make us think that the powerful are the most wretched of our kind. While this can certainly be the case, I believe that we get to choose the way power corrupts us. What if power can corrupt the bad programming and leave the rest intact?

I realized that power to me was something that we use to get through a lot of deep, personal work. It comes from setting boundaries for yourself and others and creating discipline. Power comes from the discovery and mastery of your own unique talents and from doing everything in your ability to thrive in this life. We don't get real power from lording over others or from taking it, we get true power from passion, diligence, and self-respect. Always remember, power can never be given, it must be sought out and claimed.

For the past thirteen years I have dedicated my personal, spiritual, and professional life to helping people find their power through witchcraft, psychic development, and self-mastery. In this time I have helped thousands of people overcome obstacles and fully integrate their natural gifts into their lives so they can become the person they were meant to be. Half of my practice is devoted to my work as a professional psychic-medium and witch and the other half is committed to my work as a spiritual teacher and priest. I also manage one of the longest-running metaphysical stores in the country, The Mystic Dream (Walnut Creek, CA), where I help people from all walks of life and spiritual backgrounds find whatever it is their soul craves, as well as to find commonality amongst traditions.

As a professional psychic-medium and witch I help people navigate the murky waters of life, connect to their spirit guides and loved ones on the other side, as well as prescribe and (on occasion) perform magical workings. Because the majority of my clients come from a Christian, Muslim, Jewish, or Hindu background, and much of what I do must be framed in their tradition for it to sink in, I have had to expand my spiritual knowledge base to include these faiths and have found several hidden gems that inform my personal spirituality.

In 2009 I founded the Sacred Fires Tradition of Witchcraft, which blends the teachings of Blue Star Wicca and gender-inclusive Dianic witchcraft (there are several lines of Dianic witchcraft that openly embrace men and transgender members as well as women). Through both of these teachings I received a third-degree initiation and combined with American folk magic, core-shamanic practices, ecstatic Goddess worship, and humanism, I created Sacred Fires. We place a major significance on enriching our Witch Power through psychic development, self-mastery, and alignment with the primordial forces that we call sacred flames.

We believe that if you have the ability and means to change your life for the better, then you have the spiritual obligation to do so. Because of this, our practices are centralized around obtaining personal power and influence and using them to better the world.

As witches, we have not only the drive to obtain power in this life but we have natural gifts that help us get it. In this book I share with you some of the teachings from the Sacred Fires Tradition of Witchcraft as well as some of my own personal practices for obtaining true power and influence. This book is not for the teenager who came to witchcraft seeking power; it's for the witch who has forgotten or still yearns for the power they first felt or desired. This is for the witch who knows they are capable of using magic to get what they want out of life.

In the first part of this book I will discuss the three core concepts of power in witchcraft, the springboards for our magical potential. The first section will focus on the Witch Power, a frequency of power that resides within every magical person and manifester. This form of power is responsible for your interest in magic and your connection to the unseen worlds, and is the seat of your psychic abilities. By exploring and understanding the pieces of you that create your own unique Witch Power you will be able to turn your weaknesses into incredible strengths and discover which magic you need in order to become a force of nature. Through this section you will look at the constitution of the soul and how it connects to power, as well as gain important insights about your natural talents.

In the second part of the book you will look at the frequencies of power that helped to mold you into the person you are today. By investigating your birthchart, key energetic "presets" will be identified that come in the form of planetary and elemental bands of power. Here you will discover the key components that influence your ability to effectively manifest magic and successfully achieve your goals. Using the information found in this section you will create strategic plans of magical action to bring you closer to your desires.

The final part of this book regards working with gods and spirits to gain access to power. I will introduce you to a few friends of mine whom we work with in Sacred Fires and who will act as guides for you through the incredible process of empowerment. These allies are both ancient and modern and are eagerly awaiting your arrival.

Combined, these three sections will provide you a blueprint for using your magic to gain power and influence in life. From one witch to another, I wish you the best of luck on this journey. With great power comes great responsibility.

Part One

PERSONAL
POWER

There is something you need to know that could change your life forever: You are capable of wielding incredible amounts of power and of shaping your life into whatever you want it to be. This isn't a gimmick or a sales pitch—it's a testimonial. What is it that your heart truly desires? What is it that your soul craves more than anything? Find out by putting yourself to the test.

In this first part you will explore the hidden abilities that are dormant inside of you right now. These abilities, once discovered and nurtured, will help you to fine-tune your own relationship to power and to find veins of it in your everyday life. The nature of influence will be explored and you will find your way to the ancestral lineage of witches everywhere. You will also explore the layers of the soul and discover your unique frequency and how it shapes your reality.

Once you have traveled through your divine innermost self, I will introduce you to your Crown of Sovereignty and you will make a move to restore power in your life and remove negative influences for good. This journey will require you to be selfish and to think of your best interest.

Claiming power can be a difficult process for anyone, but luckily you're a witch! The only advice I can give you at this stage is to never give up and to always choose discipline. With a little elbow grease and a lot of personal dedication, you can use the information in this section to permanently alter the course of your life. Doing this is a decision that requires you fully be on board.

Chapter One

The Witch Power

*Witch Power: A term used to describe the instinctive
drive and ability to identify, harmonize with,
and affect psychic, occult, and preternatural forces.*

As you read this there is a buzzing world just beneath your radar. There are other planes coexisting with our own, beings as old as time itself, psychic impressions bouncing off of everything we see, and allies that are waiting to show you what you are capable of. The Witch Power is that natural drive deep inside you to peer into and affect the unknown, the occult, the psychic, and the preternatural, and often the part of us that feels a sense of home when doing so. The art of stimulating that ability is what we call witchcraft.

As you will soon find, the Witch Power can manifest itself in any number of ways, but almost always there is some form of psychic ability. Because of these psychic nuances we are able to approach the development of the Witch Power as we would the development of any other psychic ability, through sensitivity and mind-over-matter training, meditation, hands-on exploration, and lots of personal development.

The Witch Power is not inherently positive or negative, light or dark, or good or evil. Like any talent it is purely the instrument through which the art is conveyed. We as witches and possessors of Witch Power decide the scope in which our magic takes shape. There is no owner's manual or rule book that comes with the Witch Power, only a drive to spring forth like grass through the pavement.

The Most Important Lesson About Witches

The most valuable of all lessons I could share with you is that words like *witch* and *witchcraft*, even *warlock* and *enchantress*, are always used subjectively. This is an occurrence not only when I am talking with the public or watching television but also when working with other magical people. The Witch Power is universal; every culture has their witches and every culture approaches the topic of how to handle them differently. Witchcraft and the use of the Witch Power are the ultimate expressions of willpower, and whatever we will them to be, they will become!

To some, picking up a Harry Potter book is blasphemous enough, let alone invoking the ancestors; to others, magic and witchcraft are about as real as the story in that Harry Potter book. I also know that to some witches the craft is a deep, religious experience that requires offerings and great scripted rituals, whereas to some witches the craft is as simple as tuning in to the environment around them. Witchcraft is a manifestation of the witch's connection to the universe and the more we practice, the more we use our tools, the stronger that connection grows. We can turn that thing that made us feel different into the thing that becomes our superpower.

To practice witchcraft is to have a love affair with the universe as you grow in your understanding of your own Witch Power. Witchcraft requires very little of us in the beginning except an open and accepting mind, but as we grow in the Witch Power we have to continue to sculpt our relationship to the craft. As we grow as people, the craft grows with us, always giving us the tools we need in that moment to move beyond the blocks between us and the other side of desire. Because of witchcraft's amazing ability to provide us with what we need in the moment, it will never look like one thing for too long. If you focus on how witchcraft feels rather than how it's supposed to look, then your Witch Power will be in control.

Before we go any further, the witchcraft that I share with you here comes from Sacred Fires and contains magic that I find to be invaluable as a modern practitioner. To get the most out of these mysteries, I recommend journaling about your own unique experiences as well as keeping track of your magical successes and not-so-successes along the way. Part of growing in the Witch Power is discovering your strengths and weaknesses and approaching the magic with absolute authenticity; journaling helps keep us authentic and can greatly impact the depth of our work. You will see writing prompts in part 1 that will help to get the magical and mundane minds to work harmoniously through this process.

Where Witch Power Comes From

Many traditions and cultures have their own beliefs about where witches and their power come from. In some, there is a sort of required soul exchange with a shadowy devil figure; in others we get our abilities from engaging in carnal pleasure with the master of evil himself, or by allowing tiny hell spawn to drink blood from our nipples. These are, of course, an outsider's best guess as to why we can do what we do and are mostly born from a medieval and colonial lack of understanding. These theories are fun and make for wonderful clichés that I think can be quite enjoyable and even empowering at times, but they only serve to muddy the collective pool of awareness when we get down to business. Today, I hold two answers to this question dear to my heart and use them both to explain the phenomenon of the Witch Power.

When viewing this subject from the perspective of parapsychology I have developed the hypothesis that the Witch Power is a form of psycho-kinesis coupled with psychic sensitivity. Psychokinesis or telekinesis is the ability to influence a physical environment without physically interacting with the environment. When a witch does magic they are essentially tuning in to their Witch Power to receive impressions and can affect the present order of things if appropriate. There is still much study needed to flesh out the bigger picture of what this could mean; however, I believe this theory to be as based in scientific method as it possibly can be at the moment.

The other is a much grander explanation as to where our power comes from and has been a treasure that my tradition holds very dear. The myth of where we come from was first introduced to me through the work of Paul Huson, a man who also introduced me to the concept of the Witch Power in his 1996 book *Mastering Witchcraft*. Later, I would find correlations to his myth in the gnostic sacred text *The Book of Enoch*, and would eventually discover my own way of telling this story through my own spiritual seeking.

The Myth of the Witch Power

When consciousness found its way to our planet our ancestors were slowly taking their first steps into the light. They hunted and gathered, they fought to survive the wilds of an untamed world, and over time they began to form families and tribes. Diana the Star Goddess looked upon them with excitement, just as a gardener looks upon the first flowers of spring. In these times humanity had not forsaken the spirits in the land or the power they possess, but lived in harmony with them.

She saw how they suffered and saw that as they did so she, too, suffered, so she convened with the first spirits of creation. "Go forth and teach them of me, their celestial mother! Give them fire and tools and show them the way to me!" In little time it was decided that mankind would begin the great exodus out of the shadows and into the light of consciousness.

Like falling stars the great warriors and teachers of Diana, known to some as Angels or Faery, came to Earth and taught humankind the ways of cooperation and survival. We learned to make tools and build fires, we learned how to read the stars and enchant the earth under our feet, we learned to fashion metals and to commune with the mother of creation.

For generations we thrived side by side, learning from the great teachers of Diana and over time they began to love us as children, some eventually falling in love with us. Soon the lines blurred and we began to mix. Daughters of humankind became pregnant and gave birth to the beings known as the Nephilim, the ancestors of the witches.

The Nephilim were a race all their own, existing in our world and in others. They had the willpower of a human and the might of a cosmic spirit but with little desire to fuse the two. Soon humanity became jealous and turned the magic and technologies upon their teachers. War began to break out among man and Nephilim alike and the world quaked.

The Goddess saw what was being done, that the worst of man and the worst of angel had mixed, that weapons were being forged instead of unity, and she called her great spirits to action. She separated the realms and annihilated the Nephilim who went to war with humankind.

The remaining Nephilim vowed to stay and guide us through our evolution and growth. Over the following generations their descendants would become known as witches and the power given to them by their ancestors, the Witch Power.

As you will see later, angels are not the winged cherubs of Romantic-era paintings but the very busy and often aggressive spirits who help run the universe. They don't belong to one religion or group of people but to the universe, and many stories of great power have been attributed to angelic acts.

The story of the Nephilim and the Witch Power at the very least gives us an outline to explore our power. In the myth, at one point there was a war between the heavens (the realms of being) and the creatures of Earth and it caused humankind and the "magical" to go our separate ways. This is seen with the story of the Tuatha De Danann of Ireland, who retreated into the mounds after the rise of humankind.

How Witch Power Manifests

The Witch Power can either be inherited through bloodlines or even past-life awareness as well as through a formal initiation where the current of power is passed from one individual to another.

In the case of genetics, like any trait, the Witch Power can skip a generation or several before independently making itself known. Many modern witches have some form of magical parentage and through genealogical research have discovered ancestral ties to magic. Though it is rare today to have unbroken family witchcraft lineages, some witches do indeed come from family witchcraft lines. The currents of Witch Power that are passed through genetic heritage are specific to that family's bloodlines. In some instances you can activate your Witch Power by studying these family ties, especially if your heritage migrated at any point in time, and by working with ancestral spirits.

Through initiatic traditions like Sacred Fires, the Temple of Witchcraft, Faery Tradition, and Gardnerian Wicca, one trains to work with psychic and preternatural abilities and later receives the current of power from a mentor. These currents of Witch Power are unique and specific to each tradition due to their mythologies, core teachings, and the sources from which they draw power. This form of Witch Power is separate from our individual Witch Power but informs, influences, and empowers it. For those of us who do not naturally have access to the currents of Witch Power, an initiatic tradition can activate and install it like code.

The Witch Power can also reside in the soul and be activated at any stage in life, just like a sleeper-cell. The belief is that in a previous life you possessed the Witch Power and it permanently joined to your soul. As you reincarnate it can be activated during times of need, spiritual crisis, accidentally by trauma, or exposure to another current of Witch Power. This explains why someone could be completely void of psychic ability and then suddenly wake up to find they are lying in bed surrounded by spirits after a major life event or near-death experience.

No two currents of power are ever the same, adding much diversity to the manifestation of ability and influence the Witch Power has.

The Witch Power in You

Those who possess the Witch Power are often energetically sensitive to their environment and possess an instinctual desire to understand and make the most of these gifts. In my opinion, those who are psychic do possess the Witch Power regardless of whether they choose to identify it or not. These gifts are one and the same, though some gifts are naturally receptive and some are naturally projective, whereas others are both! All witches possess some level of psychic ability, and discovering which abilities you naturally have is the first step in awakening the Witch Power.

Psychic Abilities of the Witch

Clairaudience (*spirit whispering*) is the ability to receive psychic insight via auditory means. Prized by some as being one of the most valuable psychic abilities when working with the spirit world, clairaudient individuals can either physically hear, as in they feel the vibration of words enter their ear canal, or they receive the messages similar to how one might hear a song in their head. Clairaudient individuals should pay special attention to their guides for help discerning information they receive. Clairaudience is considered to be a receptive psychic ability.

Clairvoyance *(the second sight)* is the ability to receive psychic impressions through visual means. Those who are clairvoyant are capable of seeing via the "third-eye" or brow chakra, and will often receive messages in the way of dreams or memory recall. Those who are clairvoyant often have an easier time performing magic as this ability is both receptive and projective. Developing this ability will aid in the witch's own ability to manifest through visualization, allowing for greater initial affect.

Clairsentience *(the knowing)* is the psychic ability that allows one to know or understand something without being given knowledge of it beforehand. Most professional psychics have some form of clairsentient ability, which is another often highly coveted gift. Clairsentience is one of the most difficult to explain, as it is often described as an extrasensory "knowing." Clairsentience is considered to be a receptive psychic ability.

Psychokinesis *(telekinesis)* is the ability to move something in an environment or affect an environment without physically being present to do so. On a small scale, psychokinesis is the process that is happening whenever we perform spell work or a healing, because we are psychically altering an environment or object. On the grander scale, psychokinesis is responsible for the floating of objects, physical levitation, and even the creation of poltergeist activity. Psychokinesis is considered to be a projective psychic ability.

Mediumship *(spirit speaking)* is the ability to communicate with the dead, spirit guides, or allies. Mediumship is often broken down into three distinct types: physical, mental, and psychic. Though all mediums are psychic, a psychic-medium possesses the ability to receive messages from spirit guides or the dead via clairsentient channels, meaning that they will simply know to give a message. A mental medium will receive messages from those who are not incarnate via mental processes (images, songs, symbols), similar to a psychic-medium; however, the mental medium usually needs to "tune in" before receiving messages. Physical mediums have the ability to receive messages through physical sensation and have been found to also produce physical psychic phenomena such as ectoplasm, which has been reported to help spirits appear in the physical. The type of mediumship will determine its classification as passive or projective. Both mental and psychic mediumship are considered to be perceptive, whereas physical mediumship can be both.

———————

The Witch Power generally works for each of us in some combination of these abilities. Even if you have never had a spirit walk up to you and start talking, chances are that you have had some message in the form of inexplicable knowledge come to you just before making a major decision, or perhaps you have felt the pull of a friend in need without knowing why. The Witch Power speaks to us individually through these processes and gives us the ability to interact with the world on a whole new level.

Revealing the Witch Power Within

Witches come from all walks of life and modern witches are just the latest in a long line descended from great beings of power. It is up to us to challenge ourselves through self-discovery and discipline in order to find where the true power of a witch lies. To do this we must face our fears, challenge paradigms, and be willing to accept that we are one tiny part of a much bigger picture.

The Witch Power guides us through fields of self-discovery and that very process is what will activate and empower our abilities. You will find that the most powerful witches are those who were willing to put aside their doubts and have moved through the blocks that were presented to them in life. A powerful witch never lets their fear get in the way and takes life head-on. It is the trust that we are being guided through these issues for a reason that strengthens our desire to move through them. What we learn in the process works like keys to unlocking hidden knowledge, and that knowledge leads to power.

We must be willing to challenge the paradigms presented to us. Liberation from negative thought patterns and behavior will only serve to bring you closer to what you truly want in life, ultimately helping you get to the person you truly see yourself to be. The Witch Power can get us there; it's all a matter of how well we study its lessons and where we tell it we want to go. We must always be willing to question the answers immediately given to us and push the envelope of possibility. When only one road appears to be present, the Witch Power can build a second, even a third with the right direction.

In this book you are going to travel through several different ways to work with and strengthen the Witch Power as a tool to get you what you want in life. Empowering it through psychic development is just the tip of the iceberg, but also a very important practice to add to your repertoire. This power grows each time we choose personal discipline over slothfulness, light a candle and chant secret names and words of power, and every time we touch the walls between the worlds; but just like lifting weights, we must work all of these angles if we are to grow strong over the whole body. The Witch Power wants you to use it, and the more you do, the bigger and stronger it will get.

Ultimately the Witch Power puts you in contact with the unseen world and gives you the ability to not only make allies there but to gain crucial insight by exploring it. The abilities that are present inside of you this very moment are the same abilities that have been evolving with humankind since we first looked up at the heavens. They are instinctual, natural, and just as much a part of you as your hair color or personality.

Though not everyone can possess the Witch Power, those who do walk a path that is never-ending and constantly unfolding. We are part of the complex tapestry that is life and our abilities can be the loom that weaves or the scissors that cut.

Journal Topics

Throughout this book you will be prompted to write your thoughts about the material in your magical journal. These prompts were added to help you get a little extra out of what you learn here. In order to take full advantage of the opportunities for empowerment found within these pages, it is highly important that you do your best to participate in these exercises.

- How do you define witchcraft and how do you embody that definition?

- How have you noticed the Witch Power in your life?

- Do you have any clue as to where your Witch Power comes from? (i.e., a certain side of the family or initiation)

- How do you manifest the Witch Power?

Chapter Two

Frequencies of Power

If you want to find the secrets of the universe,
think in terms of energy, frequency, and vibration.
—Nikola Tesla—

We are full of power. Sometimes this power is hidden from us and sometimes we are the ones hiding from the power. There is nothing more frightening to us than our ultimate potential. We are taught to give our power over for the greater good of family or community, we are taught that those who want power are corrupt, and we are taught that those with power are somehow further from the divine. The craft encourages us to challenge this power paradigm so that we can reclaim what is rightfully ours. The power paradigm comes from the desire for and fear of what power means.

Personal power is not what we get from being aggressive, it's not what we get from hurting others, and it is definitely not something that comes from an external search. Your personal power is inside you, it IS you, and in order to fully understand how powerful you can be, you have to see how powerful you already are. Take a look around you. Are you happy? Are you prepared for whatever comes next? Do you feel like others respect you? Do you respect others?

These are all subsets of something much larger: your frequency. In order to break the power paradigm we have to move from the practice of seeing power as something that is external from you or something that is given to you, and start seeing it as something that already is emanating from you. This emanation is what we call frequency and it is constantly interacting with other frequencies.

The Frequency of a Witch

Ultimately what creates our frequency is a complex layering of state of mind, connectedness to our environment, and mana levels. (*Mana* is a term used by many metaphysicians to describe the life force, spiritual energy, and power one possesses, and is generally seen as being supernatural or preternatural in nature.) When all these things are working in tandem and are present we feel powerful and capable of taking on whatever comes our way. When these aspects of life are not working together we grow lethargic and our frequency becomes quite low, making it difficult to find the next step.

A witch's state of mind is perhaps their best ally in the discovery of power. When we don't feel capable, we aren't; when we don't feel safe, we act out; when we feel lost, we stand in the fog. It is easier to stand in the middle of our lives feeling lost than it is to look for a way through, but a witch's life is not about the easy.

As a professional psychic and witch I see several hundred people each year and I find myself retelling the same story: When I was a little boy I had the most dreadful bedroom. It was full of clothes and dust, and like any little boy's room, had the distinct odor of pre-teen. My mother would tell me to clean it every day and every day I would find some excuse not to take care of it. Not because I was trying to defy her, but because there was so much to do I had no clue where to start. This would go on and on until one day she would finally have had enough and clean it herself.

When she was done I would feel shamed because I should have done it, but I also felt a sense of relief that I wasn't in such an environment any longer. By the time I was thirteen, she quit coming into my room to clean. My room after that was an unrecognizable mess until adulthood.

When I moved out on my own and began living in shared spaces with roommates I realized that my messy ways weren't going to cut it. My messes were spilling into their messes and soon we just had a huge mess that felt insurmountable. I felt the same way I did when I was a little boy, but this time my mother wasn't going to help me. Feeling hopeless and overwhelmed, I clammed up and let the mess get even bigger. It didn't matter how good of a mood or how encouraged I felt about life; when I came home and saw the messes, it all went out the door.

One day I woke up in that messy room and realized it was a giant metaphor for my whole life. The space was beautiful but I had so much junk and filth all over that the beauty was gone, and like my life, I had no clue where to even begin to fix it. In that moment of self-loathing and pity I realized it was so much simpler than I was allowing it to be.

To clean the mess (and the metaphor) I needed to not get lost turning around 360 degrees looking at the entirety of it all. That was too much and it made me feel too powerless. If, however, I picked just one corner, I would at least have a place to start. A few hours later I was sitting in my beautiful sanctuary of a room again and I had all the inspiration I needed to get my life back on track.

Sometimes the sheer volume of what we have to do in order to change is so great that change feels unreachable. We lose our power when we surrender to that perception. We are not powerless to change, we are not incapable of fixing our issues, we just don't always know where to start.

Our frequency will give us away when we aren't in a place of power. Our moods and passions and drives ooze from us like sap from a tree and everyone around us is capable of perceiving that, even if we aren't. This is how our frequency affects others and why we are affected by the frequency of others. What's even scarier is that we are perceiving these vibrations as well, absorbing them into our psyche and ultimately feeding that negativity back to ourselves. This keeps us in a loop and the power paradigm thrives.

In my tradition we value the rebellious nature of the witch and see nothing more rebellious than taking back the power of our frequency. In order to do so we have to discover how our frequency works.

Frequency Is Resonance

One of our most cherished beliefs in contemporary Paganism is that of animism. We believe everything has a soul and everything has a vibration. These vibrations emanate from us like sound waves from a speaker or a singing bowl. Much like a sound wave, this vibration carries out into the world around us, and depending on the strength of that wave it may be able to interfere with or alter other waves that are simultaneously transmitting.

Your frequency is both projective and perceptive, though. This means that not only are we transmitting those waves but we are also absorbing the waves being transmitted towards us. When we take a step back and look at all the energy transmitting from us and being absorbed by us, we get something that looks a bit like a satellite sending and receiving signals. Our Witch Power engages the universe through our frequency and transmits its influence on the waves of our frequency.

Our frequencies, like our life force, are fluidic and will take the shape of whatever they are poured into. Part of understanding the power of your frequency requires an understanding of what you are being poured into, and what is being poured into you.

Home Frequency

Your home frequency is the most perfect state of you. It is a psychic, mental, and physical state of homeostasis, which is to say that within the home frequency we have everything we need in order to thrive. Our home frequencies are ultimately the way we feel when we are not bogged down by burden, when we feel healthy and alive with possibilities, and we feel strong and capable. This state is natural for us and should be the place in which we begin all of our growth and development.

By tuning in to our home frequency we can become more aware of what other frequencies are being transmitted to us and from us and how we are being altered because of them. It is within the home frequency that we are capable of seeing the true blocks, even those we create for ourselves, and from that awareness all changes can take place. Like sonar, as our frequency transmits to the universe it bounces back off of obstacles, and by studying the feedback we can determine where our blocks are and how to get around them.

Discovering Your Home Frequency

Find yourself in a place where you can relax and be at ease. Begin by taking deep breaths and allow each breath to enter your lungs like water pouring into a cup and exit as though it was being poured back into its original container. Take time feeling the universe pour into you and spill out of you with each breath. Find yourself focusing on the points of stillness and silence between each breath and allow yourself to gently, mentally slip into them. Allow each moment of stillness to grow pregnant with potential.

Continue to do this until you begin to feel the tension slowly drain from your body. When you perceive this sensation, take it as a cue from your body that it is ready to begin its journey to the home frequency.

As you continue to breathe slow and deep, bring your attention to your heart chakra. It takes exactly sixty seconds for the blood in a healthy heart to leave, pump through the entire body, and return. Knowing this allows your focus to move from the heart to the center of your chest, to the belly, down to your sex, through your legs, and down to your feet. Allow your focus to rise back through the legs and the torso, making its way to your shoulders, down your arms, back up through the neck to the top of your head and then back down to the heart chakra. Do this as many times as you need to until you feel that you have checked in with your body. If you feel blocks or areas of discomfort, allow yourself to visualize those blocks as being merely frozen energy that will melt as your warm blood circulates.

Bring your attention now to your state of mind. Begin this by acknowledging any internal dialogue. As you acknowledge it move it to the side of your focus. See this mental chatter as a frequency all its own that has the ability to sway your focus. Instead of seeing it as the enemy, simply pause the chatter as you would pause a song on your MP3 player. Move from being aware of your states of dissonance to replacing them with the feeling of happiness in yourself. Think of how you feel when you are being generous or have had an incredible day. If this is hard for you, I recommend replacing those thoughts of dis-ease or frustration with the realization that you have already overcome so much in life. Isn't that something to be proud of? These moments are moments of perfect love and perfect trust and are aligned with your highest good.

Take that feeling of happiness in yourself and allow your consciousness to sink deep into your body. Take three deep breaths, and as you do so, allow your energy to spread out. Each breath is a pulse of energy emanating from your body. With each pulse spread your consciousness out even further until you can feel yourself taking up the entirety of the empty space around you.

Focus on your sense of identity, the real, authentic you that has been around since you were given consciousness. This you has never changed: It has always been that feeling you get when you know you are in the right place at the right time; it's the feeling you get when you listen to your favorite lyrics in your favorite song; it is the sensation that comes when you finally break the walls down and say what is on your mind. Focus on the you that you love, the piece of you that feels perfect. Send this authentic vibration out into the world with three deep breaths just as before. You are now at your home frequency.

Allow yourself to see this vibration emanate from you and see that with every pulse it is clearing away all negative conditioning and feelings of fear or dis-ease. See that each wave of energy moves from a place deep inside, through your body and every cell, and as it does so it washes away all the chains that bind you.

Spend a few moments feeling your frequency transmit to the universe; get to know this feeling of perfect love and perfect trust in yourself.

Occasionally we need to perform this exercise a few times before the full breath of its potential can take hold in our life. We spend so much time negatively reinforcing ourselves that finding this state of home frequency is not always easy. The more you practice this work, the stronger the experience will become and the easier it will be to attain the end result.

Tuning In

Possibly one of the most significant practices to the witch is the ability to use the receptive powers to tune in and adjust frequencies at will. This tuning in is similar to turning the dial on the radio to get a clearer signal or to change the station altogether. The reason why this becomes so important to us is that in its most simple form we can use this practice to quickly channel external energy to adjust our own. An example would be tuning in to the vibration of happiness by using laughter as a trigger, or listening to baroque music to help us study. We use this practice all the time without being aware of what we are doing consciously, so why not adjust our frequencies with intention?

As you will see later in this book, we can also tune in to energies, deities, spirits of place, and just about anything that produces a frequency of its own. The possibilities are endless. I prefer to see all energy as a frequency that can be tuned in to and channeled. By doing so I have the ability to increase or decrease the signal strength of those frequencies and have learned to be ever aware of when changes in those frequencies occur.

Surprisingly to some, tuning in to adjust our frequency at will can be a simple matter of creating triggers, or presets on the radio dial.

Creating Intentional Presets

Once you have become comfortable with the process of finding your home frequency you can begin building a trigger for it. This trigger, or preset, will help you enter this state in a matter of seconds versus going through the entire process, which can be lengthy, every time you need to go to your home frequency. I cannot stress the importance of being comfortable with the exercise prior to building a trigger for it. In addition, once a trigger has been made it is a good idea to "refresh" the trigger every few weeks, which is to say it is important to perform the entire meditation to reaffirm the trigger that you have created from time to time.

I find that building triggers in three parts is most effective for me. I refer to these three parts as Action, Focus, and Surrender.

Action refers to what you physically do as part of the trigger to elicit the transition. Some people will clap their hands, others will count backwards from ten, some even sing or hum. I like to do a breathing exercise, such as the four-fold breath, and/or use a "magic word" like *Kapow!* The importance here is to create a unique *Action* that is not something you do often and is not easily replicated by others. You don't want to use words that are common to your vocabulary because they will alter your trigger's ability to be effective. Each time you say that word without the accompanied action you will weaken the trigger.

Focus means to mentally clear a path for the transition to take place. During this stage you identify your end goal (the state of being your trigger is intended to elicit) and mentally connect it to your action. The instant I have performed the *Action* I visualize a lightning bolt striking my target and clearing all mental chatter and obstacles that get in the way. You don't need to void your mind of thought, but you definitely want to make sure there is no resistance between you and your ability to tune in. Use this time to focus on your intention.

The final stage of trigger building is **Surrender**. The last thing you do before you enter the intended state of mind is to surrender to it. (For this reason you need to be very comfortable and solid with how it feels to be in that state of mind.) For the trigger to work you have to fully surrender yourself to the new frequency. I like to visualize myself slipping into the new state of being. To me this feels like what I imagine a bird feels like when it jumps off a branch and into the open air. You should feel supported by the energy and comfortable enough to let go of your need to be in control of the immediate psychic experience.

Using the technique above, you'll build the first trigger to your home frequency. Follow each step with me and write down any answers or responses you may have at the end of the practice. This will allow you to edit or change any part of the process when needed. Feel free to either build your trigger along with me or create your own system if you feel confident.

The Home Frequency Preset

Before performing step one, be sure to have spent time in your home frequency prior in the day. This will allow you to build the preset from a much more familiar place.

Step One:

Action. Take a deep breath and on the exhale tonally resonate the vowel OHM and allow the vibration to carry throughout your whole body. As you inhale raise your hands up in the air as if reaching for a balloon directly over your head, and then slowly bring them down to prayer position as you tone.

Step Two:

Focus. As your hands enter prayer position, see that a tiny spark of blue electricity has been ignited. Begin to relax your body and take slow, deep, and steady breaths. As you breathe, visualize yourself moving closer and closer to your home frequency. See that each time you exhale the tiny spark grows more powerful. Notice that as you move forward the electrical spark hits any blocks or distractions, removing them from your field of thought. See that in the distance there is another version of you, a version already waiting for you at your home frequency.

Step Three:

Discover your sense of identity, the real, authentic you that has been around since you were given consciousness. Focus on the you that you love, the piece of you that feels perfect. Send this authentic vibration out into the world with three deep breaths just as before.

Allow yourself to see this vibration emanate from you and see that with every pulse it clears away all negative conditioning and feelings of fear or dis-ease. See that each wave of energy moves from a place deep inside, through your body and every cell, and as it does so it washes away all the chains that bind you.

Step Four:

Surrender to this state of being. Let go of any final vestiges of the previous state of mind and allow yourself to arrive fully. To do this, visualize yourself stepping into the body that awaits you in your home frequency.

When to Adjust Your Frequency

Because energy follows the path of least resistance, it can be difficult at times to be aware of what frequency we are tuned in to and what frequency we are emanating to the rest of the universe. The effectiveness of our Witch Power is greatly connected to where we are on the dial. Adjusting our frequency is not always easy, but knowing when to do so is more than half the battle.

Your home frequency is considered to be high-vibrational. Most frequencies that work with our highest good and self tend to be high-vibrational. Our goal is to maintain this higher frequency resonance as much as possible. Lower vibrational frequencies are negative and generally work against our highest good, altering our ability to perceive and focus and sometimes destroying our ability to manifest.

What to Look For—the Three Ds

Disease, the feeling that our natural state is ill-affected. This can be because of sickness, chemical imbalance, or any number of health-related issues. The hyphenated term of "dis-ease" is often used by energy workers to describe a state of disharmony and ill-connectedness with our home frequency as well as a feeling of being stuck in life.

Depression is responsible for many a failed magician. Depression greatly decreases the amount of mana being produced by the energy centers of the body, leaving plenty of room on the dial for low-vibrational habits and patterns to develop. These patterns build up over time and create an environment where lower frequencies that are harmful to us can thrive.

Discord is what happens when we are not harmonizing with the world around us. In my experience this is what happens when our internal and external worlds disagree with one another. In this case it is often that we are projecting a frequency that does not match or even harmonize with the frequency we are receiving from our environment or the world around us. It feels like two dissonant notes being played on the piano at the same time.

Practical Steps to Frequency Adjustment

Ironically, there is no one magical fix for low frequency. Adjustments must be made over time to ensure that our frequency stays in a high-vibrational space. These practices are simple and practical and can be done daily to ensure that you are carving the right type of path for your energy to follow.

Be aware of your obsessions. Where your thoughts may go, your energy will flow. We all obsess over the details of our life but how we obsess is what makes the difference. If you are obsessing over the lower frequency matters of life—the ones that make you feel incapable—that is precisely what you will bring to yourself. When you find yourself stuck in an obsessive loop, you must break the pattern in order to correct where that energy should be going.

The law of attraction works in all ways, so it is best to be aware of what we are focusing on and what we are attracting.

The best resolve for negative obsessive patterns is to remove yourself from those stimuli. Get out of the environment and engage in something different. I find that taking a walk, a drive through the country, or even going for a cup of coffee with the intention of that subject not being brought up can work wonders. Give yourself a new form for your energy to pour into and limit the time you spend engaged with the negative obsession. In the past, for me, that's meant creating a scheduled time each week to dive into those negative obsessions, freeing the rest of my week for positive frequency cultivation.

Be present, be in the now. There is no greater time of power than now. When we are not present in the moment we are incapable of doing the things that will bring power tomorrow. Practicing moment-based awareness will allow you to check in with your frequency and adjust it when needed.

To do this I like to set a time, or several times, throughout the day when I need to step away from what I am doing and simply check in with myself. When the time comes I close my eyes, take three deep breaths, and ask myself, "How am I doing right now?" If I don't like my response I then make a plan of action, in that moment, for how I will change my frequency. Sometimes I just need to put on my headphones and jam for a bit and other times I need to talk to someone.

Using magical timing when adjusting your frequency is always a great way to incorporate the Witch Power into your daily life. For one week try tuning in to your frequency at 11:11 a.m. and at dusk every day. Use these auspicious times as reminders to be present.

Do not invest in your inadequacy. Think about all the times you have said: "That is too hard"; "I can't do it"; "I'm not cut out for that"; "That's just the way it's always been"; or "It's never going to change." All those words and thoughts are given over to the things that make you feel like you can't do something when you could be focusing on the things that you can do. Often the worst people to be around are those invested in their own incapable nature.

Don't live under a cloud of assumptions. We can't always help it, but we assume a lot more about the world than we actually know to be true. When we live in a world created by assumptions we are unable to truly know the world we live in. When we act under an assumption we are investing our energy in something that we *think* we know but may or may not really be true. This can lead to decreased confidence and self-sabotage in the long term, and can give us false paradigms to function within in the present. To truly know something is to have its truth and from that truth we can build solid foundations. Magic that is done when we are functioning under assumptions usually ends up either not working well or creating utter chaos in the process of its manifestation.

Be aware of the company you keep. Humans are generally social beings and love to keep friends and family close. Sometimes these people make up an incredible support system; however, there are times when they create the exact opposite. Always remember that you are a sponge for energy and when you are surrounded by negative people, people who don't hold you in high esteem, people who don't respect you, or people who are more focused on themselves in your relationship with them, you are setting yourself up for a lot of extra work. Keeping people around you who genuinely believe you are capable of achieving your goals and who love you unconditionally is a sure way to keep your frequency high.

Don't let yourself get overwhelmed. If you ever find yourself feeling as though the weight of the world is on your shoulders, it's a sure sign that there is something wrong with your frequency. When you succumb to the feeling of being overwhelmed you are incapable of seeing clearly what needs to be done. Because we can't always drop everything when it comes to dealing with this feeling, it's important to take steps to actively reduce your stress load. I recommend getting out of your normal environment and engaging in something different at least twice a day during these times. Going for a walk and breathing fresh air can help put things into perspective.

Feeling like you have the weight of the world on your shoulders is often accompanied by the feeling of being punished. In fact, that saying comes from the Greek myth of Atlas, a man who was punished by the gods to carry the planet on his shoulders. The universe doesn't punish us; only we can do that to each other and ourselves.

Be aware of your addictions and the power they have over you. If you're like me and have an addictive personality, this can be highly difficult at times. Addiction happens when someone engages in an activity or substance that feels good at the time but become compulsive with prolonged engagement. This compulsive behavior then creates issues in achieving goals or performing daily functions.

It took me years to quit smoking cigarettes. It was by far the most difficult personal challenge I have faced to date and is something I struggle with daily. What I wasn't aware of until I quit smoking was how much control my addiction had over my daily life and health. When I quit engaging in my addiction I found that I had more energy, wanted to be around people more often, and slept better. Addictions are nothing to kid around about because most often, addicts live in denial. Think about the power and control you are giving over to that addiction and think about where that energy might be better used.

Spiritual Steps to Frequency Adjustment

There are of course spiritual practices that can go a long way in helping you to adjust your frequencies. Like with the practical steps, these will produce short-term benefits and long-term rewards. Further on in this book I will add to this list, but these are excellent starting points.

Begin and end every day in your home frequency. I know, I know; it seems like a lot to do on a daily basis but I promise you it will pay off! As part of your daily practice set just ten minutes aside each morning and night to preemptively address any frequency issues you may be experiencing. When we start our day off in our home frequency we are affirming our intentions of power and authenticity for the rest of the day. Think about it; when we are in our home frequency we are relaxed, feel capable, and are aligned with our true nature. By ending your day in your home frequency you will be able to release the tensions from the day and will be able to have a more restful sleep, which in return will help with the production of mana.

Empower the food you eat. An excellent way to adjust your frequency is to both watch what you eat and to eat with intention. It's a no-brainer: when we eat food that is bad for us, it has a negative impact on how we feel. When we make healthy food decisions, we provide our bodies with the good stuff they need to function at a higher capacity, again building greater stores of mana. We can take this a step further by magically empowering the food before we eat it. As we absorb the nutrients of the food we will absorb the magic and in turn our frequencies will adjust.

To do this I like to take my dinner knife (or fork, or spoon, or, in a pinch, my index finger) and draw a pentacle over the plate. I then touch every type of food and tell it what I want it to do. For example, if I have spinach on my plate I inform it that I need its iron to fortify my blood and break apart the negative vibrations absorbed that day; if I eat carrots I tell them I need them to strengthen my eyes and help me see opportunity. After I have affirmed the meal, I give thanks for any and all sacrifices made, especially if I am eating meat. I eat slowly and focus on really tasting the food and feel its nutrients being absorbed by my body.

Don't yo-yo your energy. A good friend of mine once warned me of the dangers of treating my energy like a yo-yo. If we send our intentions out to the universe we must be very careful not to pull them back in because of second-guessing. We all do this from time to time in larger ways but the act is much more dangerous in its smaller form. Take a day and pay attention to how you send intention out and pull it right back in.

Addressing the tendency to do this will cause two things to happen. First, you will find that you require a little bit more thought before sending energy out. This allows for a better-formulated approach to manifestation as it will reduce resistance. The second thing this will do is allow you to build trust in your ability to manifest, an increasingly valuable act as you grow in your Witch Power.

Create an altar to yourself. I'm a big fan of altars; I have them all over the house, but the most important altar in my possession is the altar I created to myself! The contents of the altar can change but the intention should always be the same, a place where you can celebrate and honor your own godhood. Altars are a set place where we connect to and harmonize with the divine frequencies of universe. Once built, your altar is the perfect place to perform magical changes to your frequency and to work on building right relationships with other frequencies.

Building the Altar of the Self

Some altars are meant to be big and seen by everyone, but not this altar; it should be somewhere where it won't get too much attention from outside influences. This altar needs to represent your home frequency so it should never be touched or messed with by anyone other than you. I have mine stationed atop my dresser in the bedroom so that it is not likely to be seen by anyone other than my partners; it is the last thing I see before I go to sleep. Everything in the dresser becomes imbued with its magic. This means any clothes I take out come pre-charged with all the energies I am currently working with, making it that much easier to start and end my day in my home frequency.

As you continue reading you will find talismans, sigils, and magical oils that you will add to your personal altar later, but you probably already have everything you need to get started. To create this altar you will need the following:

(One or two) Tokens of appreciation that have been given to you by another person. These can be anything from a crayon drawing given to you by a child, to dried flowers from a wedding anniversary or a thank-you note from a coworker.

(One or two) Tokens of accomplishment such as a copy of a diploma, initiation certificate, or trophy.

(One or two) Tokens of faith that symbolize your personal spiritual path. These can be a small statue of your own personal deity, an altar tool such as a wand or athame, or a picture of a beloved spiritual teacher like the Dalai Lama or Aradia.

A token of spiritual resonance. This should be something that you have that symbolizes a moment where you felt complete frequency resonance with the universe after spell, ritual, meditation, or trance work. This can be a rock from the beach that you found after performing a spell, your favorite deck of Tarot cards, or even a quote from your favorite spell written on parchment.

A picture of you. This picture should again only be a picture of you, no one else.

A mirror that no one has ever looked into (or has been ritually cleansed for magic).

Two small bowls for charging jewelry and other wearable items.

A white candle. The color can change depending on what personal development work you are doing at the moment, but white is always the default.

Other items that you might include on this altar are a small whiteboard or chalkboard for writing affirmations that correspond with your current personal development, a journal for logging personal development, and items that remind you of "where you come from," like a postcard from your hometown or shot glass from your local sports stadium.

You can arrange these items in any way you see fit. Choose an altar cloth that shows off your personality and feel free to be creative and express yourself! Even if a bunch of people will never see this altar, you will, and it should instantly feel engaging for you.

The rules of this altar are simple. Keep it clean, never let anyone touch the items on the altar, visit it frequently, and only perform magic to affect your frequency there. This means that this altar should be used as a vehicle for you to make hands-on changes to your natural state and nothing else. If you feel depressed or out of sync, visit your altar regularly and perform magic to bring happiness and positivity into your life. In the same manner, magic for healing, confidence, protection, transformation, and transcendence should be done here.

This altar is a place for you to worship your divine relationship with the universe. It is a place for you to connect to and alter the ever-present frequencies that are shaping your life as well as an anchor for those frequencies. Here the only things influencing you are those you have chosen and you are free to shape the energies in your life the way you see fit.

Consecrating the Altar of the Self

Clean the area that you will be using to build the altar. Make sure that you get all spider webs or dust, and polish any wood or metal surfaces. Remember, you are preparing this space for a god! Smudge the area and all objects meant for the altar by burning your favorite cleansing herbs, like sage or lavender.

Standing in front of the altar, take a few moments to ground and center your energy and then enter your home frequency. Place both hands palm down on the bare altar surface and focus on expanding the sensation of the home frequency outward to include the altar and the space around it. Take three deep breaths and tone or chant the vowel OHM. Then invite your allies and spirit helpers in by saying:

> *I call forth my guides and allies and all that work for my good, and banish now the negativity that here once stood. Come now allies, come to my aid, be here now, let magic be made!*

At this time go ahead and place the items on the altar in a way that is visually appealing to you; however, for now place the mirror in the center of the altar with the candle just directly in front of it. Draw a pentacle of white flame above the candle and gaze into the mirror as you slowly visualize this pentacle moving into the candle. Blow the candle a kiss and then lift your arms up so that both of your palms are facing the sky. Take another deep breath and say:

> By all that is free, by that is me, by all that is wild, by all that is tame,
> I consecrate this altar to the sacred flame! Let my light rise to touch
> the sky and may blessings come from all I try. This is my will, so must
> it be. For the good of all, but most for me!

Connect to spirit every day. It can be as simple as lighting a candle for the deities you work worth or as intense as evening trance. Every day you take a breath is a day to celebrate your divine connection. You are the product of over fifty million years of evolution and spiritual growth; everything about you is divine, and taking just a few minutes every day to honor that can make a huge difference.

The Water Cleansing Rites

Water cleansings are time-honored practices in many magical traditions. They help to purify the energy body and prepare it for spiritual work. In Sacred Fires, we use two types of water cleansings on a regular to semi-regular basis. The first is a ritual that utilizes the ancient practice of washing the hands and feet of an honored guest; the other is called Kala, a Polynesian practice that found its way into contemporary witchcraft by way of the Feri Tradition of Witchcraft.

These water cleansings can be used whenever you feel the need to let go of external energy and return to your home frequency, as well as for specific situations we'll explore later in this book.

The Bowl of Light Water Cleansing Ritual

For this ritual you will only need a clean bowl, a white hand towel, salt, and spring or distilled water. This ritual can be done anywhere at any time and can be adapted easily to fit into any witch's practice.

Fill the bowl halfway up with water and place it before you. Take a handful of salt in your dominant hand and hold it above the bowl at chest level. Say three times, "By sacred salt and purest water, with witch's might and alpha mater. I summon now the seas of change to cleanse me and help rearrange!" Gently open your hand and allow the salt to slowly pour from your fist into the bowl of water. As you see the salt enter the water, visualize this bowl glowing with white light.

Dip the white towel in the water and wipe the brow, both hands, and finally both feet. As you do this, say, "By the brow I am reborn, my senses cleansed! By the hands I am unbound, the future mine to build! By the feet I am uncrossed, my path free of obstruction!"

When you finish, say, "By the gods within and the gods without, may all evil be turned about! So must it be!"

Kala, the Cup of Light

To do this you need only a cup of clean water and a few moments free of distraction.

Initiate a steady breath. Holding the cup of water just below your navel, collect the psychic debris from your energy body as well as any feelings of frustration or fear, and send it into the cup with each exhale as you visualize the water growing thick, dark, oily, and heavy in your hands.

Breathing slow and deep, feel the light of your higher self, the glow of your own holy fire, emanate from you. With each exhale channel this light into the cup and visualize the water clearing and returning to a natural state of brilliance. See that the problems of the past are now the nutriment of the future and drink the contents of the cup up.

Frequency in a Nutshell

It is necessary to take stock of how we already impact our environment and ourselves. Part of this impact is felt receptively. How we absorb the subtle energies around us, how we hold on to those energies, and how sensitive we grow to those energies has everything to do with how we project our frequency to the world.

The other part of the equation, of course, is how we choose to use our powers of projection. Because we are beings who are constantly resonating with frequency we are both consciously and subconsciously creating impact in our lives on a daily basis. Being aware of this power and discovering its potential is a crucial first step in the direction of a well-developed Witch Power.

By creating paths to our home frequency and visiting it regularly we can carve out a path to true power and authenticity: a state of being free from the energy and impressions of others, a state that is capable of teaching us about what we truly want and need.

Journal Topics

- Aside from meditation and ritual work, when do you most often feel like you are closest to your home frequency? List any daily events or experiences that bring you close to the feeling of your home frequency.

- In what areas of your life do you most often experience one or all of the three Ds? Create a plan of action that will help avoid or isolate the interference.

- Aside from daily visits to your Altar of the Self, pick two days of the week and one time during each of those days in which you can dedicate at least fifteen minutes to personal development. List two practices that you will do during this time, such as affirmation work, mantras, uncrossing work, meditation, prayer, or trance.

Chapter Three

The Primal Soul

*The soul—which I'm defining as our capacity for these deeply
positive human qualities—is something that, in most of us,
desperately needs to be developed. Too many of us live in a fractured
state, deeply divided against ourselves—often far more so than we
are aware of or able to feel. We exist in a self-generated vacuum of
moral ambiguity, where everything is relative and our attention is
focused mainly on our emotional state. Most of us know a lot more
about what really matters than we are willing to live up to.*

—Andrew Cohen—

Your soul is an incredible thing. Some of us are brought up to believe
that there is an ancient war waging right now over who gets to claim
it once you experience physical death. In other traditions it is believed
the soul is on a never-ending quest for ascension to godhood. For many
modern witches it isn't so cut-and-dry. We believe that the soul is actually

composed of distinct parts and that these parts are actually energy centers of their own. Combined, these parts function as a complete human soul.

Three Souls

Not unlike the Eastern chakra system, the model of etheric anatomy many of us work with is comprised of three parts. These parts of the soul are said to be smaller, more specified souls known in my tradition as the primal, ego, and higher. Discovering them and building a practice surrounding them can greatly increase your ability to use your Witch Power and your connection to every other form of spiritual frequency.

This system was first introduced to me in my Wiccan training as the three cauldrons, which are overflowing into one another, always brimming with sustenance. They were briefly described to me with a list of the chakras, but I was never given instruction on how to work with them. Later they would be reintroduced to me by teachers in the Faery Tradition[1] of Witchcraft and they eventually made their way into my work in Sacred Fires. I use this model not just in my personal craft but also to diagnose and help spiritual concerns in others. At this point I couldn't imagine not using this system and have found it to be immensely beneficial. At the very least it provides a platform for spiritual diagnostic work and that alone is worth the time and effort.

I will be introducing you to the way we work with these three souls in the Sacred Fires tradition. We use several practices that help us understand the nature of these souls, like totemic associations and mythology, and later in the book the use of astrology will help us understand these souls better. We like to think of these souls as parts of our personality as well, and they are sometimes referred to as *selves,* which is used interchangeably with *souls.* Each part contains a unique frequency and a unique set of power.

---

1   Faery Tradition teachers: Storm Faerywolf, Chas Bogan, and Anaar.

The Primal Soul

Trust instinct to the end, even though you can give no reason.
—Ralph Waldo Emerson—

The primal soul sits within the lower portion of our physical being. In Indian mythology a great serpent known as Kundalini lies coiled within the root chakra, acting only out of primal instinct. Issues surrounding our impulses, drives, even our relationships to food and substances can all be attributed to the primal soul. The primal soul is concerned with the primitive needs of the human existence: to eat, sleep, make love, and to find security.

The primal soul

When we take a look at the primal soul we see that it acts as a factory, producing and sending life force through each soul and the physical body. If you have ever felt worn down, exhausted, lost, or confused in an overwhelming sense, this is usually due to your other souls being all but drained of life force, when the primal soul is forced into a state of overdrive, making us feel weak and fragile. Anxiety and depression onset when the primal soul is exhausted, which can be a lesson in just how animal we really are. During this state it is said that Kundalini the serpent will rise as your survival instincts kick in. We become sensitive to our environment, sometimes even becoming violent to those around us, all in the name of self-preservation. This feeling is a glimpse into the shadow side of the primal soul.

The primal soul is our connection to the earth, our place of origin. In many ways it speaks to us in a language that is representative of the far-off past, a time before time where simple gestures and crude drawings conveyed our thoughts. The primal soul is a remnant from the time of pre-civilization—a time when we were hunters and gatherers, making stone tools, living both in the earth and off it. This was a time when we were not the top of the food chain, when we lived solely on our animal drives and motives.

The primitive self is the truly wild part of the soul, untamed by the conditioning of society, and many of the problems we develop on a mundane level are directly related to the abuse of this soul. When society attempts to condition it, it tends to reject the oppression by driving needs even deeper into the subconscious aspects of our human experience. It is similar to wearing a corset in order to change the shape of the body. In no way is it a natural shape to take on, but in society it is the most welcomed, even worshiped and desired. This type of oppression forces primitive needs to manifest in ways that are often repressed, which can cause serious harm to us as a whole. Though we like to think of these souls as parts, they affect each other. The problems of the one become the problems of all three. A repressed primitive nature creates a restricted and inharmonic ego and can alter one's ability to perceive the divine.

The primal soul is connected to the earth and is the part of us that returns to earth when we die. In the world tree model of underworld, middle world, and upper world, the primal soul is deeply connected to the underworld. The key words and terms to remember with this soul are Feeling, Emotion, Life Force, and Survival.

The Frequency of the Primal Soul

Shown here on piano from C2 (Low C) to B3

The frequency of the primal soul vibrates the lowest of the three souls. In Western music theory this frequency resonates with notes C2 (Low C) to B3. Within these two octaves any tone played or sung by those with a deep bass or baritone voice can have an immediate effect on the primal soul. These tones can release lower-frequency energies that attach during times of dis-ease and can be used to promote life force production in the primal soul.

This frequency has the ability to physically affect an environment even if it is not in proximity to it. Additionally, this is the soul that is responsible for the production of poltergeist activity and psychic imprinting. A poltergeist is a type of psychokinesis that is generally caused unintentionally. Poltergeists are responsible for strange knocking noises in walls, the moving of objects, and even in some instances producing apparitions. In the case of poltergeist activity the energy of the primal soul is acting out on its own, generally to get someone's attention. A residual haunting, however, in which there is a reoccurring phenomenon happening, is caused by the energy produced by this soul during times of great happiness, sorrow, or trauma. This energy is absorbed by its surrounding environment and is said to be imprinted. In a way we might say that a piece of the primal soul resides within the residual haunting.

Each of our souls has its own auric emanation. Like radiation from a star, in the aura the emanation of the primal soul is the outermost layer. This is the part of your aura that is aware of your surroundings at all times and is responsible for that feeling you get when you know someone is staring at you. It can take the shape of any form you will it to be and it is in charge of collecting sensory and psychic data.

In magic you should always strive to engage each one of the souls, especially the primal soul. Not only is it the soul that is responsible for producing power but it is also the part of you that feels. It isn't concerned with what words you say in that spell but it is concerned with where you are emotionally and energetically. You should always ask yourself if you can feel your magic; if you can't then you haven't engaged the primal soul enough. Many witches focus solely on making things sound pretty (the magic of the ego soul) but don't devote time to developing a practice in which they can feel their magic. In Sacred Fires we don't move on to the next part of the ritual until everyone feels connected to the working via the primal soul. Approaching magic from this place will dramatically increase your effectiveness.

The Totemic Form of the Primal Soul

The image of the serpent is classically attributed to the deep earth. Snakes live in holes within the earth; they slither through life with their bellies in almost constant contact with land. As primitive humans saw the sweet grasses rise from the earth to provide for them, they also saw the serpent rise from the earth.

A serpent acts upon impulse only, moving from cold earth to sunny rock in search of comfort. If it is hungry, it hunts, swallowing its victims whole, often leaving nothing that is not digested. For the serpent it is all or nothing, some even dislocating their jaws in order to achieve the full consumption of prey. Beautiful and strong yet deadly, the serpent has been attributed to the mother Goddess for thousands of years. It is within the serpent's instinctive impulses that we find a sort of primitive fraternity, akin to our own primal instincts and impulses. When our primal soul feels provoked or threatened it strikes quickly out of instinct, with no rational or conscious thought, all in the name of survival.

Before it sheds its skin, the eyes of a snake will become light and look as if they have a fog in them. They retreat into a safe place and coil up in a ball, looking lifeless to those who don't know better. They also slither in and out of the ground, which is the reason snakes are said to walk between the worlds. Its consciousness leaves its body before it sheds its skin, coming back when it is time to grow, much like our consciousness becomes submersed in the underworld before returning with new perspective. We, too, shed our skins as we gain new perspectives, reaching deep into the primal self where life force is created, beckoning a new way to see the world and our environment.

For those with fear of serpents this work can be difficult and uncomfortable. In my experience you won't be able to truly receive the medicine and wisdom of an ally if it elicits fear in you. In Sacred Fires we allow our members to visualize their own version of the serpent. For some it looks like a speckled snake and to others it looks like a dragon. If you find that you are having trouble connecting to the images of the serpent do not be afraid to visualize your very own form of the serpent or to stop the practice and revisit it at a later time.

The Medicine of the Primal Soul

If something has a frequency, it has medicine. *Medicine* is a term used to describe the supplemental energies we receive through shamanic connection with various frequencies. Because our work with the souls is centered around shamanic contact we often use terms found within core shamanism to describe our experiences. The medicine of the primal soul teaches us to bring the darker aspects of our shadow self in alignment with the brighter aspects of the lighter self. The primal soul seeks harmony with its environment and in order to do this it must have internal and physical harmony.

Combining both the shadow and the lighter aspects of the primal self brings enlightenment and understanding to our true natures. This awareness must be met with love so that the root of our life force can manifest properly. Part of any act of empowerment is to embrace all of the aspects presented. We should not hold resentment for any part of ourselves because our souls are listening. Problems pertaining to the primal self seeking security or shelter truly must be met with understanding in order to remove any shame attached.

Working with the primal soul in this way teaches us to be more accepting of who we are, just as we are, and to love ourselves in spite of who or what we are. We can heal wounds by recognizing them, taking responsibility for them, and then sending unconditional love to the primal soul for them.

There are several ways to empower the primal self. One of the most natural ways is through sensuality. We often say sex releases tension and stress, allowing us to focus on things more clearly and achieve an end to the tasks at hand. Sex produces large amounts of energy that can be used to recharge and rejuvenate the primal self; the same can be said for ecstatic dancing, physical exercise, and healthy eating habits. I created the snake charming ritual with this in mind.

Snake Charming Ritual

Charming the snake will allow you to raise energy for the primal soul. Feeding your snake from time to time is an excellent way to raise vital life force and will go a long way in strengthening your other souls as well.

The ritual does require nudity. It can be done in groups, but is perfectly effective as a solitary ritual. All you need is a circle, good music you can dance to (I prefer Middle Eastern drumming or electronic dance music), and a flame. Cast a circle whatever way you see fit, and yes, the circle casting is important because you want to keep all the energy you're raising so that it can be absorbed later in the ritual. Light a candle so you can see but also because it provides important mood lighting, which will come in handy. If it is possible to do this around a fire, then by all means enjoy that privilege. Turn on the music, strip down to your birthday suit, and dance!

While you are dancing release all thoughts of how silly you may look dancing in a circle naked: The only person seeing you is yourself. When man first began there was no clothing; our oldest ancestors lived their lives in nudity. Eventually they gathered the materials needed to cover their bodies, but as nudity is our most primitive state, it is an effective way to open our primal soul. Another note on nudity in ritual: You should never be forced to be nude; however, when you are nude there is nothing to hide behind, your ego cannot tame you by putting clothes on. Many witches practice in the nude because of this.

As you are dancing connect to the primal self: Enjoy your time being naked and wild, raise the energy of the serpent and feel it wrapping around your body, writhing with snakes dancing like their master. See your primal soul take the shape of a fiery orb and become illuminated. Place your hands just below your navel and channel the energy into this orb. Send thoughts of love and healing to this orb and allow it to grow, healing any damage that has been done. Once you feel you have finished charging your primal soul, allow the fiery orb to rest back into its home, the serpent now fed, the orb now illuminated and again part of your being. Release your circle, extinguish the flame, turn off the music, and before you enter the world again, take a good hard look in the mirror—but this time, instead of seeing the ugly truths, see the beautiful truths, take three deep breaths, and ground the positive thoughts into reality. Your snake is charmed.

Basic Care and Feeding

After your first initial work with the primal soul it will be important to check in from time to time. This is because the ego soul, which will be discussed in the next chapter, has this lovely ability to consume all mental awareness and often keeps us from being aware of physical needs. Basic things like eating healthy, drinking enough fluids, and exercising can all go out the door when we are locked in the tunnel vision of the ego. Simply setting time aside each week to check in with your primal self will majorly increase your ability to strengthen it over time.

Basic things to keep an eye out for, as they might suggest issues with the primal soul, are low energy levels, dis-ease, feeling lost/helpless, and extreme cravings. If you notice yourself not moving a lot and feeling sluggish, you must get up and move! Remember, the primal self is our animal nature and animals need lots of fresh air and healthy food to eat. Properly caring for your primal self does mean you need to exercise! If, however, you find yourself in a pickle and don't know where to start the process of feeding your primal soul, begin with these meditation exercises.

Communion with the Serpent

In this exercise you will invite the spirit of serpent to join you and ask for its medicine. In shamanic cultures it is believed that all frequencies possess some sort of medicine. This medicine is a type of spiritual and energetic supplement that when given by the frequency can help us heal and empower ourselves. To obtain this medicine we must visit the totemic frequency of the serpent.

If possible this should be done outside under the cloak of a forest, in a cave, or in a basement. It is preferred to be able to totally submerse yourself in a *womby* environment like a serpent. Bring with you a candle of any color, sit comfortably with your back straight, don't hunch over, light the candle, and begin breathing three deep breaths. Go to your home frequency.

As you breathe in, allow your body to relax and remember to keep your posture. Breathe deeply, allowing your stomach to expand first, then your chest, keeping your shoulders down in a relaxed position. As you exhale through your mouth, make a "sssss" sound as if you were hissing. Again make sure you exhale completely, taking full advantage of the breath. When you feel light, calm, and grounded, silently count down from ten. As you are counting down envision pulses of light emanating from your body, cleansing and empowering the area around you. See auric steam rising from your body as if you were a light bulb burning through moisture. I call this steam-like auric radiance holy fire. Allow your holy fire to rise off your body just like steam does after you step out of a hot bath.

With your eyes shut, continue to breathe slow, calculated breaths. Visualize yourself in complete darkness with the candle you lit placed on top of a large boulder, which sits before you. All you should see is a stone with a candle burning on top of it, nothing else. Become familiar with this image and focus only on the stone and the flame. Once you feel you are comfortable and familiar with this environment, call out to Serpent: "*Serpent, I call you, I seek your medicine!*" Take a deep breath, and say again, "*Serpent, I call you, I seek your medicine!"* Follow with another deep breath: *"Serpent, I call you, I seek your medicine!"* One last deep breath, and as you release be forceful with the breath, releasing it in a controlled burst of exhalation.

See before you a serpent rise from behind the stone, coiling around the candle. This serpent is large, deep black in color with red eyes. As the serpent coils around the candle it brings with it a smell of oak-moss, musk, and deep earth, an ancient primordial smell that reminds you of your primal self. As you see it coil and smell its scent, be sure to remain calm, collected, and focused. It is within this space that you may ask Serpent to aid you in the path of empowerment. Talk to Serpent, commune with this great animal totem, inviting its knowledge and wisdom.

Once you are finished with your communication be sure to thank the spirit of Serpent for its help both in the past and the future. Again taking three deep, calculated breaths, envision the serpent uncoiling from the candle, off the stone, and back into the darkness from where it came. Take another breath, this time envisioning your holy fire being absorbed back into your body, then count from one to ten, breathing in and out between each count. Open your eyes, and with the final count of ten, use that breath to blow out the flame.

Tree of Knowledge Trance

During this meditation we will be going back to a time and place when, according to the Christian mythos, the first snake tempted the mother of humankind into eating from the tree of eternal knowledge. This story we all know well: it is said that the devil in the guise of a serpent convinced Eve to eat from the forbidden tree, and from this Eve damned all of humankind to living a life full of sin and was then banished along with her consort Adam from the garden of Eden. It is within this story that a major source of conditioning materializes: man against woman, humanity against God, God against nature, nature against man, etc. All these things surround the tree of knowledge.

In some traditions reading the Bible backwards is a practice used to release the conditioning of the church. You are doing the same in this meditation by transforming the image of your primal soul into a serpent and then visiting the garden of Eden on the astral plane. You will eat the fruit from the tree of knowledge and receive three unique and otherwise hidden personal messages of spiritual significance to you.

I recommend doing this meditation somewhere warm because it involves astral traveling and the body tends to get cold. Begin this exercise by doing the initial breath work as described in the previous exercise and visiting your home frequency. After the three deep, cleansing breaths, count again from ten to one, allowing pulses of light to come from your body, cleansing and purifying the area around you, and envision your holy fire ignite as described in the last exercise.

Breathe deeply and close your eyes. Allow the steam of the holy fire to rise as if hundreds of tiny serpents were rising from your body. Feel them as they move, and smell that ancient smell of musk and earth as you envision yourself slowly becoming the serpent. Starting at the bottom, see your feet and legs begin to fuse into what will become your tail, see your hands and arms fuse to your torso as your body elongates, see your neck become longer, and see your head transform into the head of a snake. Feel your new form, feel how the cold earth on your belly chills you, feel how your spine is no longer connecting every bone, feel how your new body moves through its environment.

See before you a hole within the earth, just big enough for your snake form to fit into, and enter it. Feel how the dry earth soon becomes cold and moist, as you travel through this hole down into the underworld. See yourself travel past roots from ancient trees, stones and mineral deposits from creation, and taste the air with your serpent tongue. Feel everything you can in your new serpent body as you travel; become comfortable with this form as you will be in it for some time to come. You see before you another hole and push through the tunnel to the edge of the opening.

As you exit the hole you find yourself in a beautiful, humid, and tropical garden, tucked away from the rest of the world. Others have been here before; this much is evident as you look around and find large stone serpent effigies. In your serpent form you slither across this trail, as large statues of great serpents mark the path on either side of you. The ground is dry yet warm, and this gives your cold blood energy that allows you to move quickly on the path.

Before you is a beautiful tree encircled by stones and you make your way to it. Above, you see that this tree has three ripe pieces of fruit just waiting for you: one apple, one pomegranate, and one fig.

You see the apple and you are hungry so you use your snake body to climb this tree. Once you reach the apple, open your mouth, dislocating the lower and upper jaws so you can swallow it whole. As you swallow this apple feel as the pressure crushes the fruit, and with your super-sensitive serpent tongue you can taste its sweet juices. As the taste of the apple fills your mouth you become suddenly aware of the true power of creation. You take within you all the knowledge of creation as the apple is absorbed into your body.

As your snake body is wrapped between the limbs and branches of the tree of knowledge see before you the second fruit: a ripe and succulent pomegranate. Use your snake body to lift off the tree and reach for the pomegranate. Swallow the purple-red fruit whole as you did before with the apple, feeling it crush in your powerful jaws, and as the juice from the seeds within spills forth from your teeth, take within you all the knowledge of death and reincarnation. Allow the fruit to move through your snake body and digest.

Looking around, you see the final piece of the fruit that the tree of knowledge offers you: the fig. This over-ripe piece of brown fruit is just right for the picking. Climb towards it, feeling the weight of the previous two pieces of fruit. Swallow the fig whole, and allow its mushy sweet, rich flavor to adjust your pallet. As you swallow the fruit, take within you all the knowledge of healing. As you begin to digest, climb down from the tree and find a safe place to rest, and coil your snake body under a sunbeam.

Allow the fruits to mix as they digest, their properties joining together. Allow your powerful senses to savor the flavors as they produce new and exciting vibrations through your body. Feel the energy pulse through you and allow any thoughts that come to you at this time to flow freely in your mind. Once you feel you are ready to return to your human body, uncoil your large snake body, and travel again upon the path that is edged with large serpent effigies. Again feel the warm tropical sun upon your snake body, giving you energy as you crawl to the hole that you entered the magical garden of Eden through. Find this hole again, and slither through it, feeling that your body is heavier now as you have recently eaten and are still digesting. Crawling through the earth, find your way back to your body. Once you find yourself there, take three deep breaths, allowing your energy to fully return with each breath, and settle into your body.

Once you have completed the trance work, allow yourself to open your eyes, and immediately journal about your experience. Remember to write about how it felt to become the serpent, how it felt to crawl through the earth into the underworld to find the garden of Eden, how the fruit from the tree tasted, and what thoughts came to you when you were coiled, digesting the fruit in the tropical sun. Over the next few days continue to journal about how you feel after the experience. You ate three fruits from the tree, giving you the spiritual knowledge of creation, reincarnation, and healing. Use this knowledge to create your own reality, one in which you are empowered; use the knowledge of reincarnation to recreate yourself, a more powerful you; and use the knowledge of healing to heal the wounds inflicted upon you by yourself and others.

Primal Soul Recap

The primal soul is the part of our being that is both physical and spiritual. It has no language to convey when it has a need but rather can only communicate to us through urges, cravings, and feelings. Connected to the deepest parts of our genetic heritage as humans, this soul is not only our connection to ancestors but to the earth itself. In the world tree model this soul is anchored in the underworld, giving us access to the subconscious and magical. Responsible for the production of life force, the energetic blood of our etheric anatomy, it acts as the powerhouse for all three souls.

Journal Topics
Describe your experience during the Snake Charming Ritual.

- How did you feel afterwards?

- How do you feel the primal soul most often cries for attention?

- What are things you can do to empower the primal soul besides the Snake Charming Ritual?

Chapter Four

The Ego Soul

The ego is the workshop where the self is made.
—Carl Jung—

Resting within the center of our torso the ego soul hangs from a thread of silk, weaving our reality. If any one of the souls could be likened to technology this one would be it. Just like a high-power computer, the ego soul processes incredible amounts of data, stores this data for later use, and executes programs and applications that use that data to construct the environment around you—or at least the way you relate to it. We construct our world based on what we know and the ego is responsible for collecting what we know.

Socially, the ego is the person people meet, your outer image, and the impression that sticks with people. The ego can be highly superficial and often requires a high level of attention throughout the day. Ego is concerned with titles, rank, social climbing, and the accumulation of power through its own special type of life force. It can be the soft-spoken old woman who is sweet and kind, or the business mogul who just couldn't be more proud of his achievements and has no problem telling you or anyone else how amazing he is.

The ego soul

The ego self is comprised of both our armor and our weaknesses. Like the Primal soul this soul has a shadow, which in our tradition is represented by the mirror. When we gaze into this mirror every flaw and detail that we mask by the ego soul can be seen. In the mirror all of the ugly truths, all of that which we couldn't bear for people to see, is reflected back to us. Sometimes, when this part of the ego soul is left to its own devices, it can wreak havoc on our lives. Instead of collecting data from the flow of the external it collects data from the deep well of the internal and can project false representations of our fears and anxieties onto our realities.

It is important for us to gaze into this mirror and see the ugly truths from time to time, because without the ugly we wouldn't be able to see the beautiful. The mirror image is sometimes the voice that tells us we are not capable, we don't deserve, and that it is never going to happen. I lovingly refer to this as the "itty-bitty-shitty-committee" and it is the cause of a lot of missed opportunities and power loss in our lives. When we react from this place of insecurity we lose control over our ego and are at its whim; we are forced into thought patterns that encourage a sense of powerlessness. This creates a need to overcompensate and in time can present itself as egotistical behavior that only serves to create dissonance in our lives.

Not only does the ego primarily make up our personalities and world view but it also is responsible for compartmentalizing and analyzing everything. As it receives information the ego absorbs it, processes it, decides what is important and what isn't, and then it logs the information somewhere in our minds or subconscious. As the primal soul instinctively knows to search for shelter and food, the ego instinctively knows to analyze and categorize. Without this ability we would not have survived the process of evolution.

The ego is a beautiful thing when it is brought in balance with the other two souls. It provides the other two with a platform from which they can express their wisdom and medicine and lays the groundwork for them to achieve their goals. Without the ego we couldn't empower our higher selves by reading books about spirituality, nor could we buy the food to feed the hungry primal soul. Because the ego has the power to build our realities it is up to us to keep it in alignment with the other two souls. Alignment will be discussed more in the next chapter.

The ego soul is connected to civilization and our humanity, which is separate and unique within the animal kingdom. It is the part of us that makes us human and not just animal. The ego connects us to one another and from those bonds we grew to build great civilizations and evolved into the dominant species on our planet. In the world tree model this soul is represented as the middle world. The keywords and terms to remember with this soul are Communication, World View, Connection, and Consciousness.

The Frequency of the Ego Soul

Shown here on piano from C4 (Middle C) to B5

In Western music theory the ego soul resonates with notes C4 (Middle C) to B5. Any note played within this range can activate and energize the ego soul, especially when chords are present. These tones can also be played to expand the aura, providing easier access to the internal energy systems.

The ego soul's frequency has the ability to create and convey multiple messages at the same time and is the only soul frequency that can freely express itself. In particular the gifts of this frequency allow for us to produce music, art, and perhaps most importantly the written word. Because of this unique ability this frequency can last forever as it is shared amongst future generations. This allows us to pass on vital information to the next set of ego souls, providing them with the platform they need in order to do their work.

In the aura, the ego soul produces the second layer as it emanates from the chest. This layer ebbs in intensity as you move throughout your day and is at its strongest when you are engaged in educational activities and deep conversation. As the frequency radiates from you it generally seeks to find harmony and informs the primal soul regarding the current harmonic state around you. The primal soul then responds emotionally or physically based on the information received from the ego.

The Totemic Form of the Ego Soul

Spider has for many cultures been a creature of interest, sometimes loved, but often feared. Spider is a powerful ally to have on your side, especially during the time when you will be working with and developing your relationship to the nature of your ego. Spider teaches us that over time we can consciously create the web instead of allowing chaos to create it for us.

———

There is a Greek myth about a woman named Arachne who was turned into a spider because of her ego. In the myth Arachne declares that she could spin wool and silk and weave them together to create a tapestry so beautiful that even the Goddess Athena herself couldn't compare. In hearing this, Athena challenges Arachne to prove what her ego has boasted. Arachne reluctantly accepts the challenge. After some time she presents her tapestry to be judged and wins the challenge!

Winning is normally a good thing; however, the topic she depicted in her tapestry was that of the inner workings and relationships of the gods themselves. Though beautiful it clearly displayed their squabbles and disagreements and this angered them. Seeing that Arachne did in fact produce a tapestry of brilliance upset Athena but seeing what it depicted upset her even more. Because of Arachne's arrogance and oversized ego, Athena turned her into a spider so she could weave the rest of her days.

In a Native American First Nations creation myth of the Hopi, Pueblo, and Navajo, it is said that Grandmother Spider wove the web of life as seven great light beings emerged from primordial darkness. She wove with her silk the doorways from which all other life emerged. As it did she attached threads of her silk to them, connecting all life to one another.

The Medicine of the Ego Soul

The medicine of the ego soul is potent and gives us a special glimpse into how we weave reality through our connections to others. Working with the ego soul in this way teaches us to be aware of how the dynamic nature of relationships affect our paths and how we affect the paths of others.

Growing up in Ohio, a state that has over two hundred burial mounds from the ancient Adena society, the precursor for the Hopewell traditions, Native American myths and beliefs were an early addition to my spiritual life. As a child I went to pow-wows and lodges, and later I would become spiritually invested in a particular burial site, the Great Serpent Mound in Adams County, Ohio, the world's largest snake effigy. While not directly descended from the First Nations people myself, I have found a deep resonance with/between their spiritual systems and my own. The exercise involving Grandmother Spider found here has been elaborated and adapted from the original stories shared with me as a child. The version here came to me during trance one night at a ritual and I present it to you as I do in Sacred Fires. I have found this deeply powerful experience to be an invaluable tool for soul development. What you read here is presented with respect for the people of First Nations from whom this mythological creatrix comes.

For this exercise you will only need a quiet environment. Find yourself seated comfortably and begin your initial breath work by taking three deep breaths and at the end of each deep breath announce to your body that you are entering a meditative trance state. Go to your home frequency. Breathe slow and deep, focusing on holding the charge of energy after you inhale, only allowing energy that carries a negative charge to be released as you exhale. At this point you may perform various breathing techniques, such as the four-fold breath, which is a simple practice of breathing in for four counts, holding for four counts, exhaling for four counts, and holding again for four counts. Practice this breath work in repetition until you have found the internal place of cosmic stillness and you feel as though your holy fire is burning steady and bright. Continue to breathe and as you do, allow your holy fire to grow and eventually encompass everything around you in pure white light.

See before you a black spider made of the absence of light but notice that within her abdomen there is a spool of silken thread that is made of light. Breathe slow and deep and allow the image of the ancient spider to meet you where you sit. This spider is older than anything you have ever known. You are not frightened, not threatened, simply fixated on the potential knowledge you can gain from her.

In the air before you, draw the sigil of the ego soul as pictured at the beginning of this chapter with the same absence of color that the great spider before you is composed of. Allow the sigil to hover in front of you and place your hands on either side of the sigil, then open your solar plexus chakra to receive the sigil. As you absorb the sigil into your solar plexus see that you are unlocking a doorway from within that leads to the very center of your ego soul. As you unlock this sacred door notice that the great spider before you begins to move closer in curiosity. Say aloud, "Great Spider, what name are you called by?" and hear the response: "I am she who stole the Sun in my silken web, I am she who wove the doorways of space and time so creation may spring forth from nothingness, I am she who weaves the threads of all things, I am Grandmother Spider." Take another slow and steady deep breath and allow Grandmother Spider to enter the doorway to your ego soul.

Grandmother Spider now resides within the walls of your ego soul as you still burn bright with holy fire. At this time give over that which you have been concerned about, perhaps projects that you have had a hard time completing, relationships that need to be healed, awareness that you have struggled to find. Give all these issues over to Grandmother Spider and lay them before her as if to make an offering. Look into her eight eyes and say, "Grandmother Spider, I have not found peace on these matters, show me how I too may weave reality with strong silken threads."

One by one discuss with Grandmother Spider the subjects that you have lain before her. The dialogue will be internal as if to ponder over the subjects with your inner voice. Take slow and steady breaths and, once finished processing the dialogue, see the spool of silken thread made of light begin to come forth from your own solar plexus, connecting you to all that you had spoken of with Grandmother Spider. Breathe slow and deep and see your holy fire burst in a blaze as if an exploding star has gone supernova. Particles of light emanate from all directions, each beam a silken thread connecting one part of the cosmos to the next. Sit in observance of this event, looking around you and taking in as much as possible.

As you come to the realization that it is time to complete this holy act of connectedness allow yourself to yet again take three deep breaths and announce to all who might dwell within this place that you are about to exit and come back to your own reality, taking with you the power of Grandmother Spider's silken threads made of light. Place your hands over your solar plexus chakra and say, "Grandmother Spider, I make space for you within, bring me the awareness I seek in all matters, bring me the ability to connect all missing pieces so that my path may be strong.

Bring to me the knowledge of foresight, insight, and inspiration. Help me to feel the tugs on the silken thread. Together may my words be gold and my tongue silver!"

Initiate a cycle of four four-fold breaths (see chapter 9 for this technique if you are not familiar). Begin to breathe in and reabsorb all the light of your holy fire back to its place of origin. Reabsorb all you have given and all that has been given to you, and on the final set of four counts, return to your body once more. Notice the feeling of your clothes against your skin, the feeling of the air that surrounds you, the sound of silence, and the taste within your mouth. Open your eyes.

Be sure to journal about your experience and how the issues and subjects you discussed with Grandmother Spider unfold in the coming days. You may also draw the ego soul sigil on a candle and light it during your time journaling or during any time as an act of reconnection to Grandmother Spider. I find that revisiting her from time to time as I work towards goals helps me understand the best course of action to take when achieving them, in some cases finding that other magic are necessary.

The idea that there are threads of energy that connect all living things is not strictly a Native American belief but can also be seen in Voudoo, Core Shamanism, and many other traditions. In Huna (a traditional Polynesian spirituality) these threads are called *aka threads* and are the lines in which energy and thought travel from one being to the next. In my own work I have found that these threads of energy do exist and magical people are quite familiar with them, whether we know it or not! In Sacred Fires we refer to them as *astral threads.*

Astral threads are like fiber-optic wires that relay spiritual information and energy in the blink of an eye. When we do spell work it travels down astral threads that are attached to all beings with which our work is either directly or indirectly associated. We don't need to cast a spell in order to have an energetic effect on an astral thread. We merely need to think about that person in order to make a connection to them via the astral thread highway.

By working with astral threads you will be able to sense changes in your relationships and connections to people. This includes the personality changes, motives, intentions, and level of attention from people around you. As one might be able to imagine this can come in quite handy in all sorts of situations. When cultivating power we must develop awareness of these astral threads as they can provide invaluable information about the current state of our reality. Astral threads are already part of the universe; we merely need to understand how to identify and work with them in order to start the process of conscious creation.

Weaving Astral Threads

In order to develop an awareness of astral threads we first must see the cords as they exist around us now. For this quick exercise all you will need is a piece of paper and some colored pencils or pens. In the center of the piece of paper write down your name, then at the top right corner write the name of a parent, on the bottom right corner write the name of a close friend, on the bottom left corner write the name of your boss (if you work for yourself just write the word CLIENTS), and on the top left corner write the name of your child, pet, or another friend or coworker.

Over the course of five days you are going to take a deep look into how you are connected to these people and how these people are connected to each other. On the first day tune in to your home frequency. Close your eyes and see an empty room where only you and the parent you selected stand. Pay attention to as much detail as possible as you are visualizing the two of you standing in this room. Ask yourself what color their eyes are, how are they standing, what color is their hair? Do the very best you can in regards to making the most true-to-life replica of them during the first part of this meditation. This will also exercise your creative visualization muscles, which are vital to the practice of witchcraft.

As you are both standing in this empty room notice that there is a thread that connects you both at the solar plexus. See this thread and by following your intuition become aware of the color of this thread. Is it blue, is it green, black perhaps, or a soft pink? Does this color make you comfortable, uncomfortable, afraid, curious? Ask yourself all of these questions. Take three deep breaths and come back to your conscious state. On the piece of paper draw a thread connecting your name to your parent's name in whatever color you saw it. If you see one that is multicolored, thick in some places, thinner in others, be sure to include this in your drawing.

When I do this exercise I use the following list of color correspondences to determine what the presented colors say about my relationships. This list can also be used to determine the frequencies of auric energy.

- **Clear/White:** Inspired, connected, aware, aligned, illuminated.

- **Gray:** Depression, anxiety, dis-ease.

- **Black:** Negative, harmful intentions, low frequency.

- **Gold:** Success, sovereignty, feeling as though they are on the "right path," talent, potential.

- **Silver:** Easily adaptable, cunning, quick-thinking, high states of energy, idealistic.

- **Bronze:** Generosity, willingness to help, co-creative, humanitarian.

- **Copper:** Love alchemy, soul-searching, honorific, soft aggression.

- **Pewter:** Deep depression, dark thoughts, possible mental illness.

- **Purple:** Responsibility, sovereignty, wisdom, respect, leadership.

- **Indigo:** Artistic, creative, emotionally deep, inspiration from subconscious.

- **Blue:** Fast-thinking, mental, intelligence, logic, willful.

- **Dark Blue:** Suspicion, assumption, untrusting.

- **Green:** Harmony, equality, strength. (Can mean sickness if dull and pea-like in color.)

- **Dark Green:** Jealousy, greed, strife, toxicity.

- **Yellow:** Creativity, searching for connection/harmony, idealism, kind, loving.

- **Orange:** Physically strong, vitality, physical in nature, pride.

- **Dark Orange:** Prideful, lack of empathy; may not be intellectually driven.

- **Red:** Passion, ambition, high sexual energy, leadership, aggressive approach.

- **Dark Red:** Materialism, anger, lust, deeper or older issues.

- **Pink:** Love for self and others, healing, successful, stubborn.

- **Brown:** Selfishness, close-minded, immovable.

Continue to do this exercise for the next few nights until you have gone through the other three names on the paper. Again, be sure to pay attention to detail each time you are recreating their image during meditation.

On the fifth night you will visualize the empty room but this time you will see all of the subjects standing around you. One by one visualize the threads that connect them to you. Once completed you should see four people (or three people and an animal) standing around you in this room with four very different and separate threads attached to you. Notice that as each one is connected to you and that you, like a link in a chain, connect them to each other. Now that all of you are connected to each other, look to see if the cords have changed. Did they stay the same? There is no right or wrong answer to this, you simply need to be aware of the threads and if changes do occur in order to document them.

This opens a brand-new doorway for most witches as we can now see what the connection between you and another person is or perhaps your connection to a group of people. When used to build group mind this exercise makes for an excellent meditation for covens or working groups.

If you wish to correct the energies between you and another person, take out the drawing you made, enter your home frequency, and then visualize the thread(s) shooting out from you to the other person(s). You can send healing energy through the astral thread at any time or perhaps even envision ivy wrapping itself around the thread to protect it. Be creative, using plant spirit allies or crystal energies to act as supplements for the threads. For those of you who are Reiki-attuned you can send Reiki down this thread to heal and cleanse the connection between you and someone else, or as an act of long-distance healing.

You may be asking yourself what you should do if you perceive during your meditation that there is something wrong with an astral thread. Perhaps the thread is sickly looking, appears to be poisoned, or the thread feels toxic. There is a way of "cutting" the astral thread if you feel it is beyond repair. In Hoodoo there is a practice called "cut-and-clear" in which the practitioner cuts the thread that connects the practitioner to another person. This is usually done when we feel the person is abusive or when we feel that they are truly no good for us. I have done this to break away from coven members who went crazy, from ex-lovers who just couldn't take no, and have recommended it for people who are in recovery and need a clean break from those who may influence them to continue negative habitual behavior.

Part of what makes this spell work is that the person performing it truly must be ready to let go. If you were to do this for a friend so they can get away from a love gone wrong, make sure they are ready for the thread to be cut and spend some time with them explaining how the concept of astral threads works.

The Cut-and-Clear Spell

For the cut-and-clear spell you will need a piece of black string that is no less than thirteen inches (33 cm) in length, a pair of scissors, two candles (preferably male or female figural candles of corresponding sex), cut-and-clear condition oil (see recipe below) or lemon oil (substitute lemon grass oil or lemon juice), and if possible personal objects such as hair, business cards, or pictures of both parties. If you are performing the cut-and-clear with the intention of cutting the ties to a habit or cycle, then you would want a personal object that symbolizes that which is to be cut and cleared (for example, if the spell is to break a habit such as smoking, then a cigarette would be the appropriate item used).

Cut-and-Clear Condition Oil

1 part black pepper oil *(Piper nigrum)*

2 parts lemon oil *(Citrus limon)*

2 parts eucalyptus oil *(Eucalyptus obliqua)*

2 parts tea tree oil *(Melaleuca alternifolia)*

3 parts carrier oil (olive, grapeseed, sweet almond, etc.)

Begin the spell by writing the names of each person on the two candles. Hold and charge each candle individually by placing your thoughts and assertions about each person or habit/cycle into the candles, say your final words about the matter to each of the candles, and then light them.

Allow the candles to burn down and, while doing so, tie a knot in the center of the black cord or string. Take the cut-and-clear condition oil, lemon oil, or lemon juice, and dress the cord or string with it. Be sure to cover the cord from tip to tip with the oil or juice. Dip the first tip of the cord in the candle that represents you or the person that you are casting for in the corresponding candle. With the melted wax on the tip attach the personal item that was chosen to represent you or the person you're casting for. Follow this same process on the other tip of the cord with the candle and personal item of the person or habit/cycle intended to cut and clear. Allow the candles to continue to burn until completely out.

Place your left hand over the tip of the cord that symbolizes you or the person you are casting for and your right hand over the person or habit/cycle you are cut-and-clearing. Take three deep breaths, exhaling over the knot in the middle. Take a second to collect your thoughts and when you are ready, speak the following words with authority: "Be ye man or beast, magic or love, be ye from the heavens or from hell, I cut the knot that binds us. Be ye oaths from my naive tongue, promises not kept or songs that remain unsung, I clear the lines that bind us." Dress your scissors with the cut-and-clear condition oil or substitute and cut straight through the knot in the center of the cord or string. When you are finished, bury the remnants that correspond to you in your backyard or in a flowerpot in your home. Bury the remnants that correspond to what you cut-and-cleared in the trash or bury them near rushing water.

Basic Care and Feeding

I have noticed that the spider energy of the ego soul is much more complex than it leads on. It connects the higher God soul (see the next chapter) and the primal soul together. In exploring this we must be very certain that we are feeding this sacred arachnid the best nourishment we can. In doing so we can have the strength and life force to weave a better and more effective form of reality, one more suited to our needs as practitioners of magic.

This also means that we cannot separate our spiritual practices from our mundane life. To truly gain the empowerment from this type of work we must always see ourselves as one working unit that is capable of performing many tasks at once. You can be a full-time mother, factory worker, PTA sponsor, and witch at the same time! I was lucky enough to learn years ago that I am a witch full-time and that even simple, mundane things like singing a child to sleep or cleaning the house can be a magical practice. The trick is to approach the mundane with a magical and spiritual mind. This is just another way to allow the weaving spider within to create a reality suited best for you. If you look for excuses to use your magic in your everyday life you will find plenty of reasons to. We often get so caught up in the web that we forget we are the ones making it.

I also find that offensive frequency adjustments are much easier than defensive magic is to perform. We can make subtle changes through spell work like protection and warding magic to keep us from receiving unwanted negative energy from threads connected to us. Remember, astral threads exist between you and anyone you have ever met. Sometimes we end up on the receiving end of some not-so-friendly energy and that can cause a lot of problems. When you make offensive shifts to your frequency you can shield yourself from unwanted energy like the evil eye, low-frequency energy attachment, and even hexes. One such way is to perform the amber spider spell.

The Amber Spider

For all intents and purposes I like to use amber when working with the ego soul. Amber is actually the sap from prehistoric trees that has hardened over thousands if not millions of years. Amber has been prized by many cultures over time for its deep brilliant color and witches have used it for protection all over the world. Amber is a stone that is not quite a stone, just like you are an ego but not quite an ego. Amber is known for its ability to trap insects, debris, and other life forms, which then fossilizes them. Once something is caught in the running sap it is near impossible to free itself, just as it is almost impossible to escape the web of a spider.

Amber is also a stone that activates the solar plexus chakra, which is the chakra in charge of our own inner light. When the solar plexus chakra is activated it projects things into our reality; thus it is the vibration that echoes into our life and work. Notice how when you are feeling down and depressed you tend to slump over, cutting off the solar plexus from shining like the brilliant golden yellow ball of sacred fire that it is.

When you are confident your shoulders tend to push back, exposing your chest and your solar plexus, projecting massive amounts of energy into your environment. (For this reason alone, posture should be something you refine in your magical practices. The more you open and project, the stronger your magic will become.)

Amber is readily available from most rock shops and metaphysical stores. I suggest making an amulet with the amber so that you may wear it around your neck and it can be close to your solar plexus. Take the piece of amber and hold it in your right palm, then lift your left palm up into the air and breathe. Focus on energy coming through your receptive left hand and traveling down to your right hand, which projects the energy back. The idea is to allow the energy to flow through you, and as it exits the body it flows through the amber and then is reabsorbed back into the body. Place it at your chest and once again breathe. Visualize a golden yellow disk spinning within your chest just at the solar plexus and allow the energy that you are drawing from the universe to flow through the amber and into the golden sun of the solar plexus.

As you are doing this place both hands on your solar plexus and recite the following enchantment: "An eye to each direction, an eye to above, an eye for below, an eye for within, and an eye for all unknown. Two legs spinning, six legs weaving, connecting all connected to me. Spider, spider, weaving spider, I feel every pulse, I feel all movement within. Spider, spider, weaver of all, I hunger for life, I hunger for things both great and small!" Envision the spider within you acknowledging this enchantment and see it stop its weaving and become still as it hangs from the great cave within. Allow the energy that is beaming through the amber to shine upon the spider as if warming it in the filtered sun. See your spider change colors as it absorbs this light, see it writhe in pleasure, extending its legs as if stretching. As it absorbs the light allow yourself to feel the effects of this as well. Your very own reality is now being charged with amber energy.

See the spider itself turn into amber, charged now with the power of resistance, protection, healing, and mystery. Once you feel that the work is done, allow your spider to sink back into your chest, now warm and strong, and allow your solar plexus chakra to close. Take three deep breaths of grounding and place the amber somewhere special or carry it with you as a talisman.

Ego Soul Recap

The ego soul is the part of our being that is responsible for creating our realities through its complex web of woven frequencies. It is the only soul that can communicate directly to other beings and is the only soul that is capable of language. The ego is responsible for interpreting the messages sent to it by the other souls and is the only soul that can compartmentalize and process direct information. It is anchored in the "realness" of the moment and is associated with the middle world. In magic it especially loves spoken word and the arts.

Journal Topics

• How do you notice your ego soul manifest in your life?

• What parts of your life do you find yourself constantly trying to organize and what do you think that means about you?

- Which astral threads felt weakest when you did the exercise in this chapter? Is there anything you can do to help repair them?

Chapter Five

The Holy One
and Alignment

You are a Divine Being. An all-powerful Creator. You are a Deity in jeans and a t-shirt, and within you dwells the infinite wisdom of the ages and the sacred creative force of All that is, will be, and ever was.
—Anthon St. Maarten—

The higher self (or Holy One, Holy Soul) is that which is connected to divinity and is the birthplace of your unique spirituality and personal gnosis. The Holy One doesn't have an instinct to seek comfort and love like the serpentine primal self, nor does it have the drive for control and separateness like the ego soul, but instead it is concerned with the drive to manifest the evolution of the soul. The Holy One wants us to be aware of our true potential and oftentimes this can cause issues within the very paradigm of self.

We see the higher self as the spark of divinity that lies within each of us. It guides us through life and absorbs the spiritual knowledge of the cosmos. It is from the higher soul that we draw down enlightenment. In times of need or stress we can access this higher part of our being to give us understanding as to the road ahead. When we see a sacred image of a saint that has a golden halo around its head we see the artistic representation of the higher soul illuminating the mind. You will have experienced this Holy Soul in action during moments of spiritual awakening. Think back to an amazing ritual experience or the first time you felt the Witch Power awaken inside you. That high you felt at the time—yeah, that is the higher soul doing what it does best!

The Holy Soul

My first experience with the Holy Soul was during my first circle casting. I was a young solitary witch lighting candles in my room in secret and I had read about this really cool thing that witches did called casting a circle. Being a real witch myself I decided it was time to do this! As I cleared the space and cast the circle for the first time I felt energy like never before coming from me! I rode the wave of energy and tried to feel all of it. I just sat in the circle, not moving, and allowed myself to feel the full extent of the experience. As I look back at that moment knowing what I know now, I see it as the first time I ever felt the energy of my higher self beaming back at me. The circle provided a barrier from which the energy bounced back instead of just radiating off of me and into the night air. That moment of connection guided me to deeper mysteries within the craft.

Describing the Holy One is as difficult as describing a newborn nebula. Brilliant and shining, made of something ancient and timeless, there just aren't enough words. It is by this soul that we are directed to our higher calling. In Sacred Fires we believe the higher soul holds the blueprint to our existence and the roadmap to our destiny. Its divine nature is an emanation of God Herself and connects us to something much bigger than humanity.

Keywords to remember with this soul are Divinity, Destiny, Karma, and Stewardship.

The Frequency of the Holy Soul

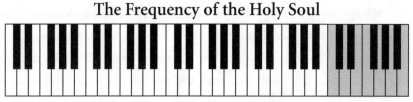

Shown here on piano from C6 (High C) to B7

The frequency of the higher self resonates the highest of the three souls and in Western music theory harmonizes with notes C6 (High C) through B7. Soprano voices can sing these notes, and when used in harmonic therapies these tones will cause lower frequencies to release from the energy body. I have found that in my work these notes can also (when softly played in chordal progressions in long durations over time) increase psychic sensitivity.

This is the part of the soul that transcends the body and ego after physical death. With all of your karmic momentum, past-life knowledge, and soul wisdom, your higher self leaves the body and moves on. On rare occasions these souls can get stuck and become ghosts that haunt our homes, cemeteries, churches, and just about everywhere else. Though an actual haunting is rare, when this soul becomes altered from its original frequency it can stay in location for quite a long time.

On an even rarer occasion these higher souls can be corrupted by traumatic experiences and their life force becomes twisted. The natural frequency of the higher self becomes so altered that it loses its ability to resonate at a high level, and without the ego's ability to process, it cannot fix the issue on its own. These are what become the demonic entities many report encountering. With a history of war, slavery, and driving indigenous people from their homelands, there are plenty of reasons these entities might exist. If you ever encounter one it is best not to engage it unless you are trained to do so. In the worst-case scenarios I would recommend working with the land spirits to help move the energy, along with a healthy dose of Archangel Michael.

Through this soul's frequency we can access inner mysteries and other realms. Spiritual and occult sciences are first inspired within this soul and then developed by the ego soul. Some shamanic practices bypass the ego soul and connect the Holy One with the primal self, producing ecstatic states. Through these states, symbols and messages are given and a language unique to the two emerges. During states of ecstasy the primal soul is guided by the higher soul to act and the ego is silenced.

In the world tree model the higher self is related to the over-world. It mimics the over-world's imagery of leaves and branches by soaking up the rays of divine light from the gods. In the aura it emanates closest to the body, though extends through the other two layers when receiving some psychic information.

Those familiar with the chakra system might see the Holy Soul as being made up of the third-eye and the crown chakras. Our spirit guides, which will be discussed a little later in the book, also commune both with and through our higher souls. Your spirit guide speaks directly to your higher self and your higher self speaks directly to your spirit guide. This allows for your guide to understand the life processes that are unfolding around you. These two have a relationship all their own. Your spirit guides will act as a middleman for information from the higher soul when we are vibrationally incapable of receiving it directly.

The Totemic Form of the Holy Soul

The owl represents wisdom in many cultures and in ancient Greece was the companion of the Goddess of wisdom, Athena. In Hindu tradition Lakshmi, the Goddess of wealth and prosperity (both physical and spiritual), light, and wisdom, is commonly seen riding an owl when not in the company of her consort, Vishnu. Lakshmi gives liberation from the cycle of life and death just as our higher soul carries the wisdom of all lives to the next.

I came across one of the most beautiful mythologies about owls from a little-known ethnic group of people from Japan and parts of Russia called the Ainu a few years ago. The Ainu are a group of people who have faced much political persecution similar to the struggles of the Rom people of Europe.

The Ainu are animists, which means they believe that all living things have a soul. They take great care to honor the spirits of their food sources like deer, game birds, and most influential within their culture, fish. This small group of people have held a very strong connection to the land even throughout the political changes brought on by World War II and the collapse of the government brought on by the changing of hands.

From these people we are given a fantastic mythological story surrounding a beloved Owl God who comes to an Ainu village and brings with him prosperity. As we explore the world of magic and look for the hidden veins of it all around us, we must not forget that there is much more than meets the Western eye.

The Song the Owl God Sang Himself[2]

The Owl God soared on the winds of a winter night, swooping through the beams of the moonlight and singing his song: "Silver droplets fall, fall around me. Golden droplets fall, fall around me." Eventually he settled on a branch that overlooked an Ainu village, where children played with toy bows and arrows on a beach blanketed with snow. He sat perched, observant of his surroundings. He was no stranger there; the village was once a favorite place for him to visit.

---

2   Adapted from a traditional Ainu myth, "The Song the Owl God Sang," translated by Chiri Yukie (2013, BJS Books). See bibliography for full citation.

As he looked around he saw that many changes had happened in the village since last he saw it. Many of those who were once poor were now wealthy and those who were once blessed with wealth were now poor. Seeing this he began to take a renewed interest in all that he saw.

The sounds of laughing children playing with their bows got his attention, and being a playful spirit himself, he jumped from the branch. Catching the air in his wings he flew to where the children played. As he flew over the children on the beach, he sang his song: "Silver droplets fall, fall around me. Golden droplets fall, fall around me." The children, who at first seemed to be in awe of the owl, soon began to shoot at him with their arrows.

Dodging arrows as they flew towards him in the night sky, the Owl God took amusement from the children as they shot at him. This went on for some time and the Owl God continued to sing his song: "Silver droplets fall, fall around me! Golden droplets fall, fall around me!"

A little boy, obviously poorer than the other boys, grabbed his bow and arrow and aimed towards the singing owl. He was dressed in pauper clothes, with soot on his face, and he held a wooden bow with bent wooden arrows. As he aimed the other boys took notice. They began to yell at him and tell him that if they had no luck with their metal arrows then he most certainly would have no luck with his old wooden ones. They started to spit on the boy and kicked him as they laughed. This saddened the Owl God as he flew above them.

The Owl God took pity on the boy and swooped down to give them a show. In an instant the Owl God and the pauper made eye contact and the Owl God knew that this boy was from a noble family, at the very least in heart. "Silver droplets fall, fall around me! Golden droplets fall, fall around me," the Owl God sang as he dove. The boy aimed his arrow towards the singing owl and shot.

The Owl God swooped right into the path of the arrow and it lodged in his stomach. As the god fell from the heavens the little boy ran to grab him, knowing that he had done something horrible in that instant. He scooped the owl up in his arms and the other boys chased after him, continuing to yell and taunt him. They began to kick him and spit on him again, this time kicking harder and cursing his name. With tears in his eyes the boy held on to the owl and curled his body around the dying owl to protect its body.

The boy jumped up and ran from the other little boys who continued to chase him for some time. Crying loudly and screaming for help, the little boy took the owl to his home. The little boy's parents came out of their hut to see what all the noise was about, and upon looking at the boy with the bloody owl they fell to their knees, begging for forgiveness. They wept as they came to their feet, knowing full well who the owl really was, and ushered the little boy into the hut. "Owl God, great lord, I plead for your forgiveness! I was once a wealthy man and now am a pauper. To bring you, such a great lord, into my home is but an honor!" the poor man said.

Once in the hut they declared to their lord that they would mend him and make him strong once again. Placing him safely next to the fire, in their best bed, they bandaged him up and went to sleep. Aware of the kindness the family had given him, the Owl God looked around the humble hut to see that this poor family was truly making the best of their circumstances. They had shrines set up and were true to their faith.

He watched them sleep and whispered, "Silver droplets fall, fall around me! Golden droplets fall, fall around me." And as they slept he flapped his wings and great treasures appeared. Golden lamps and jewels hung from every ceiling, the finest rugs replaced the tattered cloths on the floor of the hut. The Owl God sang, "Silver droplets fall, fall around me! Golden droplets fall, fall around me."

With a twist of his neck the small hut became a grand house with every room filling with jewels and the most beautiful gifts. Clothes and altars of gold and fine silk, all that were much finer than those of the rich in their village, sprang forth as he sang. The Owl God looked upon the sleeping family who were unaware of the changes that were made and smiled, knowing that he was rewarding the truly kind and faithful.

In the morning when the family woke up they found that their home was now a lavish building full of the finest things. The Owl God sat perched above the fireplace smiling and singing, "Silver droplets fall, fall around me! Golden droplets fall, fall around me."

The father fell to his knees and began to pray to the Owl God. "I thought it was all but a dream but I wake to find that you have bestowed my family with the finest of dress and treasures! Oh, great Owl God, we will hold a great party in your honor!"

The family rushed in preparation for the party to honor the Owl God. The little boy went to all the houses in the village and word spread quickly of the great changes that had taken place in the poor man's house. The little boy's mother cooked the finest food for the party and there was much merriment in the great house that day.

That night all the village showed up to see if the stories were true. Surprised and awe-struck at the lavish house and the fine food, the people of the village all joined together, the rich and the poor, the old and the young, in celebration of the Owl God's gifts. The Ainu sang to him his own song: "Silver droplets fall, fall around me! Golden droplets fall, fall around me!"

This story reminds us that if we are able to seek alignment with the highest vibrations we will be rewarded. The strong spirit who is true to its highest good will always be gifted with treasures beyond expectation. In this myth those gifts are shared even with the people who treated them badly. Like the Owl God's, these precious gifts fall like gold and silver from the wings of our Holy One.

The Holy One is capable of leading us to incredible things in our lives if we listen and seek harmony with it. Some believe that you must be poor and reject the material in order to obtain enlightenment, but the Holy Soul wants nothing more than for us to thrive. Like in the myth of the Owl God, if we seek its favor we will be rewarded. In my life I have learned if I am truly passionate about something my Holy One will find a way to make sure I can make a living doing it. This obviously comes with a lot of work and discipline but I have found power forged by the opportunities the Holy One has guided me to.

The Medicine of the Holy Soul

Owls have a reputation for being spirit heralds from the other side. Sometimes owls were seen as messengers warning of impending death; in other cultures owls were messengers of wisdom from enchanted mountains. We can work with the owl as a totem to achieve a greater understanding of our own purpose and path from all worlds. Having this knowledge is a tool that we greatly need as we walk along the path and search for a better understanding as to "Why?" and "What for?" Checking in with owl from time to time will help you to get a grip on the concepts of your own destiny, and using the totem of the great owl as the placeholder within the temple of the higher self allows you to move beyond the serpentine desires of the body, the sticky web of reality, and connect to the divine purpose of your being. I have found that once you work with the owl you begin to see that all you do has purpose and the winding road we walk on doesn't feel so daunting.

Meeting the Owl

For this introduction you merely need to allow yourself a quiet place and a comfortable seated position. Taking slow and steady breaths, allow yourself to focus on the points of stillness and silence that are at the beginning and end of each breath. As you breathe always remember to inhale, filling your stomach first, then your diaphragm, and lastly your lungs. Keep your shoulders down and free of tension. As you breathe become consciously aware of your internal world. Notice thoughts and urges but instead of engaging them, simply acknowledge them and then let them go for later examination.

Search through this internal world until you have reached the darkness that is within. Here in the darkness you are void of all light and allow the darkness to be within all of your senses, all of your thoughts, all of your urges. Within this darkness allow yourself to step forward, and even though you may not be able to see what is beneath you, know that as you step into the darkness your feet will land on solid ground. As you continue to walk, notice that before you is an elevator and as the door opens you step in.

Once inside the elevator push the button that is marked with an arrow pointing up. Feel your body become heavy as the elevator travels from its current floor to its destination. Remember to breathe slow and deep. Allow the elevator to stop and as the doors open find yourself stepping out into a room covered in star maps and constellations. As you enter this room notice that in the center, perched and silent, a beautiful owl awaits.

Move towards the owl and as you do so notice that it begins to open its eyes and welcomes you. It is here that you may ask anything, for this is the owl of your Holy Soul. The owl holds the blueprint of your life and the map of your journey. You might ask it questions such as, "What do I do next?" or "How do I…" Whatever it may be, ask it! Spend time communicating with the owl, and when you feel ready, thank this owl and go back to the elevator door.

Enter the elevator and as you do so, push the down button. Feel your body become weightless as the elevator descends back into your inner world. As the elevator stops, see the door open once again and step out into the darkness within. Continue to walk and as you walk forward, perceive your stream of thoughts and day-to-day memories flashing around you. Take three deep breaths and open your eyes.

Owl Pellets

When an owl eats, it swallows its food whole. This is usually a mouse or a frog; however, it is unique in that the owl, after eating its prey, will regurgitate any bones or fur that cannot be digested. This pellet can be used to collect negative energy that you may be carrying and remove it from your energy body. All the things that keep you from obtaining your inner wisdom or perhaps lie between you and the end of a long personal struggle can be collected in the pellet and then banished.

We are Gods, and like any God you have the option to accept or reject any offering that is made at your temple! I cannot stress this enough! When you receive negative or malicious energies into your energy body you are unknowingly poisoning yourself.

Using an actual owl pellet to collect negative energy is an extremely effective way to collect and purge your energy body of negative energy without the literal act of purging. When you get the owl pellet, allow it to be charged on your altar for a few days if possible before using it. This will allow it to sync with your energy prior to this simple ritual. From this point you can go a couple of different directions.

First, you can take a seven-inch by seven-inch square of aluminum foil and sprinkle lavender petals onto the foil, place the owl pellet (yes, it should already be foiled at the time of purchase) onto the center of the foil, then proceed to wrap it up. Rub the double-foil-wrapped pellet on your body before meditation, visualizing it acting as a magnet for the negative energies you have collected. You can use this several times, but when you feel like its job is done, bury it in the ground. For spells like this, I like to bury the remnants in a graveyard or on holy ground. What is not food for us is food for something else!

Second, you can place the owl pellet in a small charm bag (mojo bag, putsi, spell pouch) and fill the rest of the bag with herbs such as oak moss, patchouli, rue, peat, dried pitcher plant, or sage. Be sure to stuff it full as if stuffing a pillow. You might also add to the bag stones such as citrine, pyrite, lodestone, magnetic sand, or a discarded magnet from the kitchen fridge to help attract the energy. Tie the bag up and place it near your front door, or in a high traffic place. The bag will collect negative juju as people walk into your home or business.

Once a week you simply need to cleanse the bag by smudging it, spraying Florida water on it, or giving it Reiki. If you want the bag to be self-cleansing, then fill the bag no less than one-third of the way with citrine chunks during its construction. If you go this route be sure to "feed" the bag as much as possible by taking it down, bathing it in Florida water, whiskey, rum, wine, or vodka—spirits like to be fed spirits! You can also use this bag the same way you would with the pellet in option one.

The third option with this is to paint the pellets black and bury them around your property. This will act as a magical filtration system for your land as it will constantly be absorbing energies and grounding energies simultaneously. A variation on this is to place the painted pellet in a small mason jar with pieces of black tourmaline (protection), tiger's eye (warding), and fill the jar halfway up with whiskey or rum, then spit in it. Tighten the lid and light a candle on top of the jar and say the following spell: "Spirits that watch over me, aid this spell as I direct all bad straight to hell. Confuse its course, go to this jar, and so shall it be from wide and far!" After the candle burns down, bury the bottle spell in some place sacred to you.

Basic Care and Feeding

Working with the owl as a totem will only advance your connectedness to your higher self and as such will help you to seek greater wisdom and understanding of the world around you. I find that working with the owl spirit helps me when I need to know the ultimate and highest truth in a situation. We go through life only being able to perceive what we are told; however, there is an ultimate truth in every situation and sometimes it is important to find this truth so that we may act in the best interest of ourselves, our investments, and our highest good.

There are several crystals that aid in psychic awareness and "opening the communication of the higher self." I would add that in my experience all crystals bring messages and energies into our lives, but some crystals will not harmonize with your frequency as well as others. This depends on the person. Stones like wulfenite work wonders for me in this capacity; however, when my friend uses it she feels nothing.

I recommend taking time with this one and really feeling energies out before making any rushed decisions. I recommend clear quartz, angel aura quartz, celestite, aqua aura quartz, seraphinite, or selenite when working with the higher self. These crystals carry a wide ray of vibrations that are useful for this process and are easily found at your local shop.

When charging crystals for higher soul development be sure to take your time, especially if this is your first use with them. Meditate with them to unlock their hidden energies and develop a rapport with them. It allows you to establish a relationship with the crystal and it gives you the opportunity to tune in to the crystal's frequency.

Making a seraphinite gem elixir is an excellent way to utilize crystal energies before meditation or trance work with the higher self. Fill a glass jar two-thirds of the way with distilled or spring water, carefully drop the piece of seraphinite into the water, cover it, and then let it sit in the moonlight and sunlight for twenty-four hours to three days. Once the water has been charged in this way, carefully take the stone out and then drink the water. A word of caution: Never use toxic gems or minerals when making elixirs—always research!

Holy Soul Recap

The Holy One is the seat of the divine inside each of us. Through it we connect to our spirit allies and we receive the etheric wisdom to move on and grow. Resting inside this soul is all of the information that pertains to our life experiences and karma and it carries this information to our next incarnation. Throughout our lives it gently guides us to moments where we can achieve passion and ecstasy and it wants nothing but for us to thrive and to grow as much as possible in each life. Its only goal for us is to discover the living God inside.

Alignment

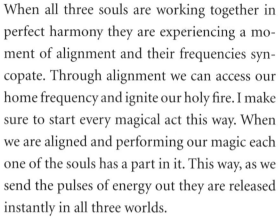

When all three souls are working together in perfect harmony they are experiencing a moment of alignment and their frequencies syncopate. Through alignment we can access our home frequency and ignite our holy fire. I make sure to start every magical act this way. When we are aligned and performing our magic each one of the souls has a part in it. This way, as we send the pulses of energy out they are released instantly in all three worlds.

All three souls working together in alignment

Find yourself seated comfortably and take a few deep breaths. As you breathe, slowly bring your awareness to the brilliant yellow flame that emanates from your solar plexus. This yellow fire is the holy flame of the ego and as you continue to breathe you see this flame consume your entire being. Take a moment now to commune with your ego.

Draw your attention now to just below your navel where a red flame begins to dance through the holy fire of the ego. You recognize this red flame as the flame of the primal self and breathe into it. With each breath the flame grows larger and eventually the yellow flame is entirely replaced by the red. Take a moment to feel your body.

At the top of your head a white flame sparks and you recognize it as the holy flame of the higher self. As you breathe this flame begins to cover your entire body and with each breath you become more and more consumed by it. When you are completely consumed in white fire take a moment to commune with the higher self.

Visualize the three totems forming in their corresponding places in the body. The Serpent just below your navel, the Spider at your solar plexus, and the Owl perched on your third eye. Take three deep breaths of power and chant, "Serpent rising, Owl descend, Spider weaving with no end!" three times. As you do this see the Owl and Serpent move to meet the Spider in the middle, then say, "We are one, the three made whole, together now, a single soul!"

Take one final deep breath of power and release any tension in the body upon exhale.

Journal Topics

- What do you think about inspiration and the Holy Soul? How are they connected?

- Are there any adjustments you can make right now to embody your higher self more?

- How did you feel when you aligned your three souls?

Chapter Six

The Pentacle and
Crown of Sovereignty

*The majority of problems on this planet are the result of the idea that
humans are not sovereign and autonomous, but property owned by
primitive Gods and incompetent governments.*
—Christopher S. Hyatt—

In witchcraft there has always been a vein of anarchy. Many witches
believe that true power comes from ownership and rule over one's
own choices and actions. The idea is that we are wild and nothing wild
likes being put in a cage or having its will broken. It would be unimagi-
nable for too many of us. Because of this we tend to reject the notion
of ownership or rulership of our minds, bodies, or spirits by outside
influences. We want to be in control of our own lives at every moment
and believe that it is our heritage and destiny to be free and forge our

own path. We believe that this is an inalienable right of ours and will do almost anything to protect it.

We call this right to self-rulership sovereignty. More than the ability to govern oneself, it also means "supreme power." One who is sovereign has both the total power to rule over themselves and the total power to impact the world around them. With great privilege, however, comes great responsibility: There is almost always someone or something threatening our sovereignty, and usually it is ourselves.

I created the Pentacle of Sovereignty to be a tool to identify and address those things that threaten my ability to maintain sovereignty. The pentacle ultimately becomes the Crown of Sovereignty, a symbol of the Witch Power and dominion over self. The Pentacle and Crown of Sovereignty are core teachings in the Sacred Fires tradition.

In the Faery Tradition of witchcraft there is a beautiful system of pentacle work that has helped me greatly in my own search for sovereignty. These pentacles are a set of metaphysical diagnostic tools for practitioners to use so that they may be aware of their own sense of self and community. Originally these tools were designed by Victor and Cora Anderson, the founding members of the Faery Tradition, and quickly became part of the foundational work for followers of Faery Witchcraft. Learning through the sheer strength of a pentacle practice I found the model to be superb when developing as a being of power.

The Pentacle of Sovereignty

The Pentacle of Sovereignty is a tool for those of us who are ready to empower our paths and take a new look at how we use our energy. Within the work of this pentacle we receive a set of five jeweled points marking symbolic frequencies of personal power. The jewels (amethyst, emerald, sapphire, tiger's-eye, and diamond) of each point will become those in your Crown of Sovereignty.

The Points

As you look at the pentacle you'll see five points of power. In the craft we generally see those points as Earth, Air, Fire, Water, and Spirit. However, in the Pentacle of Sovereignty we use a different set of points: Balance, Power, Respect, Awareness, and Divinity. Each point contains its own frequency, just like the five traditional elements of the craft. As each point is explored be sure to practice the meditations provided, keep adding to your magical journal about your experiences, and define the relationship of each point to your own frequency. This work can immediately create change if we apply ourselves.

Balance

Balance is a word often used without the resolve of truly understanding its depth. Paganism often preaches balance in all things; however, how many times have you seen someone standing on their soapbox preaching the messages of balance but then going home to an imbalanced life? How many times have you done this? The first step on our search for balance is to define what this word means to us. Open your magical journal and jot down a few words or sentences about what balance means to you. For example, I wrote down:

Balance: Fairly take and fairly give, light and dark, equality.

Now apply this definition to your life. What does it mean to personally be balanced? Skip a few lines and jot down a few sentences about what it means to be balanced. For example, I wrote:

Personal meaning of balance: For me, to be balanced is to search for and live by the principles of equality. It means that I should expect to react to any situation with an understanding of my own personal needs and interests, as well as those of other people. It means that I should give and take from my environment with equal amounts. It means that even in the darkest of times I will search for the light. Personal balance is the ability to maintain a constant flow of intake and output of my own energy.

The next step is to identify points of balance in your life, as well as points of imbalance according to your own definition of balance. Skip a few lines and write down your points of both balance and imbalance. You can have as many as you feel you have; however, I do suggest approaching this from a complete place of honesty. If not, you are only cheating yourself out of the experience. I wrote:

Balance points in my life: Career, spirituality, most friendships, family life, home life. Imbalanced points in my life: Finances, some friendships, clients.

Take a look at what you wrote down. In the balanced category I wrote that I felt my career was balanced, my spirituality was balanced, as well as most of my friendships, my family life, and my home life. Ask yourself this: Do you without a doubt feel as though these things are balanced? In my case, I, beyond a shadow of a doubt, feel like my career, spirituality, the majority of my friendships, and my home life are balanced, but my family life could use a little more attention. In this case I will move that point down to the imbalanced list.

The next step in the process is to review your imbalances. In the category of imbalances I put down finances, some of my friendships, clients, and added family life. Under the list of imbalanced points in your life, write down each of them on separate lines. Next to each imbalanced point, write down why you feel they are imbalanced and what you can do to balance these points in your life. For me it looks like this:

Finances: I have a lot of money going out and not enough coming in! I can balance this by first balancing my checkbook on a daily basis, and place 10 percent of what I earn into a savings account to cover any surprise drains on the checking account. This will help me with the feeling of taking two steps forward financially and then taking one step back when I get sideswiped with an unexpected expense.

Some friendships: I have friends who do not understand my limits. These people are oblivious to any concept of time and drain a lot of my attention on "Me, Me, Me!" I can fix this by first identifying these people and then placing larger boundaries between us. For example, when Hilary calls to complain to me for an hour about how horrible her life is, I can place a time limit on the call; instead of listening to her for an hour I can give her twenty minutes of my time before I tell her I have to get off the phone. I can define my own limits with these people and should not feel sorry for them and allow them to take over my evenings. It is draining and I don't have the time or the energy. This will help me not to feel like a bad friend when I am only trying to respect my own time and energy.

Clients: I have a lot of clients who try to get free readings from me after the in-person session. I don't mind following up with them, but I should not have to read three-page e-mails in the font of negative 6 on a daily basis from people who do not understand that I am a professional. I can place a larger barrier between me and my clients by explaining to them that I am a busy man, and even though I do find their spiritual development important I must also tend to my own soul. I can dedicate four hours each week to responding to e-mails and following up on phone calls; however, no more than that. This will help me to feel that I am valuable and will help keep my clients from running my life.

Family life: I have a hard time connecting to my family, as I end up feeling burnt-out by them. I love my family and need them in my life; however, I also need to be better at placing my own best interest ahead of their wants and desires for me. I get overwhelmed by their expectations of me, and often feel as though I am not good enough when I leave. I can fix this by remembering that I am on my own path and, even knowing that they are projecting their opinions on me from a place of love and concern, I can project back on them that I do not need that sort of help from them. I can also place energy into working on other, healthier forms of our relationship, versus the part that leaves me unintentionally wounded. I can inform them how they make me feel and leave it at that.

Now, let's say that you wrote something very big and heavy on your list of imbalances and are having a hard time trying to figure out how to make that point balanced. Divide that larger point into other smaller points and build from there. Set small goals that add to be a larger goal; be realistic, and be determined.

Over the next several days spend time putting your plan into action. Set aside time each day for at least fifteen minutes so you can meditate on the amethyst point of balance, visualize it in your head, and then project your balances and imbalances into it. Follow up your plan with determination and follow through—balance that checkbook, open a savings account, identify and place boundaries where there need to be boundaries. Don't slack off, and dedicate yourself to finding balance. Obviously, being balanced in all aspects of life is a trial all its own; the point here is to recognize your imbalances and to dedicate your time and energy into balancing them. Total balance is a rather inhuman ideology, but striving for it in every way is perfection.

When you feel you have gotten a good grip on how to find balance, and have dedicated your energy to finding and keeping it, empower yourself by invoking the amethyst point on the Pentacle of Sovereignty.

Invocation of the Amethyst Point

Go to your home frequency. Envision nothingness, empty expanses that hold neither light nor matter, simply nothingness. Before you a point of brilliant deep purple light appears. It begins to spin, and as it does, it grows larger. The point of deep purple light begins to solidify, becoming the first place along our journey—Balance. Before you now floats a perfect amethyst, polished and brightly reflecting your holy fire; it hums with the vibrations of equal proportion, equilibrium, and stabilization. Take a deep breath, breathing into this point of amethyst, and watch it shine brightly in the expanses of nothingness. Other specks of small purple light begin to flood the darkness, stars among the cosmos, the light of balance in all others.

I call to the spirits and balance makers of all worlds!
I invoke the amethyst point!
I call upon the power of God Herself!
Let balance be made!
Empower me now as I walk between all worlds!
Balance is mine!

Chant three times:

Balance, Balance, Balance, Balance!
Balance, Power, Respect, Awareness, Divinity!
Balance, Balance, Balance, Balance!

Power

Power is another one of those words that is used loosely without a full understanding of its meaning. Power means different things to different people. If I were the ruler of a country, power would mean control. However, if I were a high school teacher, power would mean the ability to help shape the future of my students. Just as you did before, open your journal and jot down the word *Power*. Underneath it write your own definition of power. For me it is this:

> *Power:* Is *a current of energy that can be utilized in magic, the ability to influence the world around me, and the ability to control a specific set of variables.*

Now that you have your own definition of power, place its reflection onto your own life. What does it mean to be powerful in your own life? What does being powerful mean to you? Skip a few lines and write a few sentences that express your own sense of power. I wrote:

> *Personal meaning of power:* My *personal meaning of power is to have as much control over the ebb and flow of my own energy as possible. Power is the ability to influence my world by causing shifts to my own energy body that will affect the world that I live in. Power is strength in my convictions. Being powerful means that I understand my own ability to affect others both directly and indirectly; it is the ability to create change (magic), and is the ultimate potential of my being.*

Take a moment to mull over your definition and how it refers to your life. Is being powerful an ability that you possess? Is being powerful something that you strive to be or something that you simply are? Okay, now the fun part: Skip a line and jot down points in your life that you feel powerful in and powerless in. For me it looks something like this:

Powerful in: voice, influencing others, career, love life, convictions.

Powerless in: the way I let others influence me, self-sabotage.

I had written down voice, influencing others, career, love life, and convictions under the list of points in which I felt powerful. After reviewing the list I believe beyond any doubt that I am powerful in those points. Now using your own definition of power, devise a plan to empower those points in which you feel powerless. Under the "powerless in" category I wrote the way I let others influence me, and self-sabotage. I know I feel powerless when I let the opinions of others overwhelm my own ideas and thoughts, often feeling that their criticism is a reflection of my voice. I self-sabotage whenever I jump the gun and start too many projects all at the same time; I also feel overwhelmed in this situation. A common theme is always something to take notice of: I feel overwhelmed quite often, and this is the root issue of my experiences with feeling powerless. For my game plan on how to empower myself in these situations I wrote:

Letting others influence me: I need to approach every situation that elicits a feeling of being powerless as a chance to promote change. When others place their criticism on my shoulders I will first look for truth in what they say, and do my best to remove all ego from the equation. If they are correct, then I will allow that message to bring clarity to my practice; however, if they are coming from a place of ego then I need to make sure that I do not allow it to affect me so deeply. I will identify positive influences and negative influences, and then treat each situation as a chance for empowerment. If the person is reflecting their opinion and is coming off as aggressive or mean-spirited, then I can seize another opportunity for empowerment by letting them know that I do not appreciate their tone, and expect to be treated like an adult.

Self-sabotage: I understand that this is one of my largest points of disempowerment. I set wheels in motion only to find myself not following through on the projects. This produces an image to those around me as someone who talks a good talk but does not walk the road to its completion. I can change this by first being more reserved in my vocalization about what ideas I have in mind. I will spend more time meditating over decisions before reacting to the impressions of inspiration in the moment. I will not decide to announce to the world my ideas until I know I can follow through.

The most challenging of all the points is to take our disempowering experiences and turn them into something that feeds and nourishes our souls. It is no easy task. I want to reiterate that you are a god and like any god you have the ability to accept or reject the offerings that are made to you. Simply not allowing yourself to accept offerings that are negative will go a long way in producing a positive shift in your life.

For the next few days be sure to support your affirmations of change by setting yourself up for success! Follow through and whenever the opportunity arises to shift that stream of disempowered energy, do so. Set at least fifteen minutes aside each day to meditate on the point of power, allowing your points of power and disempowerment to flow through you and into the emerald. When you feel that you have a good grip on the power point, empower yourself by invoking the point of power, sit in meditation after the invocation, and allow the emerald light to flood your senses and spend time simply allowing the vibration to swirl around you.

Invocation of the Emerald Point

See before you the brilliance of the amethyst point. See it shine brightly as you notice the other smaller specks of purple in the background. Breathe into this point of balance and chant to yourself, "Balance, Balance, Balance, Balance!" With each word let the light of the amethyst shine brighter until it explodes with a golden light that travels to the left diagonally, creating the first line of sovereignty. Where the line stops a beautiful emerald shining the deepest green light appears. This brilliant emerald marks the point of power. See this emerald shine in the light of your very own holy fire, and watch it spin clockwise as it soaks up its own form of being. Hear it hum the sound of creation beckoning to the cosmos with messages of energy, influence, and control. Trace the line from the amethyst point to the emerald point and see it vibrate as your energy body touches it. See that through balance, power is made. Breathe deeply and as you exhale into the emerald point see smaller specks of emerald green begin to shine throughout the cosmos, the light of power in all other beings.

I call upon the spirits and change makers of all worlds!
I invoke the Emerald Point!
I call upon the influence of God Herself!
Let power be restored!
May I be powerful as I walk between the worlds!
I am powerful!

Chant three times:

Power, Power, Power, Power
Balance, Power, Respect, Awareness, Divinity
Power, Power, Power, Power

Respect

Respect is said to be earned, not given. However, respect is also confused with fear. The interesting thing about respect is that when those around you respect you they will be loyal, but when people fear you they will almost never miss the opportunity to move on to greener pastures when opportunity arises. It may not happen immediately but when they are sick of fearing you they will find someone they can respect. As witches we have all gone through this ourselves; we are taught to fear God, so we find a god that does not want fear but respect. Obviously respect means different things to different people, so take out your journal and come up with a personal definition of respect. For me, respect means:

Respect: To hold in high esteem, regard with love, trust.

Coming up with your own definition of respect will help you identify points of both respect and disrespect in your life. Do you feel that people respect you or fear you? Do you feel you have earned respect? Do you respect others or fear others? Is disrespect something you face often from others? Take a good look at your life and pour the realizations of respect out onto the page. For me, I identified several points for both:

I feel respect: from members of my community, from most of my colleagues, and from my students. For others of the craft, for divinity, and for my family.

I feel disrespect: from some members of my family, from some of my closest friends, for those with oppressive views. Those who are consumed with ego.

This is another tricky one, as it works both ways! You can feel respected and a sense of respect for others just as easily as you can feel disrespected by others and have a sense of disrespect for others. To truly have respect in your life you must be both the respectful and the respected, as one elicits the other. As you review your lists, how do you feel you can tip the balance? For me, I realized:

Disrespect from members of my family: Remember it comes from a place of love; however, I must embody success in order to be respected in the eyes of my family. Instead of sharing all of my issues with my family, call them to share with them my successes.

From my closest friends: The closer the friend, the more they become aware of my weaknesses. This is not a bad thing; however, I do not want them to use those weaknesses against me. Just like my family I need to call them to discuss my successes, and not just my failures. People remember the bad much longer than they remember the good.

For those with oppressive views: I can keep in mind that they are working within a certain set of realities that I may not be living in. I should judge them on their actions within a specific circumstance instead of their views, realizing that I can respect their convictions as long as they respect mine.

Those who are consumed with ego: I more so need to remind myself to keep distance between those people who choose to push their weight around. If I find myself in a situation where it is unavoidable, I should shield myself and my energy more. Those with overactive egos often have them because they are bruised.

Now, perhaps you wrote down issues with self-respect. Are you self-disrespectful? Identify what triggers the feeling of disrespect. Often I find that it is not the issue but the reaction to the issue that elicits the response of disrespect. Perhaps you feel you are less than: Well, ask yourself why you feel less than and why you disrespect yourself because of it. If you disrespect yourself by putting yourself down and telling yourself you are stupid, etc., you are only perpetuating the problem because you are making poisoned offerings to your God self, and then are consuming those offerings. As you work through the Pentacle of Sovereignty, remember to identify patterns in your life that lead you to the points within the pentacle.

There will be some issues that come up where you simply cannot respect a person's decisions. For example, if you were in an argument with a religious extremist and they were vehemently disrespectful to you and your values, you wouldn't likely agree to respect them, because they most certainly aren't showing you respect. In this instance, the point of respect is showing you that there are major issues here that are causing both of you to lose your power. In my experience it is best to respect yourself and your energy more by shielding yourself and removing their influence.

Invoking the Sapphire Point

One easy way to work through the pentacle, especially at the respect point, is to embody the changes you want to make. Do you see opportunities to help others with their own issues regarding the points of sovereignty? Maybe a friend is feeling disrespected at the workplace; how might you be able to help her with the problems she faces? Set aside fifteen minutes over the next few days to work with the royal sapphire point of respect, meditate, and send your notions of disrespect into the royal sapphire; breathe into it and give it life so that it may transmute the negative into the positive. When you feel as though you are in a stable place within the point of respect, do the water-cleansing rite, such as Kala or an uncrossing bath, and invoke the royal sapphire of respect.

See before you the brilliance of the emerald point. See it shine brightly as you notice the other smaller specks of purple and green in the background. Breathe into this point of power and chant to yourself, "Power, Power, Power, Power!" With each word let the light of the emerald shine brighter until it explodes with a golden light that travels to the right diagonally, creating the second line of sovereignty. Where the line stops, a beautiful royal sapphire sparkles and a brilliant deep blue light appears. This royal sapphire is the point of power. See this royal sapphire shine in the light of your very own holy fire, and watch it spin clockwise as it soaks up its own form of being. Hear it hum the sound of creation, beckoning to the cosmos with messages of value, esteem, and privilege. Trace the line from the emerald point to the royal sapphire point and see it vibrate as your energy body touches it. See that through power, respect is formed. Breathe deeply and, as you exhale into the royal sapphire point, see smaller specks of deep blue begin to shine throughout the cosmos, the light of respect in all other beings.

I call upon the spirits and on those respected in all worlds!
I invoke the royal sapphire point!
I call upon the awesomeness of God Herself!
Let respect be found!
May I find respect as I walk between the worlds!
Respect is mine!

Chant three times:

Respect, Respect, Respect, Respect
Balance, Power, Respect, Awareness, Divinity
Respect, Respect, Respect, Respect

Awareness

Awareness is relative to all situations but once it is attained it can never be denied. We can be aware of our surroundings but also unaware of our impact upon them. To recognize your impact is to be aware of your own power, and to be aware of your environment gives you the power to change it. We also must be aware of others and their paths as they cross our own for we, too, have the power to change and to be changed. The big question is: What does being aware feel like to you? Are you happy being unaware of what goes on around you or are you someone who, like me, is constantly surveying the scenery? Take out the magical journal again and this time write down your own definition of what awareness means. After giving it some thought, I wrote:

Awareness: Perception of the current reality, enlightenment through the comprehension of my surroundings.

As you reflect upon your own sense of awareness, how does it apply to your life? What is it that you feel you are truly aware of and what is it that you feel you are unaware of? Are you aware of your own potential? Are you aware of your own impact on the world? One thing that is immensely important during the development point is to remember that our awareness is flavored by the privileges we have in life. I'm a middle-class Caucasian male living in the United States of America; I have it easy compared to almost all other demographics when it comes to my choices. Unlike women, I have a higher chance of getting a better-paying job simply because I get to tick the box next to "Male" on my applications. Even more, the benefits of my ethnicity are never-ending. I don't have to worry about being targeted by police violence because of my skin tone, nor do I have to worry about not being called in for an interview because my name sounds too Spanish or urban. Not only that, but as a white person, the majority of television shows and advertising are directed at me, which only reinforces my sense of privileged awareness. The list of comparisons could go on and on!

I think the important thing isn't to make the mistake of thinking that our privileged awareness is a bad thing or something we should be ashamed of but rather to know that it is something that functions like a frequency preset for us. Knowing that we have these presets will help us to become more conscious of how we may be letting blind spots in our awareness affect our ability to make informed and empowered decisions.

I would also like to add that it is a core spiritual belief of mine that if you have any type of privilege you also have the noble responsibility to use it to help others who are affected by it. For example, if someone from a minority race has an issue that they are trying to gain public awareness about regarding how they feel my race treates their race, I have the noble obligation to stop and listen to what they have to say. If I feel that they shared insight into this subject that I couldn't possibly have had otherwise that helps to inform me and helps me become more aware, then I have the noble obligation to help that person get their message to others who have the same racial privilege I do.

This is not by any means an easy subject to discuss for any of us. The idea of privilege is one that makes us all shudder. When I was first brought the concept I rejected it because I assumed the person trying to tell me about it was attempting to claim that I was a bad person for being born a white male. I like to think of myself as a pretty open-minded individual who helps others, so the notion that something about me that I had no control over was hurting people in the world was utterly absurd to me. Then I figured out that my privileged awareness was not only keeping me narrow-minded to the realities of other people who were not like me, but they were also supporting the status quo that created the issues that plagued the lives of those who were not like me. It was without question one of the most sobering moments of my life. I realized in that moment that I was still that open-minded individual who helped others and I had the perfect opportunity to do so by helping them with my privilege.

Skip a few lines in your journal and write down points of awareness and unawareness. I wrote:

Aware of: All the love in my life, the power of my voice, my current life situations, my privilege.

Unaware of: How I impact others unconsciously through my privilege, how others impact me, what will happen in the future.

Like with the other points, we now need to come up with a plan in which we can become aware of what we are unaware of. I am reminded of a quote from the book *The Color Purple* by Alice Walker; at the end, two of the main characters are standing next to a field and one looks over to the other and says, "I think it pisses God off if you walk by the color purple in a field somewhere and don't notice it." As you develop your plan to empower your resolve for awareness, remember to take a step back, look at the big picture, and appreciate the view; search for a greater sense of awareness. For me, the plan looked something like this:

How I impact others unconsciously through my privilege: I often forget that the way life works for me is not the way life works for other people. I have friends and colleagues who struggle each and every day in different ways than I do and I need to remember that we are all fighting to make it through to the next week. I need to make it a point to ask others about what they are most afraid of week to week so I can gain insight into the struggles of others. After listening to them I need to meditate on how the status quo might be causing these struggles and what I can do to change it so their lives can one day be better, even if that is only by becoming an advocate for their cause.

How others impact me: I need to remember my own voice and my own calling, and place them above the opinions and projections that others place upon me. I need to acquire the ability to take things at face value and spend time processing the assessment of others before taking it to heart. This will allow me the ability to accept appropriate offerings that are made to me and reject those offerings that are toxic to my greater cause. My search for acceptance by others is not an appropriate modality to achieving my own sense of sovereignty.

The future: We are all unaware of what the future holds; however, I can alter the path of the future by aligning myself with my desired course. Being grounded and prepared for the possibilities will help when I feel sideswiped by unexpected events that may potentially

alter my path. Each day I need to remind myself of what I feel is
my own calling and not allow uncontrollable events to take over
my concept of a higher calling. Everything that comes my way is a
chance for growth, I need to search for the potential of growth in all
situations, planned and unplanned.

As you search for awareness be sure to cleanse yourself often. Performing ritual cleansing like one of the water cleansing rites in chapter 2, smudging, or ritual baths for purification will help to remove the mist that keeps us from clear vision as we look around ourselves. When you apply your practice of awareness, be sure to follow through; don't deny yourself your own potential. I know I have said this a few times within the chapter, but I cannot express the importance of follow-through, for follow-through is what separates the powerful and the powerless.

To empower yourself and that which you are choosing to be consciously aware of, invoke the tiger's-eye point of the Pentacle of Sovereignty.

Invocation of the Tiger's-Eye Point

Before you the brilliance of the royal sapphire point shimmers. See it shine brightly as you notice the other smaller specks of purple, green, and royal blue in the background. Breathe into this point of power and chant to yourself, "Respect, Respect, Respect, Respect!" With each word let the light of the royal sapphire shine brighter until it explodes with a golden light that travels horizontally to the left, creating the third line of sovereignty. Where the line stops a radiant tiger's-eye sparkles and a yellow and gold light appears. This tiger's-eye is the point of power. See this tiger's-eye blaze in the light of your very own holy fire, and watch it spin clockwise as it soaks up its own form of being. Hear it hum the sound of creation beckoning to the cosmos with insight, perception, and comprehension. Trace the line from the royal sapphire point to the tiger's-eye point and see it vibrate as your energy body touches it. See that through respect, awareness is gained. Breathe deeply and as you exhale into the tiger's-eye point, see smaller specks of golden yellow light begin to shine throughout the cosmos, the light of awareness in all other beings.

> *I call upon the spirits and those who are truly aware in all worlds!*
> *I invoke the tiger's-eye point!*
> *I call upon the awareness of God Herself!*
> *Let clarity be found!*
> *May I perceive all as I walk between the worlds!*
> *I am aware!*

Chant three times:

Awareness, Awareness, Awareness, Awareness
Balance, Power, Respect, Awareness, Divinity
Awareness, Awareness, Awareness, Awareness

Divinity

The divine is all around us; it comprises the very matter of which we are made, and is the root of all things within the universe. We often forget our own divine nature as we often become consumed with trials and tribulations of life on the physical plane. The entire Pentacle of Sovereignty reminds us that we are capable of creating balance, that we have the power to change, that by respecting ourselves and others we can find a new sense of awareness, and that through this awareness we can cultivate a greater knowledge of just how divine we all are. Like all things in life we must search for our own definition rather than living off of the definitions of others that may not be suited for our own desires and needs. As you have done before, take out your magical journal and write your own definition of Divinity. My definition is this:

Divinity: That which makes all things connected to a greater thing, the potential of all things, that from which we receive our own authority.

Take a good look at your definition and ask yourself, "Do I embody this?" For me I can say that I definitely try my hardest to. However, it is so easy for all of us (including myself) to lose the wind beneath our wings. But as we move forward with a sense of awareness, in what ways can you perceive that divinity has presented itself to you, and in what ways could you project divinity into your own life? Skip a few lines in your magical journal and make a list of how divinity presents itself to you, and how you do and could project divinity. For example, I wrote:

Divinity presents itself to me: In the laughter of a child, the way the sun bursts forth announcing its brilliance and coerces life from a sleeping earth, and in the sheer ability to share with others my experiences.

How I project divinity: I project divinity by relying on my faith— faith that has been earned throughout my life. I project divinity by sharing love with those around me, and the way in which I help others find their own divinity.

How I could project divinity: I could spend more time cultivating my own sense of divinity, and could project my divinity better by allowing it to be a part of my everyday, mundane life.

Now that you have a few thoughts about you and your relationship to divinity, review the ways in which you could project divinity all around you. If the projection of energy is the ultimate goal, then what are the steps that you can take to get you there? My game plan consisted of the following.

Cultivating my own sense of divinity: I can do an alignment of my own three souls each day, perhaps even multiple times throughout the day. I can do the alignment before I speak to others about the craft, or before I teach a class. I can also spend more time connecting to my higher self.

Divinity in my mundane life: I can make a decision to include both my spiritual and mundane life as one singular practice. Why divide that which should act as one? I can be a priest in all things that I do, and I can search for divinity in everyday life.

In my experiences it is not the idea of making yourself divine that is essential, but recognizing the divine within yourself, and then bringing it to the forefront, that counts. Rediscover your own divine nature, as you are a God and we must never forget that. You have the power to affect all things, including yourself, and what could be more divine than that? When you are ready, empower yourself and your search for divinity with the invocation of the diamond point of divinity upon the Pentacle of Sovereignty.

Invocation of the Diamond Point

Before you the golden yellow light of the tiger's-eye point shines. See it in all its brilliance as you perceive the other smaller specks of purple, green, royal blue, and golden yellow in the background. Breathe into this point of awareness and chant to yourself, "Awareness, Awareness, Awareness, Awareness!" With each word let the light of the tiger's-eye shine brighter until it explodes with a metallic golden light that travels diagonally to the right, creating the fourth line of sovereignty. Where the line stops, a shimmering diamond forms. This diamond rests at the point of divinity. See this diamond shine in the light of your very own holy fire, and watch it spin clockwise as it forms its own form of being. Hear it hum the sound of creation, announcing to the cosmos that it brings authority, higher calling, and godhood. Trace the line from the tiger's-eye point to the diamond point and see it vibrate as your energy body touches it. Be aware that through awareness divinity is made. Breathe deeply and as you exhale into the diamond point, see smaller specks of white light begin to shine throughout the cosmos, the light of divinity in all other beings.

I call forth the spirits and ascended beings of all worlds!
I invoke the point of Divinity!
I call upon the divine nature of God Herself!
Let my own divinity shine!
May I find divinity in all places as I walk between the worlds!
I am Divine!

Chant three times:

Divinity, Divinity, Divinity, Divinity,
Balance, Power, Respect, Awareness, Divinity,
Divinity, Divinity, Divinity, Divinity.

Manifesting the Pentacle of Sovereignty

We now have five points upon the Pentacle of Sovereignty but only four lines. To complete the Pentacle of Sovereignty, close your eyes and take a few deep breaths, relaxing your body and releasing all tension. See before you the brilliance of the diamond point, shining iridescent and clear. See it shine brightly as you notice the other smaller specks of purple, green, royal blue, golden yellow, and white in the background, the gems of all other points of sovereignty in creation. Breathe into this point of power and chant to yourself, "Divinity, Divinity, Divinity, Divinity!" With each word, let the light of the diamond shine brighter until it explodes with a golden light that travels up vertically to the amethyst point of balance, creating the fifth and final line of sovereignty. Trace the fifth golden line with your energy body and feel its energy bring completion to the pentacle.

Silence your mind and take three deep breaths, breathing from your stomach, then your lungs, keeping your shoulders relaxed. As you exhale, send your breath into the jewel-encrusted pentacle. Envision that with each exhale you are breathing life into the pentacle and it grows stronger and brighter until it vibrates with the brilliance of sovereignty. As it begins to grow brighter with golden light, put your hands on the pentacle and spin it clockwise. See it spin furiously around, and as it does so, see it grow larger and larger until it encompasses your own being. Breathe in the brilliant golden light and allow it to feed to you sovereign life force. See the pentacle rise above you, and as it lifts, see that it is its own cosmos, a cluster of jeweled stars composing its own galaxy. This is the Pentacle of Sovereignty, your own galaxy of greatness within the universe and God Herself.

Now that you have been introduced to the Pentacle of Sovereignty and you understand the deeper and personal nature of it, we can move on to the application of the pentacle. The Pentacle of Sovereignty is a diagnostic tool for us as witches, as it allows us to have a system of checks and balances for our own Crown of Sovereignty. As sovereign beings we can put the pentacle to good use to ensure that we are meeting our greater potential and that we are responding to all that may arise from a place of authority, at the very least a place of authority over our own policies and convictions. The pentacle can be something that empowers us on all levels as it promotes not only a sense of personal possession but a view of our own sense of godhood.

Running the Pentacle of Sovereignty

Make sure you are in a comfortable standing position. If for whatever reason you cannot stand, then place yourself into a meditative state and see yourself standing. Take a few deep breaths and at your third eye see the first point of balance as a beautiful amethyst. As you see it in your mind's eye, say the word "Balance." Trace in the air a bar of gold that flows to your left foot, and upon reaching your destination, see an emerald shine and say aloud, "Power." From this point trace another bar of gold in your mind's eye from the point of power to the place of your extended right hand, see there a sparkling royal sapphire and say "Respect." Trace another bar of gold from your right hand across your chest to the place of your extended left hand, see there a tiger's-eye, and say aloud, "Awareness." From the place of your extended left hand trace another golden bar to your right foot, see there a diamond, and say aloud the word "Divinity." From here trace the final bar of gold to the amethyst point and repeat aloud the word "Balance."

Trace the pentacle saying the corresponding words as you stop at each point. You may start out slow, but eventually you will build speed. As you build speed notice if perhaps you are forgetting one of the points, or perhaps you are exchanging the names of the points with one another. As this practice becomes second nature to you, you will start to recite the points without too much thought. Keep an eye on how the pentacle unfolds for you as mistakes may be indication that the missed points, or exchanged points, are in need of some attention. If you find that you are skipping the power point as you are chanting and tracing the pentacle you might want to take a look at that point of power. Are you finding yourself to feel powerless in a set of situations in your life right now? This is where using the Pentacle of Sovereignty as a diagnostic tool comes into play.

Once you feel you have run the pentacle enough, take a moment to bask in the astral glow of it, and reabsorb that energy into your body. Remember that this pentacle belongs to you and no one else.

You may also try to do a road opener spell for each of the points as you see the need for it.

There is nothing wrong with using magic to help you reach a goal, and in the case of opening the road to find your own sense of balance, power, respect, awareness, or divinity, what better purpose could magic serve?

I recommend that you run the pentacle and allow it to empower you before each ritual. Start off by invoking your own guardians, Gods, and allies, and then run the pentacle with them as witnesses, acting as if to decree to the magical universe that you are alive and kicking! See how you feel with them present; do you discover them in a different way? When you are comfortable with this, then move on to running the Pentacle of Sovereignty in a circle with others to help boost the collective expression of both individual and group forms of sovereignty. Draw down the moon after you run the pentacle and see if you are better suited for channeling divine energy. As your own body is aligned to sovereignty, the possibilities for empowerment when using this pentacle are endless!

Manifesting the Crown of Sovereignty

The universal symbol of sovereignty is the royal crown, and no matter where you go, people know what it means. Our Pentacle of Sovereignty can be transformed into what we call the Crown of Sovereignty. In ritual, wearing your crown symbolizes your divine nature and authority over all frequencies present in your life. It is an energetic tool that we can use to assert our dominance and influence. This little piece of ritual technique has become a staple of ours in Sacred Fires.

After you have run the pentacle exercise, visualize a jeweled star before you, then place both hands on either side of the pentacle before you and grab onto the edges. Take a deep breath and spin the pentacle clockwise. As it spins in front of you, exhale holy fire at it as if your breath were a blowtorch. See the pentacle get hot and begin to glow as your breath comes to an end, and visualize the pentacle turning into a crown. As the metal cools see that all five stones adorn the crown. Reach out once again and grab the crown and place it on your head. As you rest this crown on your head, say, "By this crown forged from witches' might, I claim my power and sovereign right!"

To be sovereign doesn't just mean that we have dominion over our lives and ourselves but that we understand every other person is undergoing a similar struggle to our own. When we move through life holding the paradox of self and other as the ultimate form of truth, the way we relate to the outside world is derived from balance, instead of anger or fear, both of which weaken the foundations of power that we strive so hard to establish. Consider the Witch Power, the power of your three souls, and the power found through sovereignty as the three dynamic pillars to magical and spiritual enrichment. Each is capable of causing great change individually, but united they can alter the course of fate and the presentation of reality, taking a life that feels heavy and pointless and turning it into one full of strength, conviction, and perhaps most importantly, passion.

Part Two

COSMIC
POWER

The cosmos is a vast living body, of which we are still parts.
—D.H. Lewis—

Each of us is made of, and moves through, a complex cocktail of universal energies made manifest. Science tells us that everything we are comprised of was formed first in the belly of a star, and then over billions of years that star-stuff became us. Stars not only produce the building blocks of life but they also influence how life exists and carries on. If ancient stars were what made the clay we are constructed of, then the stars in our solar system are the tools that shape that clay.

Astrology is the practice of observing astronomical occurrences and divining the impact those occurrences have on the human experience. Just about everyone knows what their sign is and many jump at the opportunity to proudly boast about how they are the quintessential version of that sign. What a lot of people don't know, including many modern witches, is that there is an unending amount of information that can be gleaned from a deeper understanding of how we are shaped and later impacted by the way these signs interact with planets, stars, and asteroids that travel through our solar system. The only problem is that astrology is often an overwhelming and dry subject that is more acquainted with ceremonial or high magic, and most people quickly lose interest.

Besides a basic understanding of their chart, most witches never take the opportunity to explore astrology as a tool for magical empowerment. There are many ways to approach the concepts of astrology and there is more than one school of thought regarding it. For the most part, astrology is an intuitive science that invites those with the skill to peer into the kaleidoscope of energy that shapes our daily lives.

In this part of the book you will explore how the primal forces of the universe helped to shape you into the witch you are today. Among other things, you will gain insight into the magic and psychic abilities that you likely possess.

Chapter Seven

Star Power

*Astrology has no more useful function than this, to discover the
inmost nature of a man and to bring it out into his consciousness,
that he may fulfill it according to the law of light.*
—Aleister Crowley—

Today, astrology is often used for two things: to predict future events
and as a consolatory tool to help people better understand their
lives. As magicians we can take the teachings of astrology and combine
them with practical magical knowledge to produce not only a blueprint
for magical timing but vital keys to unlock our hidden magical potential.

In this chapter I will provide a lot of information about the frequency
of each zodiac sign and how transiting planets influence those frequencies. Much of this information will be used in the next chapter to help
construct what I call a Planetary Power Profile, but I felt it important
to keep all of the information together for the purpose of easy reference

later. Providing all of this information in one place will also help you gain a better understanding of how each frequency continuously works.

The Four Elemental Bands

As the planets move through the constellations they become filters for the elemental frequencies emanating from the zodiac. Each of the twelve signs (or houses) of the zodiac is a frequency and each of the frequencies falls within an elemental frequency band. Each of the four common alchemical elements (Earth, Air, Fire, and Water) rule over three houses. Each house is in turn a variation of that elemental energy (Frequency Band). These three houses are three different ways the elemental energy can be expressed. We call these forms of expression (qualities/quadruplicities) Cardinal, Fixed, and Mutable. In some schools of thought it is believed that the elemental energy matures as it moves from Cardinal to Fixed to Mutable.

When an element frequency is expressed Cardinally it is forceful, reactionary, and forthcoming. When it is expressed as Fixed it is more stubborn, rigid, and not easily moved or altered. When an elemental frequency is expressed Mutably, however, it is generally catalytic, adjustable, and adapts for optimum expression of that element's energies. It has been said that a Cardinal expression allows for the beginning of change (Active), Fixed allows for the solidifying of things (Strong), and Mutable allows for the awareness of where change is needed (Adaptive).

The Twelve Frequencies of the Zodiac

When we look at the elemental bands individually we can get a true taste of just how influential they are. Perhaps the true beauty to behold is that these are the very elements that we work with in contemporary magical systems. I have found a much greater understanding of them through my work with astrology. Not only are they expressions of elemental power, they are also expressions of planetary dominion, better carving out and establishing their energetic hold. Within each band there are three unique frequencies that have influence over our lives, our magic, and our potential.

Included with the description of each band and its frequencies is a list of corresponding attributes, allies, and traits that can be referenced at any time. Like a magical key, each reference can unlock the hidden frequencies of power found within, allowing you to directly obtain the energy from the source. Use these references like ingredients in your magic and allow the medicine of these frequencies to change your connection to the universe. We will explore specific ways to use this information in the next chapter.

The Fire Frequencies

Fire frequency strengths lie in being active and engaging. Loud and quick to respond, fire frequencies are often spontaneous, combustible, destructive, creative, and enthusiastic. Ruled by perhaps three of the most forceful, power-driven, and energetic planets—Mars, the Sun, and Jupiter—these frequencies are best described by the myths and Gods that accompany them. Mars, the bringer of war; Apollo, the virile, inspired prince; and Jupiter, the ruler of them all. Those with multiple presets to fire frequencies will be independent thinkers who possess a warrior-like energy.

The Aries Frequency

Aries is a very youthful and energetic frequency that is sharp and piercing. It is strong, impatient, reckless, aggressive, adventurous, competitive, pioneering, confident, lively, intense, productive, and powerful. Those with Aries as their Sun sign are known for being bold risk-takers who work just as hard as they play. The athletes of the zodiac, Aries people like to sweat and like making other people sweat.

Quality: Cardinal

Ruling Planet: Mars

Body Part Association: The head

Day of the Week: Tuesday

Plants and Herbs: Honeysuckle, geranium, sweet pea, thorn-bearing trees and shrubs, chilis, peppers, mustards, garlic, onions, and cinnamon.

Metal Association: Iron

Gemstone Association: Diamond, apache tears, Herkimer diamond, crackle quartz, amethyst, carnelian, malachite, and rose quartz.

Color: Red, burnt umber, pink, orange, true black, gold, and yellow.

General Magical Attributes: Magic for all purposes that require swift action or that have had no success in the past should be done under the influence of this frequency, as Aries tends to push through remaining obstacles. Spells and rituals for protection, independence, tapping into resources, and/or winning a competition are excellent uses of the Aries Frequency.

　　The Aries frequency may not be copacetic for magic being performed for concentration, selflessness, truth, or justice.

Aries Devotion: All sports, physical exercise, sweating, competitions (especially when you win), and personal discipline.

Aries Presets

Aries Rising

Those with Aries rising are spiritually drawn to battle and often wage war on outdated concepts, stereotypes, and anything that gets in the way of them exploring their spiritual side. These people tend to be loners who like to be the pillar of a small group of friends rather than being one of many in a friend group. Hard-working and dedicated, these people find spiritual enlightenment through sweat and mental discipline. Aries rising people are more comfortable in a gym or traveling the astral planes with a spirit teacher than in a temple or church, and use this time to meditate and reflect on the topics that are eating away at their souls. The higher ideals that they tend to strive towards involve equality, global spiritual evolution, and freedom from oppression.

Witches with this rising sign are excellent teachers, as they tend to bring excitement to whatever spiritual practice they are discussing. They not only love what they do with a deep passion but also are naturally gifted at the process of initiation.

Moon in Aries

Aries pulses with a very hot and aggressive frequency; however, the Moon is cool and passive. When in Aries the Moon brings about powerful internal changes and beckons us to initiate new and exciting adventures for ourselves. When the Moon enters Aries it helps us to break free from our own psychic and emotional prisons and brings about sudden changes. As the Moon exits this frequency it aids us in breaking through emotional roadblocks, bad habits, and unhealthy relationships.

Magic for road opening, freedom, to start new personal goals and disciplines, to draw good fortune, to banish or strengthen perceived weaknesses, and to get the attention of others are all excellent for when the Moon is in Aries and should be executed with much ease. In addition to being naturally gifted in the magic listed here, witches with this preset will most likely take on leadership roles within community and will make excellent wards for ritual.

Mercury in Aries

Mercury is fast and brilliant, and when partnered with Aries it adds sharpness to this already-aggressive frequency. When in Aries, Mercury brings about sarcasm and highly expressive language that can be both funny and brutal but is often necessary to bring about a shift in perspective or to remove the "rose-colored glasses" that are otherwise keeping us ignorant to important realities. As it enters Aries this planet brings with it sudden impulses and urges both good and bad, an eagerness and the ability to finish projects, and a love of writing or music. One might notice personal tastes in literature and music changing during this time. As it exits this sign it helps us clear our minds and gain valuable perspective about our motivations. We should all be wary of the urge to self-sabotage by being overly critical of ourselves and others during times when Mercury is present in Aries.

Magic for banishing, space-clearing, psychic protection, "I AM" consciousness development, the achievement of personal and group goals, identification of bad habits, and all types of magic to inspire creativity and originality should be easily executed during this time. In addition to being naturally gifted in the magic listed here, witches with this preset are usually gifted at fire scrying and have a knack for spotting negative energy within an environment.

Venus in Aries

Aries and Venus have a particularly romantic relationship that ushers in impulsiveness and flirtation with our most hidden desires. Aries, being ruled by Mars, the partner of Venus, is softened ever so slightly when Venus is present and its projective nature is turned inward, producing responsiveness and receptivity. As it enters this frequency Venus brings about changes in the way we connect sensually and sexually to the world around us and often tends to heighten our sexual desires, especially those desires we could most easily attain. As it exits, it aids us in removing bodily or sexual shame.

Magic for reconciliation, seduction, to add the "spark" back into a relationship, glamour of any kind, to start new businesses or romantic relationships, or to bring pride to one's self-image can be done unambiguously during this time. Witches with this preset are naturally gifted in the magic listed here and should be excellent at drawing any desired energy into their lives and pushing unwanted energy away from it.

Mars in Aries

Mars is most at home in Aries as it is the ruling planet for this frequency. When Mars is present in Aries its fiery potential and drive to win are exponentially increased, providing for much-needed added fuel to projects and career goals. This combination also increases the drive to succeed in all things business and life, and encourages us to get out of our own way for our own good. When Mars enters Aries, it brings with it startling realizations about what we feel we are capable of doing and how we fail ourselves by not fulfilling our potential. This also brings with it a sharpness in mind and a sudden urge to plan for battles on any front. As it leaves this frequency it aids us by increasing our desire for physical exercise.

Magic that help to start new projects, make major moves into new professional arenas, get a pay raise, for political attention, to get others to listen to you, and for protection of any kind can be easily executed during this time. Witches with this preset are not only naturally gifted in the magic listed here but are also particularly good at magic for commanding.

Jupiter in Aries

Jupiter and Aries make for quite the powerful duo when it comes to business and career. Jupiter is well-received by the frequency of Aries, which quickly puts it to work lobbying for the right kind of social and professional attention, ultimately placing your own agenda in the forefront of your professional arena. As it enters the frequency of Aries, Jupiter initiates a series of inner personal realizations that propel us forward in our professional planning and increase our likelihood to make the right kind of friends who can help us get where we need to be. As it begins to leave this frequency, Jupiter slowly removes blocks to scientific and analytical thinking, helping us to no longer be bogged down by superstitious or assumption-based living.

Magic for political gain, professional partnerships, professional independence, success of any kind, luck, or financial growth are excellent during times when Jupiter is in the frequency of Aries. Witches with this preset are not only gifted in the magic listed here but are also natural at bestowing successful blessings upon others.

Saturn in Aries

These two don't get along as well as Aries does with the others. Because Saturn is slow and stubborn it significantly decreases the initiative of Aries and the result is crossed wires and confusion. Our ability to gain influence over others is increased during times when Saturn is in the frequency of Aries; however, our ability to maintain power-based relationships is dampened. As it enters the frequency of Aries, Saturn brings about a period of mental cloudiness and a feeling of being stuck. As it exits it takes those obstacles it provided with it, leaving what is often a new and exciting playing field for personal growth.

Magic to cause confusion or to gain beneficial influence can be done with ease during this time. Witches with this preset are naturally gifted with the listed magic here and should expect a great surge of personal power in their late fifties.

Uranus in Aries

Uranus in Aries produces a quick mind and an eagerness to bring about change. Individuality is key during this time and boldness is favored over playing it safe. When Uranus enters Aries it immediately encourages us to put our own ideas into action and to not follow a predetermined path. As it begins to leave, it ushers in a period of time in which we seek clarity and truth in all aspects of life. Witches with this preset are also particularly blessed with social and political magic through activism.

Neptune in Aries

This combination ushers in a generation of new ideas and unexpected rewards through following the beat of a different drum. Those born with this generational preset will be true futurists who will propel our species into a future of unending possibility.

Pluto in Aries

Brings forth expansion, empire, exploration, and growth.

The Leo Frequency

Leo is a very strong and bright frequency. It is moody, impatient, enthusiastic, expansive, heroic, loving, patronizing, dogmatic, bossy, faithful, loyal, and creative. Those with this Sun sign preset are known for being philosophical and prideful. The showmen of the zodiac, Leos are more comfortable being in the center of attention than being on the sidelines. Witches with this preset possess great personal strength that shapes their magic.

Quality: Fixed (Strong)

Ruling Planet: Sun

Body Part Association: Spine, heart, and back

Day of the Week: Sunday

Plants and Herbs: Bay, all palms, all sunflowers, rue, sweet pea, saffron, mint, corn, honey, passionflower, hazel, juniper, laurel, dahlia, and marigold

Metal Association: Gold

Gemstone Association: Ruby, danburite, jasper, kunzite, sardonyx, sunstone, diamond, crackle quartz, garnet, citrine, amber, and onyx

Color: Yellow, gold, mustard, bronze, cyan, scarlet, emerald, purple, and magenta

General Magical Attributes: The Leo frequency is creative and dominating and is best harnessed when the desired ruling planet passes through the fifth house. Leo is excellent for magic that needs to be creative as well as insightful. Spells and rituals for loyalty, sovereignty, money, passion, pride, vanity, the creation of big ideas, domination of one's will, overcoming challenges, to find inner strength, to take control of a situation, to remove someone's influence, and to influence others are powerful during times of Leonian influence. Witches with a Leo Sun preset will be naturally gifted in the magic listed here.

The Leo frequency is not good for magic regarding trust, equality, justice, or sacrifice. Leo devotion: Perform in a stage play or drama, publish a blog post or article with a Leo theme, meet new people, partake in networking events, be artistic, and perform the magic listed above.

Leo Presets

Leo Rising

The Sun blesses those with Leo rising with a bombastic personality that inspires a positive outlook on life. These people are showmen by nature and have a knack for drawing attention to themselves. Luckily they are spiritually determined to inspire others to do better in life and rise above the perils of suffering. Their spiritual journey will take them to large institutions where they will quickly rise in influence. Those who don't find themselves involved in large spiritual institutions will likely discover an urge to connect to large amounts of spiritually like-minded people via the Internet. They value tradition but enjoy playfulness and will revolutionize spiritual education systems. Witches with this preset are likely to become priests and priestesses of power deities that encourage freedom.

Moon in Leo

The flamboyant and thrill-seeking frequency Leo meets the Moon in the heavens and produces an atmosphere of idealism and optimism. The Moon is warmed as it transits Leo and its emotional influences are directed at helping others feel better about themselves during tough times. As it enters the frequency of Leo, the Moon makes us feel like we don't have enough and may lead us on a spending spree. As it exits, it lays the groundwork for networking and social gatherings where we can be seen.

Magic to gain influence, to make your feelings be heard, to heal from emotional trauma, to purify the heart, and to bring about change in leadership are powerful during this transit. Witches with this preset, in addition to being naturally skilled in these magic, will possess a propensity for scrying and have excellent leadership qualities.

Mercury in Leo

During this transit Mercury and Leo create one of the brightest and most enjoyable atmospheres that we could ask for. This is a fantastic time for writing, social networking, parties, and coven meetings where big decisions need to be made regarding the future. As Mercury enters the frequency of Leo it adds fuel to the already bright and fiery sign. As it exits this frequency, Mercury helps to build bridges to the future and helps to clear any mental fog that might be standing in the way of obtaining empowerment.

Magic for eloquence, networking, inspiration, and to gain attention are particularly powerful during this transit. Witches born with this preset will be naturally gifted within these magical arts and will also find that they possess a particular command of the voice in magic.

Venus in Leo

Venus is full of love and devotion to give and Leo is more than willing to soak it all up. When Venus travels through the frequency of Leo it adds an amorous pull on almost everything we do. We become pleasure-seeking and allow ourselves to indulge a bit too much, perhaps out of a need to feel as full and bountiful on the inside as we do on the outside. When Venus enters Leo it immediately quickens our emotional responses to those with whom we are in personal and professional relationships. As it leaves, however, Venus lays the groundwork for self-love work. This transit in general produces a lot of drama.

Magic for self-love, to attract a lover, to heal previous emotional scars, and to gain dominance in a relationship are done with ease during this transit. If you have this preset you will find that you are particularly blessed at glamour magic in addition to the previously mentioned forms of magic.

Mars in Leo

The fire of Leo is accentuated when Mars enters this frequency. Double the fire means double the passion and enthusiasm. The air becomes full of potential and we find ourselves wanting to be surrounded by beautiful and lush scenery. Our need and drive for sex is also increased (especially if you have a fire-dominant chart). When Mars enters this frequency it makes us aware of our primal instincts to seek attention from potential mates and partners. This can make you needy, so you are just as likely to attract a hot fling as you are to annoy your boyfriend of nine years. As it exits this frequency Mars clears the path of blocks related to how you express yourself.

Sex magic of any kind as well as those magic that are employed to find a partner, to be heard in large crowds, to take dominance in the bedroom or the boardroom, and for clearing obstacles are powerful during this transit. Witches with this preset will find that in addition to being gifted in these magical areas they will also make excellent ritual wards and would likely find great empowerment through sex magic.

Jupiter in Leo

The combination of Leo and Jupiter produces a bright and buzzy atmosphere where anything is possible. During this time you are likely to gain positive attention from a boss or coworker, come up with big ideas to propel yourself forward, and are prone to moments of serendipity. When Jupiter enters the frequency of Leo it ushers in a period of good luck, especially in gambling and games of chance. As it leaves it helps to connect us to greener pastures in our career sector.

Magic to gain public awareness or attention, for luck in gambling or money, and to remove curses are powerful during this time. Witches with this preset will note that in addition to being talented in the previously mentioned magic they are also likely to be gifted at finding lost objects.

Saturn in Leo

These two don't get along as well as they could and perhaps that is because Saturn puts a dampener on things with its overbearing ways. During this time we are likely to develop a coldness towards those we love as we begin to question and even retaliate against any parts of our connections that don't serve us. As Saturn enters Leo it slows the otherwise confident and fiery frequency by changing the way it presents itself entirely, adding an earthy element. Think of the energy changing from a campfire to lava. It becomes sluggish and clings to just about everything it touches. As it exits Leo it will leave emptiness behind in its wake, which might leave you feeling a bit weak and confused.

Magic during this time will go smoothly as long as they are not for obstacle removal. Witches born with this preset should keep the sigil of Leo on their Earth altar to help bring balance.

Uranus in Leo

The connection between Uranus and Leo is strong and flows pretty smoothly. When transiting through the fiery and energetic frequency of Leo, Uranus brings a need for heroism as well as a need to be seen being the hero. This is generally okay because it also brings luck in just about every arena in life. As it enters, Uranus instantly starts broadening the influence of Leo on our lives and ushers in a period of seeing things that we were unable to see before. As it exits it gives a chance for sudden opportunities to develop from current or past love relationships.

Magic for love, sex, to gain the truth from anyone, to be heard or seen by anyone, and those magic to bring about sudden change are powerful during this transit. Witches with this preset are likely to be blessed with enhanced psychic perception through omens, in addition to the previously mentioned magic.

Neptune in Leo

This combination brings about a time of dignity, generosity, and courage. Those with Neptune in Leo are likely to be great leaders who bring about enormous change through sacrifice. Witches with this preset are also likely to be great healers.

Pluto in Leo

Brings about love of power and aggression but also change through seeking pleasure and enlightenment.

The Sagittarius Frequency

Sagittarius is a regal and commanding frequency. It's known to be daring, jovial, independent, tactless, superficial, sophisticated, restless, optimistic, and straightforward. Those with this as a Sun sign preset will possess all of these traits and will have the good fortune to reap major reward from them in life. Likely to attract others to their inspiring ideas, these people make natural leaders and pioneers with an intuitive knack for knowing when to show up at just the right moment. These people value humanity's bright future more than its past.

Quality: Mutable (adaptive)

Ruling Planet: Jupiter

Body Part Association: Thighs and hips

Day of the Week: Thursday

Plants and Herbs: Birch trees, lime, sage, bilberry, oak trees, ash trees, anise, moss, cinnamon, honeysuckle, aster, vervain, deer's tongue, and dandelion

Metal Association: Tin

Gemstone Association: Topaz, beryl, lapis lazuli, citrine, emerald, Iolite, labradorite, sugilite, and zircon

Color: Dark blue, red, dark cyan, purple, gold, emerald, black, and royal blue

General Magical Attributes: During times of Sagittarian influence, magic should be big and allowed to make a splash. Spells and rituals for growth, opportunity, to assist friendships into becoming more, to produce spontaneity in lovers, to protect personal freedoms, expansion of any kind, to aid in multitasking and versatility, aid in comprehension, for social justice, and to lift one from depression are powerful during the time of Sagittarian influence. Witches with this Sun sign preset are likely to be naturally skilled in the magic listed here.

The Sagittarian frequency, however, may not be copacetic with bindings, control, or love spells.

Sagittarius Devotion: Engaging in stimulating conversation, moderating a debate, laughing until your belly hurts, helping others, acts of leadership, and performing any magic listed above.

Sagittarius Presets

Sagittarius Rising

Jupiter, the ruling planet of Sagittarius, blesses those with Sagittarius rising by providing them with a restless spirit and a love of living life to the fullest. Those with this preset are likely to travel a lot and are not likely to live in one location for too long. Spiritually they idealize humanitarianism and egalitarian principles and often find themselves in a fight over injustices, especially those done to spiritual groups and minorities. These people are likely to become leaders in their spiritual communities, as they are capable of inspiring large amounts of people and having sway over public opinion. Those with this preset are also likely to revolutionize magical systems and update outdated practices.

Moon in Sagittarius

In the bright and shining frequency of Sagittarius the Moon loses its shy nature and becomes more outwardly expressive. During this transit we become more capable of processing sensory information and are capable of transversing astral planes with ease. As the Moon enters the frequency of Sagittarius it ushers in a lighter mood and a jovialness to tasks at hand and urges us to give back to society. As it exits, however, the Moon is likely to cling to its independence in this frequency and might leave us feeling vulnerable to assimilation.

Magic during this time for independence, emotional freedom, to change outlook, gain insight into hidden truths, and all shamanic practices are done with ease. Witches with this preset are likely to posses skill as mediums and empaths in addition to being naturally gifted with the magic listed here.

Mercury in Sagittarius

This combination makes for a fast and seemingly restless period as Mercury travels through the frequency of Sagittarius. During this time expect sudden opportunities to travel, moments of serendipity, and heightened fear of censorship. As Mercury enters the frequency of Sagittarius it ushers in an outspoken need for freedom and a certain awareness of limitation. As it leaves, however, it prepares us for bigger and better things that lie just beyond our field of view. Allow yourself to prioritize the finishing of any projects that might bring you money.

Magic to encourage freedom of expression in oneself and in others, for honesty, for eloquence, or for inspiration are particularly powerful during this transit. Witches with this preset will be naturally gifted in these magic and are likely to make gifted cartomancers.

Venus in Sagittarius

During this transit we romanticize the impossible, lose ourselves in the chase, and discover the fiery lover within. This undoubtedly produces a wild and exciting time that will bring on confusion if we aren't diligent in addressing emotional issues as they arise. Venus, the bringer of harmony and love, ushers in a period of time in which we fall in love with the idea of love and begin to compare our relationships to idealized Hollywood versions of perfect love. If we aren't careful we can bite off more than we can chew as this transit does not have the staying power to prolong these comparisons. As it leaves it provides ample opportunity for us to bring the spark back into relationships we thought long dead.

Magic to entice a lover, to bring about harmony through collaboration, to encourage honesty between lovers, and magic for eloquence when speaking from the heart are powerful during this transit. Witches with this preset will note that in addition to possessing skill in these magic, they also likely have great skills at teaching the craft.

Mars in Sagittarius

This combination produces an atmosphere full of limitless possibility and a sensual outlook. Mars, the great bringer of new beginnings and action, pairs nicely with independent Sagittarius, inviting us to challenge our perceived boundaries. As Mars enters Sagittarius it brings with it a period of strong personal motivation for success in our careers, as well as an increased libido. As it leaves, it takes with it the remaining vestiges of self-doubt, making the future a bright place.

Magic that involve manifestation through the law of attraction, to increase motivation and stamina, and those magic that involve the removal of obstacles are exceptionally potent during this transit. Witches with this preset will posses natural ability in these magic as well as a natural ability to gain dominance over others.

Jupiter in Sagittarius

Jupiter is quite at home here in Sagittarius as it is the ruling planet associated with this frequency. During this transit we will be blessed with an industrial mind and a generous nature, which is likely to bring us luck in limited partnerships. As it enters the frequency of Sagittarius, Jupiter is known for bringing good fortune into our lives and increases our intuitive ability to make cash. As it leaves it paves the way for future career changes or advancement.

Magic to get a new job, for success of all kinds, for eloquence, for luck, and for manifestation through sympathetic work will be done with ease during this transit. Witches with this preset will possess natural skill in these magic in addition to making great teachers and engineers of magic.

Saturn in Sagittarius

This transit produces internal struggle between our need for structure and security and our desire for excitement and adventure. We are likely to talk ourselves out of new experiences that would otherwise bring us great happiness. During this transit we are likely to become shy and will feel as though time is moving slower than usual. As Saturn enters Sagittarius it decreases the momentum of projects, delaying success until we have learned a lesson or two in patience. As it leaves, however, it releases hidden pressures related to long-term goals, freeing up much-needed mental space.

Magic involving the law and to gain insight into the unknown can be done with ease during this transit. Witches with this preset are likely to make great magical advocates and counselors, in addition to being naturally skilled in the magic mentioned here. Magical acts involving luck should be avoided during the first week of this transit.

Uranus in Sagittarius

Uranus and Sagittarius join forces to produce a remarkably pioneering and inventive atmosphere during this transit. Originality and independent thinking yield fast reward and recognition during this time. As Uranus enters Sagittarius it ushers a period of luck in the areas of business, science, and philosophy. This is an excellent time to build your financial portfolio. As it exits the frequency of Sagittarius, Uranus paves the way for prophetic vision.

Magic for success of all kinds, to increase psychic sensitivity, and uncrossing are done with ease during this time. Witches with this preset will make excellent psychic-sensitives in addition to being naturally skilled in these magic.

Neptune in Sagittarius

The combination of Neptune and Sagittarius produces a long-lasting and compassionate period of time. Those born with this preset are known for their higher mental processes and profoundly spiritual relationship to humanity. Magically, those with this preset are likely to be excellent channelers.

Pluto in Sagittarius

Brings about change through the development of foreign relations, philosophy, and spiritual understanding.

The Earth Frequencies

Earth frequency strengths lie in stability yet stubbornness. This band of frequency is known for its perseverance and practicality as it ushers in moments of growth and stimulation to productive efforts. It is motivated by the material and generally seeks to find harmony with its surroundings. It can be bring order or chaos depending on how it is being directed.

Domineering and compassionate, those with multiple presets (planets, asteroids, comets, nodes, etc.) to Earth frequencies carry the energy of the working masses.

The Taurus Frequency

Taurus has a warm but shy feeling to its frequency. It is stylized, persistent, clingy, reliable, steadfast, patient, routine-oriented, shy, glamourous, possessive, resentful, and also placid. Those with a Taurus Sun sign are known for being hard workers who have a sensible approach to life. These people tend to be emotionally sensitive and giving but sometimes have a difficult time expressing themselves. Taurans need to feel secure and are likely strongly connected to home and family.

Quality: Fixed (strong)

Ruling Planet: Mercury

Body Part Association: Throat, neck, and thyroid

Day of the Week: Friday

Plants and Herbs: Violet, poppy, roses, apple, crab apple, fig, cloves, spearmint, beans, wheat, mugwort, lovage, sage, cardamom, patchouli, and heather

Metal Association: Copper

Gemstone Association: Emerald, azurite, agate, coral, rose quartz, kunzite, selenite, and diamond

Color: Pink, pale violet red, magenta, orchid, pear, mauve, blue, and gold

General Magical Attributes: The Taurus frequency is strong and solid. Magic for anything requiring extra foundational energies or stronger group-mind connection are especially easy during this time of Tauran influence. Spells and rituals for acquisition, patience, virtuous growth, long-term projects, tying of one's nature, binding, stability, and magic to convince someone conception is a good idea are ideal for this time. Witches with this Sun sign preset will be naturally gifted in these magic.

Magic for creativity, charitable donations, new friendships, reconciliation, and personal awareness may not be successful when employing this frequency.

Taurus Devotion: Shopping (especially antiques), beauty treatments, massage, balancing bank accounts, and work around the house and home.

Taurus Presets

Taurus Rising

Venus, the ruling planet of Taurus, governs over beauty and esthetics and brings its desire to harmonize with both into the mix. Those with Taurus rising spiritually explore and express themselves through art, decorating, poetry, and the creation of the visually pleasing. These people tend to find wealth and material possessions to be quite important in life and measure how successful they are based on how much they have amassed. Another equally important part of life to them is love, as those with this preset tend to obsess and agonize over it but are likely to be quite blessed in this department. These people strive to embody the higher ideals of cleanliness both spiritually and physically and are also likely to seek out others with whom to do deeper spiritual work.

Witches with the rising sign of Taurus are particularly gifted in the arts and will most likely incorporate them into their magical practices.

These witches should also pay special attention to the home as they are likely to attract helpful spirits there.

Moon in Taurus

Taurus is strong and unchangeable but the Moon is the exact opposite. Exalted by the frequency of Taurus, the Moon is at its strongest when influenced by the earthy and stable energy that resides there. The result is that we get all of the power of the Moon without the changeability. When the Moon is in Taurus we have access to stable lunar energy that heightens our sensory perception as well as our ability to send and receive psychic phenomenon. When the Moon enters Taurus it brings with it an instinctual urge to seek out what is real and tangible in our everyday beliefs and banish what is not. As it begins to leave Taurus, the Moon forces us to examine the impractical beliefs surrounding how we spend our money, spiritual resources, and emotional energy.

Magic for self-love, romantic love, glamour, beauty, the clearing of lower frequencies, as well as any magic that is done in the name of compassion should be executed with ease during times when the Moon is in Taurus. Witches with this preset not only are naturally gifted with the magic listed here but are also likely to excel at channeling.

Mercury in Taurus

When the swiftness of Mercury meets the earthiness of Taurus the result is a productive mind and an eagerness to be busy. When in Taurus, Mercury's otherwise cool intellect is transformed into a rigid system of checks and balances that must be met with a keen eye in order to take full advantage of all it has to offer. As it enters this frequency, Mercury ushers in a period of know-it-all behavior that can cause more than its share of communication problems. As it begins to leave Taurus, however, it strips away our impractical beliefs about money and gives us insight into a better way to budget and manage it.

Magic for long-term financial success should be started during this time. Magic for glamour, eloquence in speech, and to get a good deal on a large purchase can be done with ease during Mercury in Taurus. Witches with this as a preset are not only naturally gifted at the magic listed here but will also excel at psychic protection and would make excellent wards in ritual.

Venus in Taurus

Venus is quite at home here as she has rulership over this frequency. This connection here may be strong but it ushers in a period of slow emotional understanding and processing. Sexual desires grow into needs as we search for someone to hold on to and feel a physical bond with. As Venus enters Taurus it reminds us that love is necessary in life and it forces us to look at our romantic relationships, past and present. As it begins to leave it stirs up our primordial need for connection and encourages us to seek it out.

Magic for love, lust, dominance, and connection are easily performed during this time, as well as sex magic and Tantra. Witches with this preset will find that they are naturally good at the magic listed here as well as with all money magic.

Mars in Taurus

Mars is fiery and passionate and Taurus is earthy and romantic. Put the two together and you get fireworks! Our drives to succeed in the material world are doubled under this influence and we change the way we measure what it means to succeed altogether. Our motivations change and we start chasing two things: sex and money. When Mars enters Taurus it brings with it a burst of physical energy that leaves us craving a night on the dance floor and a chance to impress a new (or current) lover. As it leaves it takes with it our unseen strategies for financial success.

Magic for love, lust, to take control of a situation, and to remove obstacles can be done during times of Mars in Taurus with ease. Witches with this planetary preset are not only naturally gifted at those magic but are also talented crystal healers.

Jupiter in Taurus

These two go together quite well as Jupiter rules over abundance and Taurus over money and the material. Combined, these two pulse with secure potential and create a foundation for powerful changes in our luck with money and our relationship to it. As Jupiter enters the frequency of Taurus it almost instantly brings with it a sense of universal abundance and our eagerness to connect to it heightens. As it exits it helps us to remove the blocks that are keeping us from secure financial living.

Magic when Jupiter is in Taurus will go off without a hitch if they are for security, protection, long-term financial growth, or for securing an easy transition to a new promotion. In addition to being naturally skilled in these magic, witches with this preset also often possess the musical or poetic skill through which their magic is strongly conveyed.

Saturn in Taurus

The heavier aspects of Saturn are highlighted when it travels through the frequency of Taurus. It brings us abrupt awareness as to our current ability to access resources as well as our ability to provide. When Saturn enters Taurus it is a good idea to finish large transactions, buy stocks and bonds, and cash in on large investments. As it leaves it will increase your urge to donate to the less fortunate or help out a friend in need.

Magic centered on the protection of home, family, or assets as well as magic to help increase your savings like "money stay with me" are excellent during this time. Witches with a preset of Saturn in Taurus are naturally gifted at these magic as well as the gifts of karmic healing.

Uranus in Taurus

Uranus in Taurus produces a strong willpower as well as a desire to build, create, and ultimately expand one's own empire. Our sense of determination is heightened greatly during this time. As it enters Taurus, patient Uranus ushers in a period of time in which we are asked to reevaluate modes of self-dedication as it stirs our deeper desires to obtain more in life. As it enters the last ten degrees of its transition we are urged to replace the old and worn out with the new and energized. Witches with this preset are likely to be great at money magic and manifestation through visualization.

Neptune in Taurus

This combination ushers in a deeper understanding of what is really important in life. Those born with this preset carry with them a need to explore their psyche through spiritual quests and are most likely born with heightened psychic ability.

Pluto in Taurus

Brings forth greed, materialism, division of class systems, and revolution.

The Virgo Frequency

The Virgo frequency is passionate yet modest. It's known for being driven by perfectionism, shy, diligent, analytical, conservative, as well as reliable and meticulous. Those with this Sun sign preset are likely to possess great attention to detail and to have an investigative and inquisitive personality. These people make excellent teachers, counselors, and scientists.

Quality: Mutable (adaptive)

Ruling Planets: Mercury (and Earth)

Body Part Association: Stomach, abdomen, and nervous system

Day of the Week: Wednesday

Plants and Herbs: All nut-bearing trees and low-growing flowers such as periwinkle, clematis, fern, anise, lavender, bergamot, rosemary, peppermint, valerian, and marjoram

Metal Association: Nickel and mercury

Gemstone Association: Sardonyx, rhodochrosite, zircon, carnelian, moss agate, amazonite, turquoise, gold, and apatite

Color: Dark blue, earthen brown, cobalt, steel, pink, violet, purple, and white

General Magical Attributes: This frequency is particularly helpful for any magic that requires details to line up in specific ways to produce the desired results, and for multi-action spells. Spells and rituals for longevity, manifestation of thought into physical form, protection, exorcism, the building of infrastructure, spirit channeling and karmic clearing, and to assist in weight loss are powerful magic in this frequency. Witches with this Sun sign preset will be naturally gifted in the magic listed here.

   The Virgo frequency, however, isn't the best for chaos, sex, or love magic as the tendency for this frequency to become obsessive can get in the way of potential outcomes.

Virgo Devotion: Solving crossword puzzles, playing chess, completing puzzles, diet and exercise, home improvement, volunteering with organizations that build homes for the poor, and performing the magic listed above.

Virgo Presets

Virgo Rising

Mercury, the ruling planet of Virgo, bestows upon you the blessings of a highly analytical mind that will steer you well in this life. Those with this preset are likely not to consider themselves to be overtly spiritual but will likely play a valuable role in the spiritual development of others. One of the interesting things about this ascending frequency is that it will attract to you those who seek practical advice on matters of the heart and soul. The conversations that ensue may not have much significance to you but to these people they are likely to bring much-needed grounding to otherwise turbulent waters. People who feel lost or overwhelmed will be naturally drawn to anyone with this preset. Travel and property are likely to be a large part of life for those with this rising sign preset and they will also be inclined to find spiritual inspiration when abroad.

Witches with this preset will be gifted in green magic involving herbalism and the healing arts. Though not likely in any rush to become leader of the pack, these witches will be the steady force behind many progressions when involved in covens and spiritual community.

Moon in Virgo

The Virgo frequency is a stabilizer for the Moon as it travels through. The Moon, now given structure and integrity, gives us an opportunity to take off the rose-colored glasses and see ourselves as we really are. Luckily, this isn't so much destructive as it is supportive, so there is a strong chance we will find avenues to personal empowerment during this transit. As the Moon enters Virgo it grounds our emotional selves and provides much-needed level thinking. During this time we are likely to lose confidence in matters of the heart, so this isn't a good time for romance. As it leaves, the Moon inspires us to apply common sense to anything that has been bugging us. Those with this preset will likely not trust people easily.

Magic during this transit will be powerful if it is for emotional balance, freedom from bad relationships, to gain insight into the motives of others, and/or for truth. Witches with this preset will be naturally gifted in these magic and will also make great psychic counselors and ritual wards.

Mercury in Virgo

The mind is sharpened and our mental processes become more rigid during this transit. Mercury, the ruler of thought and intellect, takes on the structured and sometimes overly analytical properties of Virgo, producing an atmosphere of eagerness and tension. As Mercury enters Virgo it immediately begins to change our relationship to human weakness. We become hypercritical of others and perceive weakness as failure and we will also find ourselves being less emotionally responsive than normal. As it leaves the frequency of Virgo, however, it lays the mental groundwork for scientific process and increases our observation skills.

Magic for uncrossing, to find new ways of moving through issues in life, herbal work for memory retention, as well as all magic observing strict protocol are done with ease during this time. Witches born with this preset are likely to be gifted in these magic and most likely possess excellent visualization skills.

Venus in Virgo

This particular transit is known for bringing about scandal involving sex and/or relationships, especially if you have this as a preset. Venus, the ruler of love, beauty, and harmony, exaggerates the untrusting nature of Virgo, producing fear around emotional exploitation. As Venus enters Virgo it ushers in a time of intelligent emotional responsiveness; just be careful not to think yourself out of love or passion but rather use this time to evaluate and plan. As Venus exits the frequency of Virgo, it makes the air ripe for mentorship and partnerships based on mutual understanding. Those with this preset should note that they may have difficulties with power dynamics in love. It is very important that they demand reciprocity and equality in relationships to avoid the negative aspects of this preset in life.

Magic for ending a relationship that is past its prime, to remove unwanted influences from your life, and to protect those you love are done easily during this time. Those with this preset will notice that in addition to being naturally skilled in these magic, they also possess a natural propensity to teach.

Mars in Virgo

The fiery and determined influence of Mars is refined and given instruction during this transit. Virgo, being a frequency of planning, organization, and quiet stability, lends its structural integrity to Mars during this transit, bringing order to chaos. When Mars enters Virgo it is likely to cause us to feel overwhelmed by detail and bogged down by the amount of work we perceive to be on our plate. As it spends time in this frequency it helps us to organize and empower new systems of approach to that which brings us anxiety and stress. As Mars leaves, it encourages us to build stronger foundations.

Magic involving energetic support, bringing order to chaos, for empowering us before new projects or to reinvigorate during long projects, and all glamour should be done with ease during this transit. Witches with this preset will notice they are skilled in these magic as well as those magic that require secrecy.

Jupiter in Virgo

Jupiter, the big and jovial protector of our solar system, turns his influence over success and blessings inward during this transit and produces an atmosphere of intellectual desire. The usually heady Jupiter pairs nicely with the down-to-earth Virgo because it grounds the otherwise too intellectual by adding common sense to the mix. This allows for us to find real-world answers to our problems surrounding manifestation. When Jupiter enters

Virgo it is likely to increase the odds of being noticed by others for hobbies and pastimes. It is also likely that business opportunities can come from your hobbies and special interests. As it leaves, Jupiter establishes intellectual connections to others, which can fuel success in life.

Magic for wishes, to bring dreams into reality, to help others grow in success, and for harnessing unseen potential will be executed with ease during this time. Witches with this preset will find that, in addition to discovering they are skilled in these magic, they possess skill at teaching the craft and other spiritual systems to others.

Saturn in Virgo

Unlike when Saturn transits the other frequencies, bringing chaos and confusion, he is quite at home in earthy and practical Virgo. Heightening Virgo's powers of intellect and organization, Saturn stokes the flames of goal-based desire. As it enters Virgo, Saturn stirs the cauldron of practicality and encourages us to deal with long-term dark clouds that have been following us around in life. This generally happens by a bit of obsessive thinking, so do be careful not to pick yourself apart without having the intention to immediately put yourself back together. As Saturn leaves it makes us vulnerable to overreacting when we feel we aren't being understood by others, and could bring wisdom through vision and trance work.

Magic for money, weight loss, achieving goal-based desires, long-term career frequency adjustment, and to gain wisdom are done with ease during this transit. Witches with this preset will note that in addition to being naturally skilled at these magical forms they are also likely to possess great skill in the divinatory arts of Tarot and runes.

Uranus in Virgo

Uranus in Virgo creates a period of time in which allegiance and unity are replaced with independence and eccentricity. During this time there is an extreme desire to better the world through healthful adjustment. When

Virgo enters Uranus it brings luck through sudden changes in career or spiritual community. As it leaves it paves the way for changes in diet and exercise.

Magic for psychic protection, secrecy, to aid in health changes, and to break from restrictive routines can be done with ease at this time. Witches with this preset are likely to naturally posses skill in these magic as well as all forms of divination.

Neptune in Virgo

This combination ushers in a time of great change from the status quo and great medical advances. Those with this preset are known for their work in the civil rights movement, for being fiercely challenging of outdated concepts, and for being psychically gifted. Magically, those with this preset are capable of swaying large numbers of people to their side of an argument.

Pluto in Virgo

Brings about revolution through exploration, service to others, and by actively identifying threats to progress.

The Capricorn Frequency

This frequency is solid and communal. It is known for being ambitious, stubborn, patient, careful, prudent, disciplined, practical, conventional, and at times rigid. Those with this Sun sign preset are likely to be devoted to a cause and possess a hungry desire for success and money. This desire comes from a never-ending yearning for stability and the ability to provide for yourself and others. They are conservative and can be a little standoffish at first or put off a cold vibe, but they are more than willing to help a stranger in need, even to their own detriment.

Quality: Cardinal (activating)

Ruling Planets: Saturn

Body Part Association: Knees, bones, and teeth

Day of the Week: Saturday

Plants and Herbs: Pine, marijuana, poplar trees, hemlock, henbane, pansy, yew, willow, comfrey, ivy, jasmine, rue, and honeysuckle

Metal Association: Silver and lead

Gemstone Association: Amethyst, turquoise, garnet, cat's eye, onyx, boji stones, bloodstones, beryl, malachite, smokey quartz, and tourmaline

Color: Dark brown, deep grey, true black, hunter green, navy blue, indigo, and champagne

General Magical Attributes: Energies under its influence help to stabilize energy, making Capricorn great for long-term magical projects. Spells and rituals for generosity, to defuse emotional situations, to lower emotional sensitivities, to affect someone's confidence, to make overwhelming obstacles move forward, and all magic related to the underdog are powerful during times of Capricorn influence. Those with this preset are naturally gifted in the magic listed here.

    The Capricorn frequency isn't the best for magic dealing with love, management, or sex.

Capricorn Devotion: Putting your hands and/or feet in the earth, taking classes in martial arts or yoga, building something, helping the less fortunate, and performing the magic listed here.

Capricorn Presets

Capricorn Rising

Those with Capricorn rising are blessed by Saturn to have a cautious demeanor that will serve them well in life. Those with this preset are known for being shy and sometimes hard to connect with, but once connection has been made they are sure to be warm and inviting. This preset disposes its natives to have a quiet spirituality that is more about service and less about ecstasy and rapture. Their spiritual journey will lead them to deep spiritual wells that will shake their foundations to the core and long treks through a dry desert where they will feel spiritually isolated. Those with this Capricorn rising are likely to want to take on the burdens of others out of an instinctual feeling of responsibility for their fellow human. Spirit for these people is best nurtured in a garden or amongst a forest than in a grand temple. Likely spiritual development can be gained through martial arts and yoga.

Moon in Capricorn

When the Moon transits the restrictive frequency of Capricorn it gains support but suffers from an inability to fully express itself. During this transit we are likely to become more persistent when seeking answers from others and will require more attention from our partners. Even with this need for reassuring affection we are still likely to be emotionally distant. When the Moon enters the frequency of Capricorn it brings reassurance to false perceptions and can make it difficult to distinguish reality from fiction. As it exits this frequency the Moon is molded into a stronger vessel capable of withstanding great pressure.

Magic for psychic and physical protection, to bring stability to unstable relationships, to end affairs and scandalous behavior, and to inspire commitment from partners are exceptionally powerful during this transit. Witches with this preset will possess great skill in these magic and will likely make great herbalists and healers.

Mercury in Capricorn

Swift and impulsive Mercury is made patient and logical as it travels through the frequency of Capricorn. During this transit we can expect to find ourselves feeling the need to slow down and remove irrational thinking that could be inhibiting us. It is likely that we will experience a mental shift toward calculated strategy and we will relinquish impulsive thought process, if only for a moment. When Mercury enters Capricorn it heightens our authoritarian processes but shortens our patience in regards to the patience of others. As it exits this frequency, Mercury paves the way for new foundational infrastructures that will allow you to better convey your intentions to the world. Those with this preset should be aware of their potential to dismay others by being too dictatorial when communicating.

Magic to gain authority in all matters, to aid in the clearing of blocks towards meditation, to remove energetic blocks in the chakra system or three souls, as well as all magic involving cunning or rootwork are potent during this transit. Witches with this preset are likely to be skilled herbal healers in addition to being naturally gifted with the magic listed here.

Venus in Capricorn

Venus and Capricorn share a passionate bond during this transit that escalates our drives to fulfill the primal roles of courtship and partnership: to provide, to nurture, and to protect. During this transit these ancient roles become the primary focus in our love sector. When Venus enters Capricorn it increases our capacity to maintain space for others who are healing from emotional trauma but will also increase our capacity to receive energy empathically. Witches with this preset should especially be aware of their natural ability for empathy. As Venus exits Capricorn it helps us to introduce better boundaries to our relationships.

Magic to add stability to old relationships, for emotional healing after major trauma, and to summon the attention of a potential lover are all done with ease during this time. Witches with this preset are likely to possess an acute ability to psychically identify the physical pain of others in addition to being naturally gifted in the magic listed here. I highly recommend that these witches do regular cleansings as part of their spiritual practice.

Mars in Capricorn

During this transit the roaring energy of fiery Mars is harnessed and turned into a creative tool that can bring about great change if met with proper discipline. Imagine taking a wild fire and turning it into a forge; all of the potential energy that would otherwise be left unfocused now has the chance to burn with steady intention. As Mars enters Capricorn it heralds a time when we start to develop or reinforce systematic structures that will provide current and future stability. As it leaves it heightens obstinacy and sets the stage for potential problems brought on by stubbornness.

Magic to bring order to chaos, to aid in the cultivation of personal discipline, to uncross or unhex a business or family, and to inspire strategy are all done with ease during this time. Witches with this preset are likely to possess great skill in manifestation and creative visualization and, in addition to being naturally gifted in these magic, their magic will likely pack a punch.

Jupiter in Capricorn

Jupiter brings great success through ambition and hard work during this particular transit. Capricorn, being a frequency of business and romance, inspires Jupiter, the planet of success and expansion, to bring focus to our desires. During this transit we can expect to have luck in our careers and covens and will likely notice adjustments to the way the culture functions in these areas. People in general will become more passionate about the same things as those around them. As Jupiter enters the frequency of Capricorn it encourages us to take a serious look at our finances and to begin the process of long-term financial planning. As a result, Jupiter will bless any wealth that accumulates with abundance. As Jupiter leaves the frequency of Capricorn it inspires us to budget for daily expenses better so we can spend generously later.

Magic for business success, to bring about change in intimate social structures, to uncross and/or unhex oneself in the areas of money and entrepreneurship, as well as magic to inspire passion in ourselves and others is done with ease during this transit. Witches with this preset will be naturally gifted in these magic and are likely to make excellent leaders in their spiritual communities.

Saturn in Capricorn

The frequency of Capricorn is ruled by the planet Saturn, making it feel quite at home here. Both positive and negative aspects of Saturn are empowered during this transit, so we are likely to discover a rejuvenated need for independence at this time. When Saturn enters Capricorn it makes us less likely to seek help from others or be willing to take much-needed advice. Be careful during this time not to push close friends away. As Jupiter exits, it leaves behind a feeling of melancholy.

Magic to bring about independence are done with ease during this transit. Witches with this preset are likely to make excellent herbal healers but should work on their bedside manner.

Uranus in Capricorn

Uranus, the planet of originality and change, enjoys its stay in independent and focused Capricorn. This transit produces a constructive atmosphere and a strong will to succeed. As Uranus enters Capricorn it ushers in a time of idealized leadership where we are invited to step up to the plate. At this time it is likely that we will experience a great need to break away from the norm. As Uranus leaves, it brings us deeper to our inner desires and helps us to manifest them in our reality.

Magic for psychic development, to inspire leadership, to bring change in leadership, and for removing obstacles that stand in your way are all done with ease during this transit. Witches with this preset will be naturally gifted in these magic and are likely to possess great skill at manifestation through creative visualization.

Neptune in Capricorn

This combination brings about a change in how we relate to the natural resources both within the planet and within ourselves. Those born with this preset are destined to bring about great change by remodeling old ideas and allowing them to inspire new ways of thinking. Witches with this preset are likely to be great mediators between our world and others and have a knack for spotting false spiritual paradigms.

Pluto in Capricorn

Brings revolution through a change in work ethic and a heightened sense of responsibility.

The Air Frequencies

Air frequencies' strengths lie in the mental plane. The arts and all forms of communication are governed over by these frequencies, and when channeled with skill they can be used to bring about an enemy's change. These frequencies are untouchable yet they can touch us, allowing us only to know they are there when they choose to let us know. Air frequencies inspire those they touch to be free spirits and to rise above all conflict and search for higher ground. Those with multiple Air frequency presets will be sometimes difficult to understand when they are excited and often verbally process their deeper thoughts and emotions.

The Gemini Frequency

The Gemini frequency is highly adaptable and capable of bridging the mental and the material. Known for being eloquent and lively, this frequency is versatile, swift, cunning, charming, superficial, tense, youthful, communicative, and restless. Those who have this Sun sign preset are known for having skills in multiple areas of life, for having varying interests, and for possessing a quick wit. These people make excellent teachers and politicians and are excellent at dealing with others.

Quality: Mutable (adaptive)

Ruling Planets: Mercury and Uranus

Body Part Association: The nervous system, shoulders, and upper arms

Day of the Week: Wednesday

Plants and Herbs: Lily of the valley, all ferns, lavender, all nuts, all nut-bearing trees, anise, carrot, and bittersweet

Metal Association: Mercury

Gemstone Association: Agate, citrine, tiger's eye, fluorite, sapphire, topaz, lodestone, jade, green jasper, and peridot

Color: Yellow, neon, amber, lavender, orange, cobalt, silver, violet, and turquoise

General Magical Abilities: All magic requiring an external social component that requires speed, spells, and rituals for adaptability, survival (especially survival through wit), glamour, politics, social climbing, truth, to gain keen insight, and to heighten perception are all powerful when under the influence of Gemini. Those with a Solar preset here will be naturally gifted in these magic.

Magic for completion, wholeness, stability, and internal questing may not be at its best when this frequency is being channeled.

Gemini Devotion: Debates, reading, attending lectures or workshops, playing games of mental skill, working with technology, and performing any magic listed above.

Gemini Presets

Gemini Rising

Mercury, the ruling planet of Gemini, instills a quick mind, fantastic sense of humor, and a love for audiences. Those with this preset are likely to take on positions of power easily, as they are good at navigating social circles and are also likely good at getting people to listen to them. Their spiritual journey often leads these people to enter larger organizations, take on positions of power, and then later change the status quo. These people are spiritual revolutionists, at least when it comes to the way we think about the roles of spirituality in everyday life. They are likely to be skilled in multiple spiritual practices and techniques, though true masters of few, if any. They are diverse in interests and will often sway from moments of deep spiritual introspection to moments of spiritual avoidance. They like to keep busy and should watch out for spiritual burnout.

Witches with this preset make excellent seers and diviners who more than likely have a knack for teaching, leadership, and conveying spirit through poetry and song.

Moon in Gemini

Gemini is fast and intellectual and the Moon is slow and emotional and also likes to take its time processing. The Moon's sway changes into something more mutable and we are suddenly capable of responding from a collected analytical place rather than an emotional one, and our ability to respond to stimuli is heightened. As the Moon enters Gemini it brings with it a sense of fierce personal independence and a need to be a freethinker. During this time we are most likely to crave deep, philosophical conversation that can actually inspire us, instead of sitting at home in front of the television. As it begins to leave it helps to clarify our outlook for the road ahead and sparks our imagination.

Magic for freedom from that which does not serve you, balance, to calm emotional upheavals, or for bringing new opportunities into your life can be done with much ease during this time. Witches with this as a natal preset will be gifted intuitives, as well as possessing skill in the previously mentioned magic.

Mercury in Gemini

This combination makes for a fast and exciting period of time where we move quickly through the mental plane. Speedy and intellectual Mercury is quite at home here in the frequency he rules, making them a perfect pair. When these two partner during a transit they usher in a period of great mental questing when we become interested in many different subjects all at once, seeking to obtain a true understanding of one's place in life. As it enters Gemini, Mercury brings with it an intense hunger for knowledge and adaptability. We are invited to reevaluate the way we think and to find updated beliefs during this time. As it leaves it takes with it our ability to complete projects and may leave us feeling that we have bitten off more than we can chew.

Magic to aid in memory retention (such as study spells), for truth, to bring balance, and for inspiration are done with ease during this transit. Those witches born with this natal preset are likely to be gifted seers.

Venus in Gemini

When Venus is in Gemini the world is lush with the potential to meet new and exciting people who are more than likely going to redefine the way you connect with loved ones. This combination brings about the need to have an intellectual anchor in relationships, and you may find that your lover is no longer as attractive to you if you haven't connected in this way recently. The mind becomes sexy and appealing to you and you crave connection. Those born with this as a preset are likely to have multiple lovers for this reason. When Venus enters Gemini it ushers in a cool attitude towards life and eases up the stresses of our careers. During this time we are gifted with extra versatility in love and work, so go with the flow! As Venus leaves Gemini it strips away the rose-colored veneer of superficial relationships and leaves us wanting more.

Magic to call forth a true soulmate or kindred spirit, to ignite passion in a group or individual, to reconcile, and to clear auric threads to past relationships are especially easy during this transit. Witches born with this preset will be naturally gifted with these magic and are also likely to possess heightened skill in magical arts of Hoodoo and cunning work.

Mars in Gemini

This combination produces an exuberant mental plane that is capable of shattering outdated concepts to the ground. Mars is fiery and passionate, Gemini is airy and intellectual; when combined they make the air sizzle with electricity. As Mars enters Gemini it brings with it brilliant ideas and new concepts that are likely to revolutionize the way you do things. This also affords you the opportunity to take full advantage of new short-term educational opportunities. As it exits Gemini, Mars clears the path ahead of mental roadblocks and insecurities, and instills pride and vitality to the tired parts of our psyche.

Magic for inspiration, to find new friends of like mind, to clear out stale energy, to be heard in a crowd, and all initiations are performed with ease during this transit. In addition to being naturally gifted with these magic, witches with this preset are also likely to possess skill in warding and make excellent teachers.

Jupiter in Gemini

Jupiter, who rules over success and blessings, gives abundantly when it exists within the frequency of Gemini. As the two pulse together they give us optimism and a positive attitude, which attracts adventure and a willingness to fulfill our ultimate potential. As Jupiter enters Gemini it ushers in diplomacy and a desire to connect to people from all walks of life. As it leaves, it helps to establish a better way forward rooted in awareness of the past.

Magic for eloquence, seership of all kind, communication between the worlds, to bring about change of any kind, and to open the door for shifts in career are done with ease during this transit. Witches who have this preset are likely to be natural teachers and community leaders, in addition to being gifted in these magic.

Saturn in Gemini

This combination creates an atmosphere of intellect and study, coupled with a desire to know more and dig deeper. During this time we are susceptible to problems while traveling and should be aware of how our own cynicism may impact others. As it enters the frequency of Gemini, Saturn brings distraction through music and old habits. As it begins to leave it stirs up feelings of being unprepared or ill-educated.

Magic that help with memory retention (like study spells), for advances in career, and all seership are done with ease during this influence. Witches born with this preset will make excellent profits in addition to being gifted in the previously mentioned magic.

Uranus in Gemini

Uranus in Gemini produces a period of time where inspiration and the imagination run wild. Together these two produce an atmosphere of playfulness and originality that draws others to you. When Uranus enters Gemini it brings with it a desire to travel, learn new languages, and explore the mystical and preternatural. As it leaves it brings you a deeper understanding of the unseen world and a craving for more knowledge.

Magic for psychic development, secrecy, truth, eloquence, and spirit contact are done with ease during this time. Witches with this as a preset will be skilled in shamanism and ecstatic witchcraft.

Neptune in Gemini

This combination ushers in a time of off-the-wall thinking, scientific advancement, and advances in engineering. Those born with this preset are imaginative, magnetic, and even hypnotic at times, magically capable of expressing themselves through invention and the development of new techniques that bridge the spirit world and the mundane.

Pluto in Gemini

Brings about revolution and change in technology and transportation.

The Libra Frequency

The Libra frequency is flirtatious and sympathetic. It is known for being harmonious, diplomatic, self-indulgent, romantic, changeable, charming, chivalrous, indecisive, and easygoing. Those with this Sun sign are capable of bringing balance to any situation, though rarely feel that they themselves are in balance. These people make excellent counselors, mediators, and judges, as they have an innate sense of fairness.

Quality: Cardinal (activating)

Ruling Planets: Venus and Saturn

Body Part Association: Kidneys

Day of the Week: Friday

Plants and Herbs: All roses, cornflower, coriander, ash trees, spearmint, cayenne, vine, poplar, hydrangea, foxglove, thyme, and apple

Metal Association: Copper

Gemstone Association: Sapphire, jade, smokey quartz, tourmaline, ametrine, beryl, kunzite, rose quartz, Iolite, desert rose, and agate

Color: Ultramarine, pale green, steel, blue, dusty pink, cerulean, lavender, and primrose

Magical Abilities: This frequency is capable of changing stable energies into unstable energies, making it perfect for clearing and obstacle removal. Spells and rituals for protection, peace, diplomacy, to slow a process down or stop it all together, legal matters, reconciliation, forgiveness, to gain friends and allies, and to gain favor among peers are extra potent when this frequency is employed. Those with a Solar preset here will be naturally gifted in these magic.

Avoid magic for independence, speedy endings, to bring final outcomes, or banishment when working with this frequency.

Libra Devotion: Performing the magic listed here, creating beauty through art, flower arranging, attending a court hearing or rally, and mild self-indulgence.

Libra Presets

Libra Rising

Those with Libra rising, thanks to the blessings of Saturn, are born with an innate sense of right and wrong that will ultimately color their entire lives. They are naturally drawn to the arts as a way of expressing their spiritual path and are more comfortable in a studio than in a church, unless they are the ones leading the service. These people are greatly impacted by cruelty and violence and easily grow depressed by the sight of it. Though they seek harmony and balance instinctively they are likely to polarize when it comes to being attracted to the lighter or darker aspects of spirituality. Clues for this can be found in their Uranus placement.

Witches with this preset make excellent teachers, counselors, and mediators within the occult system, and are often thrown into unwanted positions of power and leadership. This is because Venus naturally gives them a spotlight, and Saturn, the wisdom to use it!

Moon in Libra

When the Moon is in the frequency of Libra, presentation is just as important as passion. The Moon's ability to shift without notice is heightened by Libra's pendulous search for balance. During this transit we can expect to be more indecisive and easily changeable. As the Moon enters this frequency it invites us to be more playful with our identity and step out of our comfort zone for a bit. When it exits, it shifts our amorous attention from being predominantly emotional to predominantly analytical. People with this preset do not like emotional games.

Magic to attract a life partner or lover, to add passion and spark, for cleansing, as well as those magic for beauty and glamour are powerful during this transit. Witches with this preset are naturally gifted in these magic and possess a high potential for service to the Goddess.

Mercury in Libra

Mercury in Libra produces an atmosphere of cooperation and comparison. Mercury, being the planet of intellect, and Libra, the frequency of balance, marry well together as they invite us to gain wisdom through the weighing of options and by seeing every side of a situation. Both airy in their nature, this transit places more emphasis on the mental struggles to trust one's own intuition. As it enters the frequency of Libra, Mercury enlivens the mental centers of the creative mind, providing insight to old problems. As it leaves it brings about better communication skills when in groups and encourages connections with others that might bridge you to the next phase in life. Those with this preset should be careful not to overanalyze their intuitive senses.

Magically speaking, all work done for cooperation, to find balance during upset, to ease the stress of mental disorders, and to bring eloquence will be executed with ease. Witches with this preset are likely to be gifted in these magic as well as those that involve attracting others to you.

Venus in Libra

The combination of Venus and Libra fills the air with the intoxicating aroma of love and the rituals we have surrounding love. During this time we become so concerned with feeling wooed and wooing others that anything that is too representative of reality easily distracts us. It is likely that those who haven't felt 100 percent secure in their relationships will begin to have a wandering amorous eye. Those with this preset are likely to have multiple lovers, even simultaneously. When Venus enters Libra we become enamored by the thrill of chasing love, sex, or anything else that we are passionate about. We rediscover the need for those tiny little rituals that bring us closer in connection with others and our need to be desired. As it leaves it helps to cushion the pain from past relationships.

Magic to gain the attention of others, for love and lust, or to enchant objects are done with ease during this transit. Those witches with this preset are naturally gifted with these magic and are likely to be good at swaying others.

Mars in Libra

Mars, the bringer of motivation and war, and Libra, the seeker of balance, create internal challenges during this time. The frequency of Libra causes the energy of Mars to fluctuate, making it hard to be consistent in mind and body. Sex drives will likely increase during this time and playfulness will enter the bedroom. Unfortunately the Martian ability to initiate sex is muted, and frustration will likely ensue. It is important to not think too hard about the primal instincts but rather spend your attention on finding a consenting partner to play with. During this time, playing by the rules becomes increasingly important in love, war, and of course, career. As Mars enters airy Libra the flames of passion and desire are fanned and our energies shift to strategies that aid in attaining whatever is at the end of this desire. As it leaves it is likely to clear a path through unhealthy body image issues.

Magic to aid in supporting physical health, to start a new routine, to bring lovers to you, and to weaken existing systems of oppression are done with ease during this transit. Witches with this preset are likely to be gifted in these magic as well as magic that involves the breaking of curses and uncrossing magical victims.

Jupiter in Libra

The energies of love and harmony pierce the veil of over-calculated emotional response. Jupiter, the planet of blessings and success, bestows a particular luck on all marriages and partnerships that are formed during this transit. As Jupiter enters Libra it encourages us to use whatever natural skills we possess in the field of networking and party planning to bring our friends and allies together in a laid-back atmosphere. Think tanks and collaborations of all kinds are likely to happen during this transit.

As it leaves the frequency of Libra, Jupiter quickens the speed of our social endeavors and meetings with influential people are likely to come from unexpected places. Those with this preset are highly influenced by marriage-type relationships and are likely to find partners easily.

Magic for love, success, luck, networking, and bringing people together can be done with ease during this transit. Witches with this preset should note that in addition to being naturally gifted in these magic they also possess great skill at teaching the craft to others and counseling people through karmic lessons.

Saturn in Libra

Saturn in Libra brings about a positive shift in our judgment; however, the challenges we find here are likely to bring about major change and more than likely a bit of heartache. As the challenges present themselves they are also likely to come with many blessings. Libra's propensity to cause fluctuation is heightened during this time. When Saturn enters Libra it immediately affects our judgment positively, making it more likely for us to make choices that will bring unforeseen benefits later down the road. As it leaves, however, Saturn shakes the foundational relationships in our lives, even bringing about the end of those relationships that are not good for us. Witches with this preset should spend extra time studying the techniques of Core Shamanism as this form of magical soul development will greatly benefit their ability to make decisions and feel secure in them afterwards.

Magic to cause great change in our lives, to help us remove the outer skin so a fresh face can be presented to the world, to rejuvenate or bring revolution, and magic to bring luck and success will all be done with ease during this time. Witches with this preset will find that in addition to being naturally gifted with these magic, they are also naturally gifted seers and psychopomps.

Uranus in Libra

During this time we choose to express ourselves and challenge the accepted norms. Uranus, the planet of originality and change, invites us to think outside the box and take a walk on the wild side. It is likely that you find yourself becoming a bit more daring than usual during this time but are also likely to reap great reward from getting out of your comfort zone for a bit. As it enters the frequency of Libra, Uranus increases your charm and helps you sweet-talk your way in and out of situations. As it leaves this frequency, however, it lays vital groundwork for future partnerships that will help you expand your career and help you carve out a unique niche that will bring great future reward through independence.

Magic for independence, to financially support small business and entrepreneurship, to bring about change of any kind, and for eloquence will be done with ease and strength during this time. Witches with this preset will naturally be gifted in these magic and will likely be great mediators for humankind and the beings we call faeries, angels, demons, and other potential spirit allies.

Neptune in Libra

This combination brings an atmosphere of love and free will that will undoubtedly produce major challenges to aggression of any kind. Those with this preset are creative and fun-loving but are willing to put aside fun and play in order to create real change. Witches with this preset are likely to possess the power to create peace and diplomacy.

Pluto in Libra

Brings about change through harmony and partnership.

The Aquarius Frequency

The frequency of Aquarius is intense and idealistic. It is known for bringing the energies of independence, honesty, loyalty, humanism, originality, vision, idealism, and professional friendship. Those with this Sun sign are creative free-spirit types who have a flair for individualistic expression and loathe feeling confined. These people possess great people skills and likely have a love for the far-off past and distant future.

Quality: Fixed (strong)

Ruling Planets: Uranus and Saturn

Body Part Association: Ankle, shins, and circulatory system

Day of the Week: Saturday

Plants and Herbs: All fruit trees, pepper, orchid, mandrake, parsnip, pine, frankincense, patchouli, pomegranate, sorrel, and moss

Metal Association: Aluminum, lead, and silver

Gemstone Association: Aquamarine, hematite, onyx, opal, clear quartz, amethyst, garnet, jasper, fluorite, and zircon

Color: Turquoise, sea foam, indigo, silver, violet, ocean blue, cerulean, and saffron

General Magical Attributes: Solitary magic of any kind benefits from the Aquarian frequency. Spells and rituals for originality, career development, starting a business, sex, power, the making of new friends and allies in business, to gain respect from others, to heal generational wounding, any and all divination, to bring hope to helpless situations, and to speed up decisions are done with ease in the Aquarius frequency. Those with a Solar preset here will be naturally gifted in these magic.

Magic may be negatively impacted by the Aquarius frequency if it is employed for partnership, cleansing, and/or truth.

Aquarius Devotion: Going to museums and gallery openings, making new friends, dating, attending think-tanks, going to poetry readings, and performing the magic listed above.

Aquarius Presets

Aquarius Rising

Uranus, the ruling planet of Aquarius, bestows his blessings by making those with this preset easily likeable and quick-witted. These people possess originality and magnetism that will shape their lives and spiritual practices. Their spiritual journey will take them through several different philosophies and schools of thought before finally settling upon the realization that they must develop their own unique connection. Although easy to theorize, this is not easy in practice. Those with this preset are natural leaders and often are capable of creating great rebellion in life. They are likely to reform any spiritual system they do involve themselves in.

Witches with this preset make excellent seers and diviners with a knack for teaching the occult and metaphysical.

Moon in Aquarius

When Aquarius, the frequency of individuality and expression, meets the intuitive and impressionable Moon, the air becomes ripe with sensitivity and open perception. During this transit it is likely that we will become enamored with the unknown and will direct our personal time to exploring odd topics. As the Moon enters the frequency of Aquarius it quickens our imagination and we easily become entranced by the spiritual realm. As it leaves, the Moon uses Aquarius to unlock doors to the unconscious.

Trance work that involves shamanism, soul retrieval, and all ecstatic practices is done with ease during this transit. Those with this preset will possess a natural affinity for ecstatic witchcraft and shamanism.

Mercury in Aquarius

During this time, quick and mental Mercury glides through Aquarius, the frequency of originality and inspiration, and produces an inventive atmosphere where a quick and inquisitive mind can reap major reward. It is likely that during this time our quirks, odd hobbies, and strange interests will inadvertently be pushed into the light of day, gaining the attention of others. As Mercury enters Aquarius it heralds a time of eccentricity and intellectual discussions. As it leaves the frequency of Aquarius, however, Mercury brings inspiration from the distant past and the limitless future. Witches with this preset will likely find they possess great skill in the occult sciences.

Magic for inspiration, out-of-the-box thinking, to aid in memory (such as study spells), for the discovery of lost objects, and to discover the truth are quite powerful during this transit. Witches with this preset will be naturally gifted in these magic as well as make great predictive psychics and teachers of the occult.

Venus in Aquarius

Venus, the planet of attraction and beauty, rests nicely in the freedom-loving and magnetic frequency of Aquarius. During this time we are likely to step out of our shell a bit in order to see what else is out there that we haven't seen yet. We will be likely to seek a deep, spiritual love affair that will be more of a hot flash and less of a steady burn. As Venus enters Aquarius it turns up the charm and we all become a little flirtier and we notice an increased need for sexual expression in our lives. As it exits, Venus increases our star power and we are likely to become more popular in certain circles during this time. Those with this preset should note that they possess a particularly immense magnetism and are the perfect type to become the next big star. Everyone is watching them and will be interested in what they do; secrecy may be a problem.

Magic to attract the attention of others or that involves the raising of sexual energy, and all magic for confidence, can be done with ease during this transit. Witches with this preset are likely to possess a high degree of practical spiritual wisdom early in life, in addition to being naturally skilled in the magic listed here.

Mars in Aquarius

The initiatory influence of Mars is made mental during its transit through Aquarius. We develop a need to become invested in multiple possible ventures. It becomes more important to feel intellectually committed to an action before you embark on any new endeavor. As Mars enters the frequency of Aquarius, it may make us feel high-strung and can make the air ripe for unpredictable activity. We will also likely become fiercely independent at this time. As Mars exits, it helps to remove the psychological blocks we possess that keep us from freely expressing ourselves as creative and sexual people.

Magic for sex, freedom, and inspiration are all done with ease during this transit. Witches with this preset should note that in addition to being skilled in these magic they are also likely to make excellent shamans and astral warriors.

Jupiter in Aquarius

Jupiter, who rules over success and optimism, accentuates the Aquarian frequency's capacity to bring about opportunity and luck through others. We may find that we are able to help others bridge to the next phase of their lives, find a new job, or even break free from old cycles and patterns.

As it enters the frequency of Aquarius, Jupiter strengthens our resolve to predict future trends in our own lives based off of previous behavior and will undoubtedly notice increased intuition. As it leaves it shifts our focus from the acquisition of money to the manifestation of higher ideals. Those with this preset will likely make excellent musical magicians.

Magic to remove blocks between the three souls, to bring new and fresh energy into our lives, for inspiration, and all magic that involves ancestral allies is powerful during this time. Witches with this preset are likely to have great skill as seers and prophets, in addition to being naturally talented in the magic listed here. These witches will also naturally possess skills in ecstatic witchcraft.

Saturn in Aquarius

Humanitarianism and self-discipline become increasingly important during this transit. Saturn, the planet of hard work and responsibility, places emphasis on the Aquarian frequency's ability to deal with tough subjects and we become inspired to move through upsetting subject matter and make change in our lives. As it enters this frequency, Saturn activates our rational mental centers and encourages us to look to the past for answers. As it leaves, however, it redirects us towards the future and forces us to make tough decisions to ensure future security.

Magic to bring change to foundational practices and foundational relationships is exceptionally powerful during this transit. Witches with this preset will be naturally gifted in these magic and posses keen leadership skills.

Uranus in Aquarius

Uranus, the planet of change and individual expression, is completely at home here in the frequency of Aquarius for which it rules. The Uranian propulsion towards independence and originality is exaggerated during this transit. As it enters Aquarius, it is likely to make us stubborn and hard to communicate with. This is due to a possibility for dense mental processes. Quickly, though, once we have reached our maximum the mental strain lifts and we feel inspired. As it exits Aquarius, Uranus can bring unexpected success.

During this transit, magic for originality, independence, to gain the attention of others, to bring about change in corporate culture, and for recognition is done with ease. Witches with this preset will possess natural skill in these magic and will make excellent teachers of the occult.

Neptune in Aquarius

This combination ushers in a time of social justice and humanitarian change. Those born with this preset are known for being intuitive, caring, emotionally wise, and most importantly, capable of seeing false power paradigms in society. Witches with this preset will possess a high psychic aptitude.

Pluto in Aquarius

Change will be made through major scientific advancements and humanitarianism. It is expected that those with this preset will bring an end to world hunger.

The Water Frequencies

Water frequencies' strengths lie in emotion and feeling. Each of these frequencies brings about feelings and emotional responses and, depending on the particular frequency, that emotion is either raw or refined when expressed. Known for bringing about spiritual awareness and clarity, water frequencies are often employed for divination. Those with water frequency presets are often psychically gifted and make great caregivers.

The Cancer Frequency

This frequency is known for being responsive and heavy. It is emotional, empathic, imaginative, sympathetic, caregiving, moody, changeable, protective, gullible, anxious, shrewd, and clingy. Those with this as a Sun sign are known for being incredibly giving and for loving deeply. They make excellent caregivers and teachers and are generally quite artistic and intuitive. These people tend to have strong connections with their mothers and generally posses great matrilineal power.

Quality: Cardinal (activating)

Ruling Planet: Moon

Body Part Association: Chest, breasts, and lower arms

Day of the week: Monday

Plants and Herbs: All trees that produce sap, all white flowers, lotus, lilies, acanthus, lettuce, verbenas, myrrh, catnip, poppy, violet, jasmine, and datura

Metal Association: Silver

Gemstone Association: Pearl, moonstone, beryl, calcite, selenite, zircon, sapphire, and opal

Color: White, silver, grey, navy, eggshell, violet, ocean green, and deep purple

General Magical Abilities: All magic requiring a feminine touch or that are aimed at making a deep impression are excellent magic for this frequency. Spells and rituals for healing maternal relationships and/

or negative maternal family patterns, attracting someone to help in times of need, recollection, bindings of all kind, deception of any kind, protection, banishment, and divination of all kinds benefit from the Cancer frequency. Witches with this Sun sign preset will be naturally gifted in these magical arts.

This frequency does not usually go well with magic for independence, focus, stability, or forgiveness.

Cancer Devotion: Going to see a romantic drama or comedy at a theater, going out on dates, spending time on the water, having a heart-to-heart conversation, caring for the elderly.

Cancer Presets

Cancer Rising

Those with Cancer rising spiritually express themselves through acts of charity, compassion, caregiving, and service. These people tend to have an incredible intuitive sense and have impeccable magical timing. Instinctively finding the motives of others, those with this rising sign are also known for making excellent counselors and karmic healers. They intuitively discover the Goddess's nurturing influence and tune in to it at a young age. Those with this preset should also be weary of their tendency towards self-martyrdom and holding a grudge.

Witches with this preset make excellent clergy people but will more than likely have issues maintaining spiritual balance and are generally very sensitive to magic and psychic phenomenon.

Moon in Cancer

The Moon, ruling planet of the frequency of Cancer, fits perfectly here and is personified exponentially. During this transit these two produce a very psychic atmosphere that is charged with the need to feel and experience each emotion or connection as they rise. When the Moon enters

Cancer it ushers in a short period of emotional upheaval that quickly fades into a post-drama glow. With this new release of emotional tension you are free to let the healing waters flow through anything else that might have been getting you down. As it leaves it creates new avenues of emotional freedom and psychic vulnerability.

All magic for healing, psychic cleansing, uncrossing, as well as magic that involves past-life memory work, the Goddess, or soul retrieval are exceptionally powerful during this transit. All lunar work during this time must be specific to the moon phase. In addition to being naturally skilled at these magic, witches with this preset are particularly gifted empaths and psychic healers.

Mercury in Cancer

Mercury in Cancer produces a highly charged psychic atmosphere, which skilled sensitives can use to gain access to hidden or harder-to-find spiritual realms. Mercury is fast and intellectual and the Moon is energetically impressionable and intuitive; combined, they shake the veils between the worlds and psychic phenomena ensue with ease. As Mercury enters Cancer it heightens our psychic abilities while simultaneously making us vulnerable to acts of emotional sabotage. As it exits, it removes obstacles that stand between you and your ability to adapt to new situations.

All psychic work and development is done with ease during this time as well as magic for adaptability, transformation, and protection. In addition to being naturally gifted in these magic a witch with this preset will also likely be a skilled at spirit-summoning and evocation.

Venus in Cancer

When Venus is in Cancer we crave romantic connection and fall in love with the idea of being in love. We suddenly become enamored with the idea of finding that special someone, but just before we get too excited the realities of future security creep up on us. This energy produces a sway between desire and insecurity that can get the better of anyone. When Venus enters Cancer it brings with it a strong awareness of how love has shaped us and how it might potentially shape us in the future. During this time it is normal to want to be more of a homebody. As it leaves the Cancerian frequency, Venus opens up new possibilities to find love in unexpected places.

Magic for love, reconciliation, all glamour, to heal emotional rifts between people, to find new friends, and to cleanse a new home of past energy will be powerful during this transit. Witches with this preset will be skilled in sex magic as well as the previously mentioned forms of magic.

Mars in Cancer

Mars is hot, focused, but temperamental, while the frequency of Cancer is emotional and always changing. This combination dulls the aggressive nature of Mars and makes us cling to relationships that are not good for us. During this time any heavy emotion felt or large sway of emotional attention should be noted and dealt with softly. It will be hard to keep composure at times. As Mars enters Cancer it increases our ability to be harmed by those closest to us as well as harm those closest to us. As it leaves Cancer, however, it gives us strength to forge through new emotional barriers.

Magic that involve energy clearing, to sway a group of people in your favor, to bring a lover near, or to tie one's nature are done with ease at this time. Witches with this preset make natural sex priest/esses and are often highly skilled intuitives, in addition to being gifted in the previously mentioned forms of magic.

Jupiter in Cancer

This connection produces an atmosphere that is brimming with luck! During this time we find the things that bring us pleasure have the potential to now bring us fortune. When Jupiter enters the frequency of Cancer it ushers in a period of jovial temperament and lighthearted connection. As it leaves it opens new doorways for successful relationships and partnerships.

Magic for luck in gambling, success, and abundance of any sort as well as magic involving ascension techniques are powerful during this time. Witches born with this preset will be lucky in life and possess great skill at blessing others. They will be naturals at the previously mentioned forms of magic.

Saturn in Cancer

This combination produces a depressed and easily irritated atmosphere that can make it hard to feel comfortable around others. In Cancer, Saturn personifies the darker and clingier aspects of the frequency, leaving us feeling vulnerable and alone to emotional attack. As it enters Cancer it heightens our need to feel connected to others as well as a higher purpose, pushing us to react out of emotional discomfort when dealing with these areas of our lives. As it exits it softens our ability to make reason out of difficult relationships and makes it hard to gauge personal emotional health.

You may find love spells difficult during this transit. Magic for emotional healing and self-preservation can be done with ease during this time. Witches with this preset will make excellent shamanic healers.

Uranus in Cancer

During a Uranus transit through Cancer intuitive abilities are heightened and access can be gained into hidden realms with much ease. We are likely to encounter mystical people, strangers who come with opportunities, and even to have hypnotic exchanges with the other side. As Uranus enters Cancer it ushers in a lengthy period of psychic adjustment, which often leaves us desiring spiritual cleansing and/or alignment. As it leaves Cancer, Uranus produces an unpredictable atmosphere that will undoubtedly lead sensitive types to new and exciting spiritual realms.

Magic that involves the contact of spirits, the summoning of matrilineal ancestors, or spiritual cleansing is exceptionally powerful during this time. Those witches born with this preset will find that, in addition to being naturally gifted in these magic, they also possess a skill for soul retrieval.

Neptune in Cancer

This combination ushers strange and unseen phenomena into our lives and provides a mystical quality to much of what is experienced. Those born with this preset are known for being idealistic and spiritual in nature and for possessing psychic skill.

Pluto in Cancer

Brings upheaval to family values and the status quo, inspires the forming of unions and other labor-based organizations.

The Scorpio Frequency

The Scorpio frequency is sexual and elusive. It is known for being emotional, forceful, responsive, dynamic, passionate, secretive, jealous, exciting, obsessive, and resentful. Those with this Sun sign preset are passionate and determined people who never miss an opportunity due to lost focus. These people love sex and generally have more than their fair share of it in life; however, as a result, they often don't find true happiness in love until later in life. These people can also be manipulative if they feel crossed and generally have their way when all is said and done.

Quality: Fixed (strong)

Ruling Planets: Pluto and Mars

Body Part Association: Sexual organs and reproductive system

Day of the Week: Tuesday

Plants and Herbs: Catnip, blackthorn trees, aloe, blackberry, lady's mantle, vervain, geranium, garlic, and cinnamon

Metal Association: Steel and iron

Gemstone Association: Opal, jasper, amber, beryl, agate, rhodochrosite, obsidian, larimar, malachite, bloodstone, and amethyst

Color: Deep red, maroon, mauve, black, gray, crimson, dark green, and indigo

General Magical Abilities: Magic that requires a sexual component will find success here as well as magic that cultivates life force. Spells and rituals for love, attraction, fixation, enchantment, the bending of one's will, seduction, to create jealousy or end jealousy, emotional healing, to find ways when all else feels lost, getting to the root of an issue, and to stimulate action are powerful during a Scorpio transit. Those with this Sun sign preset will likely be naturally gifted in these magic.

The Scorpio frequency may not be best for magic regarding sobriety, forgiveness, and/or weight loss.

Scorpio Devotion: Acts of self-preservation, having a deep love affair, winning at games of chance, sex, and performing the magic listed here.

Scorpio Presets

Scorpio Rising

Pluto, the planet of death and regeneration, bestows upon those with this rising sign the ability to connect to ancient worlds and formidable will-power. Those with this preset are known for putting the entire force of their personality behind all that they do and do not believe in, fulfilling the minimum obligation. Spiritually these people have a life-long inner knowing and are called to service later in life once they have learned to trust their impressions. These people are prone to extremes in spiritual awareness, one moment feeling completely plugged in, the next not at all.

To balance this, they strive to live with sacred principles and carry these values through every lesson presented.

Witches with this preset are likely to make gifted seers and prophets who will undoubtedly have an unquenchable thirst for gnosis.

Moon in Scorpio

This combination produces an atmosphere that is buzzing with emotion and spiritual awareness. During this time it is likely that you will become more sensitive to the impressions of those around you and should also be aware that at this time you are apt to hide your feelings from others. As it enters the frequency of Scorpio the Moon increases your self-reliance and empowers your ability to sift through doubts that have been getting in your way. As it exits it increases your influence over others and you will notice you have an easier time convincing people to do what you want them to do.

During this transit magic for psychic development, psychic cleansing, spiritual protection, mental clarity, and for empowerment are quite powerful. Witches with this preset are likely to be gifted karmic healers in addition to being naturally skilled in the magic listed above.

Mercury in Scorpio

Scorpio alters the influence of Mercury as the two join together in suspicious connection. The air becomes charged with preternatural energy and our psychic responses heighten. Scorpio's questioning nature significantly increases the likelihood that the unknown will surface during this time. Be aware that you are susceptible to emotionally responsive outbursts and mean sarcasm when challenged. Think before you speak during this transition. As Mercury enters the frequency of Scorpio it almost immediately alters our powers of perception and we find ourselves being invited to play with the unknown behind the veil. As it leaves, however, it has the potential to draw you into unneeded drama that likely has little to do with you. If you were born with this preset you likely possess major psychic ability.

Magic to find hidden objects, to void yourself of suspicion, to cover your tracks, to entice a lover, as well as all magic that involves the primal soul will be done with ease during this transit. Witches with this preset will be skilled in these magic as well as make for excellent mediums and ghost hunters.

Venus in Scorpio

Being in love is the most important thing when Venus and Scorpio meet in the heavens. The frequency of emotionally intelligent Scorpio deepens the vibration of beauty and love-seeking Venus, altering our perception of love and widening our propensity to share it. Those with this preset may be prone to fear-based emotional outbursts when their love is left unrequited. While this may be true they are also vibrationally drawn to relationships that have the potential to bring financial comfort and possible excess. Those with this preset are known for a profound emotional intensity. When Venus enters Scorpio it encourages emotional connection with others who you think might "get you." During this time you are likely to make new long-lasting connections or reconnect with old friends. As it leaves the frequency of Scorpio it has the potential to leave you feeling empty and longing for deeper psychical and psychic connection.

Magic for psychic development, advancement in career, to create enchanted artwork, and for any kind of love work will be executed with ease during this time. Witches with this preset will find that they are already gifted in these magical areas and also possess the potential to become great spiritual leaders, as they tend to make anything they are passionate about a spiritual experience, and vice versa.

Mars in Scorpio

During this transit we become touchy and a little standoffish. Emotional Scorpio, which contains the potential for deep suspicion, meets the aggressive and always busy Mars and as a result we become persistent and ardent in our thinking. This transit has the potential to intensify your sex life as well, heightening your ability to connect deeply with others. As Mars enters Scorpio it ignites any emotional powder kegs that have been left to fester due to lack of appropriate processing. As it leaves it increases your motivation to invite an element of danger into your life in order to increase the likelihood of life-affirming experiences.

Magic to gain the attention and adoration of audiences, to remove unwanted and hidden influences, and all magic for love will be extra powerful during this time. Witches with this preset are likely to be skilled in these magic and have the potential to make excellent karmic healers and astral warriors.

Jupiter in Scorpio

Jupiter, the planet of success and luck, gets along quite nicely with the frequency of Scorpio and during this transit we are presented with a fantastic opportunity to do love magic, specifically to attract a partner that is a match in regards to financial goals and need for emotional responsiveness. Scorpio, with its deep and artistic nature, is likely to produce brilliance when Jupiter enters this frequency and our artistic endeavors become fruitful. As it exits Scorpio, Jupiter leaves clues for picking lucrative investments behind. Those with this preset are likely to be good at investments.

Magic for success, to turn a failing business profitable, to attract the right kind of investors, and magic that involves attracting the perfect match are done with ease during this transit. If you have this as a preset you are likely skilled in these magic and also possess a high capacity for soul healing and soul retrieval.

Saturn in Scorpio

Saturn's ability to stir up problems produces a scandalous atmosphere whenever it is in Scorpio. Because Scorpio has an endless well of emotional intelligence it increases Saturn's likelihood to extenuate the less desirable traits of this frequency, like jealousy, emotional sabotage, and overactive imagination. The good news, however, is that this chaos can bring about great change in your relationship sector. As Saturn enters Scorpio, it adds mud to the already murky waters found there. It can almost instantly make us feel our relationship problems (romantic or otherwise) with increased sensitivity and we should be careful not to overreact. As it exits it helps us to realign with our greater sense of purpose in matters of the heart.

Magic for love and sex should be avoided during this time unless other astrological phenomena can help to ease the troubles of this transit. Witches with this preset are likely to be energy healers and possess a high shamanic aptitude.

Uranus in Scorpio

This combination produces an air of intensity and a stirring within to be heard. During this transit we are likely to experience bouts of animal magnetism and our powers of persuasion are increased tenfold. When Uranus enters Scorpio it brings with it deep concentration and other-worldly intuition. As it exits it expands your capacity to manifest anything you want through determination.

Magic that involve psychic development, sexual attraction, and to gain the attention of others will be particularly powerful during this transit. Witches with this preset are likely to become skilled seers later in life in addition to being naturally gifted in these magic from an early point in their development.

Neptune in Scorpio

This combination produces an interest in the occult and an intuitive understanding of the preternatural. Those born with this preset are likely to possess some psychic skill early on that will continue to grow with care. Magically those with this preset are likely to possess skill in the areas of high magic.

Pluto in Scorpio
Brings about change through scientific advancement, spiritual regeneration, and psychic development.

The Pisces Frequency

The Pisces frequency is highly intuitive and selfless. It is known for being compassionate, sensitive, escapist, impressionable, sympathetic, unworldly, and imaginative. Those with this Sun sign preset make great artists and counselors with an affinity for helping those less fortunate. They are sympathetic and are easily led to see both sides of a situation. Passionate yet playful, those with this preset are likely to find recognition through acts of kindness and visual art.

Quality: Mutable (adaptable)

Ruling Planets: Neptune and Jupiter

Body Part Association: Feet

Day of the Week: Thursday

Plants and Herbs: Water lily, willow, fig, apple, pumpkins, all melons, lime, moss, lotus, honeysuckle, jasmine, sage, lavender, and rue

Metal Association: Platinum and tin

Gemstone Association: Moonstone, bloodstone, mother of pearl, jasper, sugilite, sapphire, aquamarine, amethyst, ruby, and cat's eye

Color: All pastels, cornflower, deep ocean blue, sapphire, teal, sea foam, and turquoise

General Magical Abilities: The Pisces frequency is excellent for all matters of trance and astral projection. Spells and rituals for divination, spirit contact, to elicit sympathy, to create internal conflict, cleansings of all kinds, inspiration, to bring adventure, to break repetitive cycles, and to make contracts with spirit allies are powerful under this influence. Witches with this Sun sign preset are likely to be naturally skilled in these magic.

Magic, however, may clash with the Pisces frequency if it is for organization, focus, or grounding.

Pisces Devotion: Psychic development, artistic expression, having a good cry, laughing until your belly hurts, all acts of divination and occult practice, as well as the magic listed above.

Pisces Presets

Pisces Rising

Neptune, the planet of mystery and illusion, imparts upon those with this preset the blessings of psychic and preternatural abilities. Jupiter, the co-ruler of this frequency, bestows the gifts of keen intuition and luck in exploration. Together these blessings combine to produce an incredibly spiritual being. Those with this preset are naturally tuned in to the preternatural forces in our universe and will likely shy from traditional religious structure as they will find this to be too rigid. On their spiritual journey they will be forced to bring art and emotional expression with them as tools to convey the wisdom they receive while developing their souls. These people should also expect to use their psychic abilities to help others.

Witches with this preset not only make excellent psychics but they also make quite skilled healers. In addition, they will likely find themselves taking on leadership roles in covens and communities.

Moon in Pisces

The frequency of Pisces and the Moon get along nicely during this transit. Pisces, the frequency of emotional depths, provides extra gravity to the water's tides of lunar influence. During this time we are more susceptible to being let down by others or have a tendency towards masking sorrow through indulgence. Those with this preset are notorious for possessing psychic ability from an early age that, if left untrained, can cause much discomfort in life. As the Moon enters Pisces it activates our emotional centers and empowers the primal soul to begin astral travel while sleeping. Be prepared for insightful dreams. As it exits this frequency the Moon encourages us to take a look at the impressions we make on others.

Magic for psychic development, psychic healing, psychic protection, for the cultivation of long-term inspiration and life changes, to escape from unhealthy situations, and for spirit contact are all powerful during this transit. Witches with this preset will likely make excellent leaders in occult communities and possess heightened psychic abilities in addition to being naturally skilled in the magic listed here.

Mercury in Pisces

The combination of Mercury and Pisces produces mystery and increased psychic perception. During this transit it is likely that you will be prone to sudden insights and bursts of unexplained knowing. It is also likely that during this transit you will be more sympathetic to the mistakes and failings of others and will have increased empathic ability. As it enters the frequency of Pisces, Mercury stirs the mental and psychic energies around us, awakening the subtle knowing that rests deep inside. By the time it exits Pisces, however, Mercury has amassed so much psychic emotional energy that it leaves us feeling drained and sensitive to the opinions of others. Those with this preset have natural psychic abilities.

Magic for psychic development, spirit communication, creativity, soul retrieval, and any act of astral travel will be done with ease during this transit. Witches with this preset will note that in addition to being naturally skilled in these magic, they also possess a propensity for prophecy and will have strong bonds with familiar spirits.

Venus in Pisces

Generosity and tenderness fill the air when Venus transits through Pisces. During this time we long to be passionately devoted to someone or something and begin to expect devotional reciprocity from others. The sometimes-shifting energy of Pisces is brought into harmony when Venus enters the frequency, which provides us with special insight into our true needs and desires. We have the capacity to romanticize or idealize love by comparing it to other things, and this can cause trouble as we grow in our understanding of our own needs. As it leaves this frequency, Venus helps us find deeper connection with those we feel in tune with and provides opportunity to heal the vibrational riffs between those we were once in tune with but no longer feel as strongly connected to.

Magic that harnesses deep and emotional love, calls forth a new partner, or magic to inspire devotion or to gain insight into matters of the heart are done with ease during this transit. Those with this preset are likely to make excellent clergy members who service the Goddess and will be naturally gifted in the magic listed here.

Mars in Pisces

The fiery spark of Mars accentuates the turbulent waters of Pisces during this transit. Likely we will experience this in two ways. The first is that we will be more susceptible to emotional outbursts and may even feel that our lives are unrecognizable for short moments of time. The second is that all of this stirring up of emotional sediment provides for the release and surrender of negative energy and emotional baggage. As it enters the frequency of Pisces, Mars activates and clarifies the perceptive centers of our mind, heightening our senses. As it exits, Mars clears a path for emotional and psychic freedom. Those with this preset are likely to gain powerful friends in life but may experience moments of physical mediumship.

Magic for emotional release and healing that involves the employment of spirits for "low magic," and all psychic or spiritual acts of protection, are immensely powerful during this time. Witches with this preset are naturally gifted in these magic and will likely have great skill at the removal of curses and the banishment of low-frequency entities.

Jupiter in Pisces

During this transit we become more aware of the needs and societal limitations of others and make a move to help those other members of the human race. From the acts of generosity and kindness we are likely to make influential connections or gain new opportunity. Those with this preset are likely to thrive in a non-profit career. As Jupiter enters Pisces it encourages us to think of what we can do to cause great change through increased apathy. As it exits the frequency of Pisces, Jupiter carves out new and exciting adventures that will bring benefit to you and your community.

Magic to increase charitable donations, to bring attention to religious communities or institutions, to gain employment in the non-profit sector, as well as all magic to gain the favor of those in charge are all done with ease during this time. Witches with this preset will notice that in addition to having a natural skill in these magic they possess a propensity for possession and trance work.

Saturn in Pisces

During this transit we all feel the pain of the starving artist. Internal development is favored over material success as change-bringing Saturn cannonballs into the deepest parts of the elemental frequency band of water. While here it asks us to make personal sacrifices for the greater good, which can make us feel responsible for the actions of others. As it enters the Piscean frequency, it teaches us harsh lessons about how we get in our own way and forces us to form new rules to live by. As it exits, however, Saturn increases the velocity of negative emotional patterns and can make us vulnerable to addictive behavior.

Magic for self-improvement should be done via shamanic and ecstatic practices during this time. Witches with this preset will make excellent psychopomps, in addition to being skilled in shamanic practices.

Uranus in Pisces

The bombastic nature of Uranus is turned inward and made emotional by the watery frequency of Pisces. During this transit we become sensitive to emotional expression of any kind and develop an increased awareness of the spirit world. As Uranus enters this frequency it activates the psychic centers of the mind and makes us more artistic. As it exits the frequency of Pisces, however, Uranus can leave us feel psychically drained and in need of a recharge. Those with this preset are intuitively drawn to the occult, where they will find much success.

Magic that involves trance or possession, for activating latent psychic abilities, to draw strength from ancestors, or to make contact with the spirit world is all performed easily during this time. Witches with this preset will note that in addition to being naturally skilled in these magic they are also likely to make excellent psychic-intuitives.

Neptune in Pisces

This combination brings forth a time of great spiritual evolution and awakening. One of the heralds of the age of Aquarius, this transit helps set the stage for a major psychic shift. Those born with this preset will be harbingers of great spiritual change, likely to possess great connection to familiar spirits. Magically speaking, these witches will be responsible for ending suffering and bringing forth a new age of enlightenment.

Pluto in Pisces

Brings spiritual ascendancy through the mutual respect of life, as well as metamorphosis, and by bridging the scientific and spiritual worlds.

Chapter Eight

Planetary Power

For all its complexity, however, astrology remains fundamentally simple. It offers a time-honored system of symbols that sum up key aspects of human life while providing profound insights and practical guidance.
—Anne M. Nordhaus-Bike—

It might surprise you to know that you did come with an instruction manual, of sorts. When you were born the planets, stars, and asteroids surrounding Earth were in just the right places to usher in the amazingness that is you! Depending on where they were at that exact moment can determine everything from what type of person you are to become to how you will interact with the rest of society and culture, to what karmic debts you might need to repay in this lifetime. Astrology gives us the ability to see which energies and patterns will be attracted to us in this lifetime and allows us to see which influences are on the horizon. We can use it as a tool to find our Achilles heel and turn it into our superpower.

In addition, astrology allows us to find the hidden meanings and root causes to these different experiences and, when approached for personal development, can give us an immensely deep understanding of ourselves.

That manual I mentioned can be found written in between the lines of what we call a birthchart. Your birthchart contains a snapshot of the astrological atmosphere during the exact moment you were born. If we are a cocktail of astrological influence, our birthchart is the recipe book the cocktail came from. Essentially, the information in your birthchart provides you with a list of planetary frequency presets. Your planetary presets will determine how you carry the energies of the universe within and you'll get a good idea of what you can do with those energies. This can be exceptionally beneficial for those who have reached a place where they don't know where to look for spiritual development, for those who have mastered the basics of witchcraft but are longing for magical direction, and for solitary practitioners who lack the benefit of guided magical study. Within the pages of this manual you will also get a glimpse at the areas in your life that cause you to lose power so that you can stay in peak working condition.

The modern astrologer now gets to spend more time studying the frequencies of each sign rather than spending all their time drawing charts, thanks to the advent of computers. Now all we have to do is type some basic information into an application like Solar Fire or Time Passages and a detailed report is provided in seconds.

Before you go any further, please flip to the end of this chapter and go to one of the websites listed under the heading "Birthchart Resources." You will be able to use the wonders of modern technology to draft a free copy of your birthchart. Once you have printed up a copy of your chart keep it close by for reference. You will use it as you go through this section.

Creating Your Planetary Power Profile

By this point in your craft evolution you are familiar with the basics of astrology: Some of the information provided here might look like a refresher but don't let that get in your way of learning something new.

I designed this profiling system to act as a magical formulary for witches who were looking for a digestible version of astrology specifically suited to them as magical people.

This profile will break down your energetic makeup and you will discover where you are likely to shine and where you are potentially vulnerable.

Your birthchart should provide you with all the needed information to complete this form. At this point I am going to enlist the help of an imaginary client to take this to the next level.

Let's say that this person provided me with their birthdate, time, and location and has a birthchart that looks like this.

When you look at your chart for the first time it can be a little overwhelming. The trick is to look at it in sections rather than trying to understand it all at once.

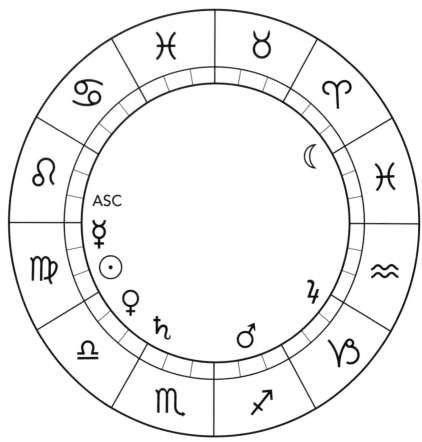

Creating your own planetary profile

Time of Birth: 5:09 a.m.

Date of Birth: September 12, 1984

Birth Place: Cincinnati, Ohio

Which yielded the following information:
Sun 19 degrees Virgo
Moon 12 degrees Aries

Rising 23 degrees Leo

Mercury 2 degrees Virgo

Venus 13 degrees Libra

Mars 14 degrees Sagittarius

Jupiter 3 degrees Capricorn

Saturn 12 degrees Scorpio

Uranus 9 degrees Sagittarius

Neptune 28 degrees Sagittarius

Pluto 0 degrees Scorpio

Now, here is the worksheet you're going to fill in. This chapter will take you through the process of filling out your Planetary Power Profile.

Planetary Power Profile

Birthdate: Day of Power: (Day of the Week

Birth Time: Associated with Your Ruling Planet)

Birth Place:

Planetary Presets

Personal Presets

Solar Frequency:

How do I present myself to the world?

Lunar Frequency:

How do I connect to the world?

Ascending Frequency:

What do I strive to bring the world?

Mercurial Frequency:

How do I communicate with the world?

Venusian Frequency:

How do I seek harmony in the world?

Martian Frequency:

What motivates me in the world?

Secondary Presets

Frequency of Jupiter:

How will I grow in the world?

Saturnian Frequency:

How does the world shape me?

Uranian Frequency:

How am I different from the world?

Neptunian Frequency:

How do I build my own world?

Plutonian Frequency:

What do I hide from the world?

Ruling Planetary Frequency:

Elemental Bands

Fire: total: Strongest:

Earth: total: Moderate:

Water: total: Weak:

Air: total:

My Preset Strengths Are:

My Preset Weaknesses Are:

Magic I Am Most Naturally Gifted at:

Personal Three Souls Incense:

Personal Sigil of Cosmic Alignment:

Incense to Repel Negative Effects of Mercury Retrograde:

My Planetary Power Seal Looks Like:

Before you give up too easily I want to invite you to think of this like filling out a *Cosmo* quiz; you have nothing to lose and you might find out how to make people like you more! In all seriousness, though, give this a try. Fill out the section for birthdate, time, and place.

Planetary Presets

Every planet has its own vibration and frequency whether it is in our solar system or not. When these frequencies interact with other natural vibrations in the atmosphere they create changes in the overall flow of energy around us. Depending on which system of astrology you follow the influences of the specific planets will change. Each planet in our solar system contains unique archetypal energy and that energy is filtered and changed in presentation depending on which sign it rests in.

Each of these rules over a specific set of principles and determines how the frequencies of each sign will be expressed within our psychological and magical makeup. For the purposes here, you will only be looking at each of the planets in relation to your power. These planets are the filters through which the twelve frequencies of the zodiac emerge, each ruling over specific aspects of life. As the planets move in their natural orbit their influence over us ebbs and flows like the ocean, affecting our ability to influence the world.

The Big Three and the Three Souls

There are three presets in your birthchart that you should understand even if you skip the rest of this chapter and never look back. These three presets are known as the Sun, Moon, and the Rising (or Ascendant), and because of their strength of influence compared to the other presets, they can contain more information about you than the rest of the chart entirely. Each of these presets correlates to one of the three souls and when properly observed can deeply impact the way you understand your etheric makeup.

When someone asks what sign you are, you most likely respond with your Sun sign. The preset of the Sun sign is the most identifiable sign out of the three and in Western astrology is determined by the then-current placement of the Sun during the time of your birth as it travels through the different signs of the zodiac. For example, I have a Sagittarius Sun sign because when I was born the Sun was traveling through the sign of Sagittarius. This sign determines how you will approach new situations, interact with others, and how society will receive your works. Our Sun sign is the most outwardly projected aspect of our personality and represents our most basic attitudes towards life. In the three souls model the Sun sign is the sign that represents the ego soul. This sign will tell you a lot about your magical ability to manifest, attract energies, and remove obstacles.

The preset of your Moon sign is determined by the placement of the Moon as it traveled through the signs of the zodiac during the time of your birth. The Moon sign also governs over the internal world of the psyche and subconscious. It rules over the aspects of emotion and intuition and has a lot more to do with how you feel about yourself and life than any other sign. In addition, the Moon sign teaches us about our needs and our desires and quietly guides us to seek and find comfort. If you have ever met someone with the same Sun sign and thought, "You are nothing like me," their Moon sign would be why. In the three souls model the Moon sign corresponds to your primal soul. Many clues as to your magical abilities for divination, trance, spirit communication, and enchantment can be found by studying this sign.

The third preset or sign that you should be aware of is your Rising or Ascendant. This sign gives you glimpses into your destiny, life purpose, how you will choose to become part of the world, and your psychological motivations. Information about your Holy Souls, or higher selves, can be found here. Magically speaking, this is where you might discover information about hidden or clerical abilities, karma, sacred contracts, past lives, and divine attributes.

Take a look at these three presets in your birthchart and add them to your planetary profile. Be sure to reference back to these chapter sections when the appropriate planet is transiting to gain magical insight regarding each movement.

The Sun
—Self-expression, Idealism, and Strength—

The Sun is not just the ball of burning gas that each of our planets is bound to by gravity, it is also the bringer of light and the producer of all the building blocks of life. In astrology the Sun represents the way we express ourselves to others and how we consciously create the world around us. Its energy is one of the strongest expressed in your birthchart.

As it filters the frequencies of the zodiac it rules over how they will be expressed as ideology, motivation, and strength of character. As a witch you could also say that this is the seat of magical expression, the place from which you project your magic. When the Sun transits a frequency it brings great strength to certain forms of magic found within that frequency. Each solar preset contains clues to the forms of magic in which we will be dominantly skilled.

The Moon
—Emotion, Intuition, and Instinct—

The Moon has just as much sway over you as the Sun and is expressed just as strongly. In astrology the Moon rules over the internal world, the subconscious, and the way in which others impact you the most. I like to think of this as our "squishy center."

As it filters the frequencies of the zodiac it governs how they will be expressed as psychic and magical abilities, instinctual motivations, maternally, and through intuition. This is the place where witches are most receptive to external energies. When the Moon transits a frequency it brings great strength to certain forms of intuitive magic found within them. In addition to each solar preset the Moon contains clues to the forms of magic that we will be dominantly skilled in.

ASC

The Ascendant (Rising)
—Spiritual Idealism, Values, Expression, and Path—

The Rising sign (Ascendant) has immense sway over how you reconcile what you see in the world and how you reflect it back as you spiritually progress through this lifetime. This is the sign that is responsible for expressing the needs of the higher self and is the mouthpiece for your particular spark of divinity.

Identify the Sun, Moon, and Rising signs in your birthchart and reference chapter 7 to discover how each of these presets manifested at your birth. By gathering what you have read there, fill in the corresponding sections in your Planetary Power Profile.

In addition to the Big Three there are a few other planets that are referred to as your "Personal Planets." These planets also have a major sway over how energy will manifest in your life, but do not have the same connection to the soul and the Big Three. These presets will affect not only your magic but you personally and will give greater insight to where potential weaknesses may lie.

Mercury
—Communication and All Things Mental—

Mercury is in charge of communication, inspiration, sibling and near-relative relationships, and perhaps most importantly, comprehension. In astrology Mercury is seen as both the winged messenger and the bringer of chaos, as it tends to bring changes in mental temperament as it moves through each frequency.

As it filters the frequencies of the zodiac it is responsible for how the frequencies are expressed in our thoughts, mental cycles, which personalities we choose to make friends with, and how we integrate technology into our lives. For a witch, Mercury guides our ability to predict the future, understand the natural signs around us, change the course of events, and start new beginnings.

Mars
—Physical Ability, Aggression, and Motivation—

Mars has dominion over action, discipline, and the mechanical world. In astrology Mars is the boot that smashes anything in its way and the general who commands the legions.

It is the antithesis of Venus and creates disharmony through aggression.

As it filters the frequencies of the zodiac it is responsible for how those frequencies manifest through our deeds and actions, what forces we oppose, and our core values surrounding violence, conquest, and punishment.

For a witch, Mars has influence over our ability to engage the magical world around us with confidence and daring.

Venus
—Love, Business, and Harmony—

Venus is the ruler of all matters of the heart, lust, and how we either harmonize with other frequencies or don't. In astrology Venus is seen as the lover who seeks to find resonance and the never-ending search for beauty.

As it filters the frequencies of the zodiac Venus directs how those frequencies manifest through our sexual desires, how deeply we feel connected to those closest to us, and how we express beauty.

For a witch, Venus is the planet that has influence over our ability to be open to the universe.

Identify the placement of Mercury, Venus, and Mars in your birthchart and reference chapter 7.

By gathering what you have read there, fill in the corresponding sections in your Planetary Power Profile.

————————

The next set of presets to explore are referred to as "Secondary" because their influence is not as strong over us as others.

The transit duration of each of these planets takes longer so their influence is felt generationally, or more psychically and less physically.

4

Jupiter
—Expansion, Growth, and All Things Intellectual—

Jupiter is the ruler of the heavens and controls all matters of expansion and territory. Mythologically, Jupiter is the father who had his finger in everyone's business and who wasn't afraid to throw his weight around. In astrology Jupiter is seen as the father of language, travel, loyalty, and justice.

As it filters the frequencies of the zodiac it is responsible for our ability to grow and adjust to changes, how we view politics and authority, and how we view worldly possessions. For a witch, Jupiter influences our ability to grow authentically.

Saturn
—Control, Restriction, Order, and Law—

Saturn is all about control and ushers in deeply stabilizing energies. In astrology Saturn is seen as a stubborn planet that doesn't like to budge when pushed and one that encourages us to lay down our own boundaries.

As it filters through the frequencies of the zodiac Saturn is responsible for how the frequencies manifest in the areas of structure, integrity, and our need for control. For a witch, it is the planet from which magical discipline springs forth.

Uranus

—Change, Independence, and Sexual Deviations—

Uranus controls matters of independence and escapism. In astrology it is known for encouraging out-of-the-box thinking, nervous disorders, mental escapism, phobias, and in some cases, sexual excessiveness.

As it filters the frequencies of the zodiac it is responsible for how the frequencies are expressed as hidden passions, our ability to be original, and how eccentric we can be. For a witch, this planet influences the development of the shadow self.

Neptune

—Idealism, Artistic Expression, and States of Reality—

Neptune is the king of the depths and the ruler of arts. In astrology Neptune guides the steady hand of poets and artists and encourages the type of deep trance-like state that comes from artistic expression.

As it filters the frequencies of the zodiac Neptune is in charge of how the frequencies manifest as our sensitivities, the ways in which we deceive ourselves, and our ability to escape into the inner worlds. For a witch, Neptune is responsible for our ability to enter altered states.

Pluto

—Subconscious, Endings, Transformation—

Pluto rules over the underworld and is the bringer of endings. In astrology Pluto is most seen as being concerned with the subconscious and the planet that encourages us to move through obstacles.

As Pluto filters the frequencies of the zodiac it influences how the frequencies manifest in our lives on a spiritual and transformative level. It also governs what we become secretive about. For a witch, Pluto is the planet that aids in our ability to receive and give spiritual medicines.

———

Identify the placement of Jupiter, Saturn, Uranus, Neptune, and Pluto in your birthchart and reference chapter 7. By gathering what you have read there, fill in the corresponding sections in your Planetary Power Profile.

Remember the imaginary client's birthchart at the beginning of this chapter? At this point my imaginary client's Planetary Power Profile looks like this and yours should be filled out similarly.

Planetary Power Profile
Birthdate: Sept. 12, 1984   Day of Power:
Birth Time: 05:09 am
Birth Place: Cincinnati, Ohio, USA

Planetary Presets

Personal Presets

Solar Frequency: Virgo

Lunar Frequency: Aries

Ascending Frequency: Leo

Mercurial Frequency: Virgo

Venusian Frequency: Libra

Martian Frequency: Sagittarius

Secondary Presets

Frequency of Jupiter: Capricorn

Saturnian Frequency: Scorpio

Uranian Frequency: Sagittarius

Neptunian Frequency: Sagittarius

Plutonian Frequency: Scorpio

Ruling Planetary Frequency:

The Ruling Planet

There are several ways to determine your ruling planet, and again, depending on the school of astrology you come from, the technique for discovering it could be different than others seen elsewhere. When a planet has rulership over a frequency it means that it governs similar energetic properties and has sway over the way those properties are embodied by other planets that transit that frequency.

As you might have noticed in the previous chapter, each frequency of the zodiac is ruled by at least one planet. In traditional Western astrology the planet that rules over your rising sign is considered to be the ruling planet of your birthchart. This planet bestows upon you blessings or gifts at birth that you embody as sacred attributes.

You will likely have a particular affinity for working with the energies of this planet and the frequencies it governs. Another perk is that when this planet shows up as a preset elsewhere in your chart its power is intensified and those attributes are strengthened in us. Using this method, in the case of the imaginary client, their ruling planet would be the Sun because of the rising sign preset being in Leo (ruled by the Sun).

Another way to see if a planet may have a particularly strong influence over you is to see if you have multiple presets to one particular frequency. If one frequency stands out more than others in your chart then the planet that has rulership over that frequency will likely have great influence over you as well. Generally, I would expect to see this frequency show up more than four times before I would consider it able to provide a strong planetary influence.

By referencing chapter 7, determine which planet has rulership over you and fill in the corresponding space in your Planetary Power Profile.

The next step is to determine which elemental presets you carry and how they influence you. By separating your planetary presets by elemental band your elemental makeup can be broken down, which will provide extra insight into your strengths and weaknesses. To do this, use your birthchart and reference back to chapter 7 if you need to and divide your eleven planetary presets (minus your ruling planet) into their corresponding elemental frequency bands and total the number of planets in each. For our make-believe client it looks like this:

Elemental Bands

Fire: Aries, Leo, Sagittarius (x 3)	total: 5	Strongest: Fire
Earth: Virgo (x 2), Capricorn	total: 3	Moderate: Earth
Water: Scorpio (x 2)	total: 2	Weak: Water and Air
Air: Libra	total: 1	

Elemental Presets

You will have noticed by now that one or two of these elemental frequency bands have the majority of attention in your chart. In the case of the fictional chart the Fire frequency band has the most presets with five, Earth is second with three presets, then Water with two, and finally Air with one. Because Fire has the most presets, this person would be called *Fire Dominant.*

If you happen to have two frequency bands that express themselves as dominant, meaning they are tied for the greatest number of presets, you would acknowledge both as being dominant. For example, someone with four presets in Earth and Water would say that they are *Earth and Water Dominant.*

Being dominant in one or multiple frequency bands means that you have the capability to hold those currents of energy with ease. Your natural talents, interests, intuition, magical abilities, and even your home frequency will be highly influenced by these bands. Because this person is Fire Dominant they are most likely to be excellent at magic involving creativity, passion, sex, destruction, alchemy, and love.

The frequency bands that are expressed the least, in the above case Air and Water, are the passive energies. These frequencies are softer than the others and though they do have some form of influence over us, they represent the areas in our lives where we are the weakest. Our fictional birthchart suggests that this individual would be most likely reserved and probably not a great communicator. The properties of Air and Water are diminished in this instance, making this person *Air and Water Passive.*

The passive frequencies aren't just where we as individuals have reduced character but are also where we will be most vulnerable magically. Seeing where we are weakest allows us to know where we need to work and where we need to strengthen ourselves. Because our fictional chart suggests this person is Air and Water Passive they would be most susceptible to magic regarding emotions, sensitivity, communication, and mental clarity.

Though rare, you may find that you have a pretty equal smattering of presets in each frequency. This means that you are elementally balanced. You most likely will be good at many different things but not feel that you are great at any one thing. Your interests will vary and your magical strengths will best be determined by your "Big Three" presets.

If you have elemental frequency bands that are not present in your chart you have a special relationship to that missing energy. In Vedic astrology it is believed that the absence of an elemental frequency suggests that in a previous life you mastered the lessons of that frequency. Those missing frequencies are not presented as presets because they come included elsewhere in the package and are considered to come standard in your model.

Though I do not believe that the goal should ever be to strive for perfect elemental balance I do think it is important to understand YOUR elemental balance. If you notice that there are energies that should be present in your life according to your Planetary Power Profile or you are interested in developing strength in your relationship to the bands, then see the devotional suggestions under each frequency you wish to better align with. Listed there are magic that when performed can help to better tune you to these frequencies.

I should also mention here that if you read the information provided under each zodiacal frequency associated to you and you discovered that you have a preset with particularly negative attributes (as is the case generally when Saturn gets involved), don't sweat it! Performing the magic listed in the corresponding frequency, doing acts of devotion like those listed earlier in each section, and actively tuning in to the frequency during the corresponding day to perform these acts will significantly decrease any negative influences these frequencies may have over you.

Now, you will use all of this new information to give you better magical understanding of yourself and what you are capable of. Referencing chapter 7, determine the following:

My Preset Strengths Are: *(See Strengths under Elemental Bands for the Element(s), and zodiacal frequencies that appear more than four times in your birthchart.)*

My Preset Weaknesses Are: *(See Strengths under Elemental Bands for the Elements that appear the least in your birthchart. These attributes will likely cause interference with stronger presets.)*

Magic I Am Naturally Gifted at: *(See the General Magical Attributes section for your Sun sign preset, Moon sign preset, Ascendant preset, as well as your Jupiter preset.)*

After you have done this, your profile should be close to completion. In the case of our imaginary client this section turned out like this:

My Preset Strengths Are: *To be active and engaging.*

My Preset Weaknesses Are: *Emotions and feelings in relation to the mental plane.*

Magic I Am Most Naturally Gifted at: *Multi-action spells, manifestation of thought into physical form, Karmic cleansing, banishing weaknesses, inspiration, to bring blessings, to open roads, to gain attention, for success in business, and hex removal.*

The next time you feel stuck on the wheel of magical progression and aren't sure where to put your attention visit this portion of your Planetary Power Profile. Often when we enter a spiritual plateau and feel disconnected from our path it is due to blockages and stale energy. Simply by turning to this part of your profile you can find any number of magic that will help ignite the Witch Power.

Personal Planetary Power

Lastly, you'll use your Planetary Power Profile to help you immediately add what you have learned to your witchcraft. This final portion of the profile is dedicated to four magical practices that will bring your thirst for power instant planetary gratification. Follow the instructions listed and use the correspondence tables in chapter 7 to complete each section.

Personal Three Souls Incense

Each frequency of the zodiac associated with the "Big Three" has its own herbal correspondences. Build this recipe by combining a frankincense or a resin from the herbal list under your Ascending frequency, a bark or wood from the Lunar frequency correspondence list, and a flower from the Solar frequency correspondence list in equal parts.

Personal Sigil of Cosmic Alignment

Stack the sigils for your Solar, Lunar, and Ascending frequencies on top of each other like a totem pole. Draw a line connecting each sigil ending in an arrow at the bottom.

Incense to Repel Negative Effects of Mercury Retrograde

Mix two-parts dried rosemary, one-part copal, and one-part of any herb from the correspondence list that can be found under your individual Mercury frequency preset. Pray to Mercury while burning for harmony, protection, and anti-calamity during retrograde. (I felt the need to include this as many of us feel powerless during Mercury retrograde and have a difficult time maintaining focus during this time. Burning this incense the Wednesday before Mercury goes retrograde and during its retrograde has shown to be quite effective.)

In the case of the imaginary client this portion of their Planetary Power Profile looks like this:

PERSONAL THREE SOULS INCENSE:
Equal parts frankincense, rue, and cinnamon

INCENSE TO REPEL NEGATIVE EFFECTS OF MERCURY RETROGRADE:
Two-parts rosemary, one-part copal, and one-part bergamot

Personal Cosmic Sigil of Power

The position of the planets in your birthchart also makes a design that can be empowered as a magical sigil. This sigil is particularly powerful as it represents the shape of the cosmos when you were born and is a unique moniker that displays your planetary presets. You can use this sigil in different ways to tap into the power of your presets; the sky is the limit! By placing this sigil on anything you instantly connect it to your energy.

Draw or paint this magical sigil on your magical tools to mark them as your personal objects of power. This charges them with your cosmic essence and they should not be shared with other people once they have been used in this way. Repeat the chant used to seal the sigil below when empowering any object with this sigil.

Incorporate this sigil into your meditations. Draw it on the ground beneath you with holy fire once you have tuned in to your home frequency. Repeat the chant below to seal the sigil and each time you revisit your home frequency visualize it beneath you. By doing this you will further anchor the sigil to your frequency.

You can in some cases use this method to create a sigil to gain power or influence over someone for magical purposes. As long as you have their birthchart information and can produce the wheel image this is actually quite easy. Simply create their cosmic power sigil and then use it in spells and magic as a symbol that represents their strengths and their weaknesses. When you do this visualize the sigil diminishing in vibrancy. You can also use this sigil as a substitute for hard-to-obtain personal items.

What you need

The wheel image from your birthchart

Pen and Paper

Ruler

High John the Conqueror Condition Oil

(Substitute honeysuckle, rose, rue, or dragon's blood essential oils.)

Begin this process by going to your home frequency. Place the wheel image from your birthchart in front of you and familiarize yourself with the position of the planets. First, find your rising sign and draw a straight line connecting it to the Sun. Second, find where the Moon is and draw a line from the Sun to it. Next, draw a line connecting the Moon to Mercury.

Using the example of our imaginary client to create this sigil, currently it should look something like this:

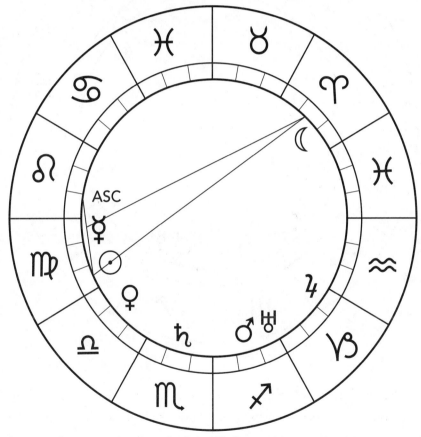

Personal cosmic sigil of power part 1

Now draw a line from Mercury to Venus, and then from Venus to Mars. Continue by drawing a line from Mars to Jupiter. It should now look something like this:

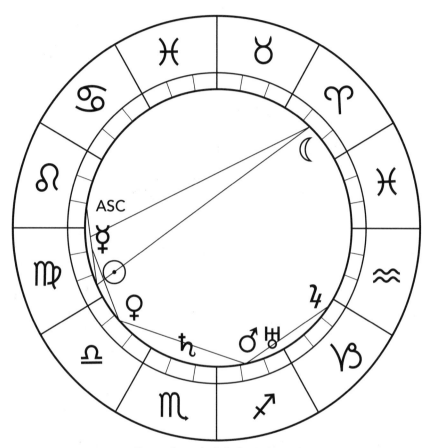

Personal cosmic sigil of power part 2

Draw a line from Jupiter to Saturn, from Saturn to Uranus, then from Uranus to Neptune, from Neptune to Pluto. Lastly, draw a line from Pluto back to your rising sign. Extrapolate the line-drawn image you have drawn and redraw it in your Planetary Power Profile.

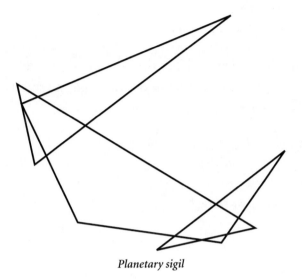

Planetary sigil

This effectively is your sigil, but now you need to empower it—until then it is just a doodle. Draw the sigil on a separate piece of unused white paper. Dip the tip of your finger in the oil and trace the sigil from beginning to end. Be sure to cover the sigil completely. Run the remaining oil on the palms of your hands and rub them together until a slight heat is produced from the friction. This warmth should invigorate the scent from the oil. Open your palms and gently fan them towards your body. Take a deep breath and as you exhale resonate the vowel OHM.

Grab the edges of the paper and lift it into the air as if you were presenting a work of art to a roomful of people. Repeat the following chant:

Ascendendo, Sol, Luna, Mercurius!
Venus, Mars, Jupiter, Saturnus!
Uranus, Neptunus, Pluto, Ascendendo!

Now place the paper down in front of you and then draw the sigil with your fingers in the air in front of you with holy fire.

By the power of planets I bid you rise,
I weave this sigil across the skies!

Visualize this sigil ascend into the stars above you and become one with the universe. Place your hands over the sigil and seal it by sending holy fire into the symbol while chanting three times:

A conjured symbol, that is my mark,
A shining light against the dark.

And finish this working by saying,

This is my will, so must it be, for the good of all but most for me!

Take the piece of paper that has the final copy of your sigil and has been dressed with oil and place it in your book of shadows. By placing it there the sigil will be empowered by the book and the sigil will empower the book, acting as a synching cord between you and your own personal mysteries. On your next and following birthdays redo this magical working to realign with the original energies.

In my time as a practicing witch there have been peaks and valleys of understanding and connectedness. There have been times when I felt like I was at the right place, at the right time, feeling that I had been clearly guided to that point for a reason. Other times I have felt lost and alone and that I had no direction. This is a perfectly normal part of the process but for some people can be the thing that frustrates them so much they lose faith in their own process and gnosis. As a witch, knowing what steps to take next along your path can be very difficult, with or without the support of a community. For me, the study of astrology and how it influences me has been a giant help along the road to self-mastery.

By looking at the default energies of your existence as shown in your birthchart, you can begin to map a course and plan of action for personal development. What is provided there is a detailed look at the basic energetic components that have been pushing you along your whole life. Knowing what your default tendencies are can help you master your ability to wield true power. Power is most often lost when we sabotage ourselves, so being aware of when and in what situations we are most likely to do that is critical. No one can make a map without knowing what the terrain is going to look like, and thanks to astrology we can forecast the influences of the future and detail the influences of the past.

Regardless of your chart you can always make the changes you need. If you have discovered that you are all Fire and no Earth then you have also discovered that in this life you need to develop the ability to keep yourself grounded. If you have found that you have a lot of Water in your chart, then you more than likely have found the reason for your emotional sensitivity and are looking for ways to bring openness into your life. If you have a lot of Air then you are going to be full of ideas but have little follow-through and may have discovered that by working on developing discipline that you could really take yourself to the next level. If you have a lot of Earth you probably have realized that your stubborn nature keeps you from living the big, bold life you secretly want and that it might be time to think outside of the box.

Perhaps the best hidden secret in witchcraft is that your weaknesses are actually strengths just waiting to be used for the right purpose. You can find the way to make them into your superpower if you look in the right places.

Birthchart Resources
For Mac Users
Time Passages (Professional Application), www.Astrograph.com

For PC Users
Solar Fire (Software), www.SolarFire.info

www.Alabe.com/freechart

Other Astrology Technical Resources
APPLICATIONS (APPLE AND ANDROID)

For Planetary Hours—Hours, www.Lunarium.co.uk

Birthchart and Personalized Horoscope—Time Passages
(Professional Application), www.Astrograph.com

Find more links and resources for astrology
at my website, www.DevinHunter.net.

Part Three

ALLIES IN POWER

In this last portion of *The Witch's Book of Power* I share with you some of the most powerful magic that I could impart to another witch. I will discuss the great creator God of my spiritual tradition, known as the Star Goddess. There is more that I would like to share about her than I could fit into one chapter; however, I am able to give you at least some of the good stuff! Through her we learn about ecstasy and becoming one with the universe to harness the powers of rapture and restoration.

In chapter 10 I will introduce you to the two halves of the Star Goddess, Diana and Dianus. Along with their daughter, Aradia, we will explore the powers of the Gods of the craft. These ancient powers are older than we might think and just as alive in the twenty-first century as they have ever been. In this chapter we take an updated look at the queen and king of the witches and join their daughter as advanced students on the path.

In the final chapter I discuss the allies of the witch, their benefits, and how to get their attention. I couldn't imagine my witchcraft without the spirits described there. I hope that you find power in the relationships forged there.

Chapter Nine

The Star Goddess
and Ecstasy

The first peace, which is the most important, is that which comes
within the souls of people when they realize their relationship, their
oneness with the universe and all its powers, and when they realize
that at the center of the universe dwells the Great Spirit, and that
this center is really everywhere, it is within each of us.
—Black Elk—

Some traditions like to think that God is a man who sits upon a throne strategizing as he fights an ancient war against evil and chaos while he simultaneously creates and judges humanity. In these traditions there tends to be a perpetuated separateness from God. He is a maker but once something is made it's on its own. It is then the job of the creation to find its way back to its maker, and religion often happens to be the best way to do that. Though separate from their maker, the followers of these traditions agonize over moral codes that keep the chaos away. They use these codes to justify harming those who they see as being representative of the chaos, non-believers, and then use those codes to justify war. They see themselves as being part of an army that was created to fight the forces their God protests. To us God works very differently.

A core tenet in many religions and spiritual philosophies is that everything is one. It's a big concept to get our heads around sometimes. To say "everything" implies the things we can see, study, and understand as well as all of the things we have never seen and that which we may never understand. It is the knowledge we have gained since birth and the science that waits undiscovered. It is consciousness, it is matter, it is light, it is time, it is the laws of physics, all that has ever been and all that will ever be. Everything is limitless and omnipresent. We believe that the everything is one and that the one is what we refer to as God Herself or the Star Goddess.

The Star Goddess

The Star Goddess is the being that contains all of existence: The entire universe and its different fascinations. We refer to the Star Goddess often as either God Herself or Goddess Himself. There is no gender assignment that is appropriate as this being is pre-gender and needed no consort to reproduce.

The Star Goddess

To us the Star Goddess is something that we are part of. We believe that she uses the experiences of individual sentient beings to examine, find purpose, and express her own nature. In this we carry an understanding that we are made of the substance she is and therefore we are divine ourselves. All that we experience and struggle with in our lives is a part of the process of this omnipotent being growing into its ultimate potential.

In several witchcraft traditions the priesthood involves years of devotion and study dedicated to the Star Goddess. We learn the cherished practice of discovering right relation to oneness and learn to bring our home frequency into resonance with the divine numinous.

The Charge of the Star Goddess[3]

Hear now the words of the Star Goddess!

I am the source of all things who is known by many names.

Diana, Mari, Kuk, Nuit, Isis, Astarte, Elohim.

I am space. I am time. I am infinite and forever. I am the one who is made of many.

From me all things proceed, and unto me all things must return.

Within my expanses there are divine secrets to behold. I am the mysteries of life and death, order and chaos, light and darkness, emptiness and fulfillment. I am the force that holds all things together and the force that pulls them apart. I am the Alpha and the Omega, the void and that which lies beyond. Within me thine innermost divine self shall be enfolded in the rapture of the infinite.

As I exist, you exist. As I breathe, you breathe. Your thoughts and discoveries are my own and your intentions are made clear through me. As you grow, I grow. As you evolve, I evolve. You are the pebble and I am the mountain.

---

3   As inspired and adapted from Doreen Valiente, beloved foremother of modern witchcraft.

*Let my worship be with the heart that rejoices, for behold, all acts of
love and pleasure are my rituals. Therefore let there be beauty and
strength, power and compassion, honor and humility, mirth and
reverence within you. For as you feed your tired soul you feed mine.*

*Know that if you search for me but do not find me you have not
looked within. I have been with you from the beginning and I am
that which is attained at the end of desire. You are never alone. You
are never without power. For behold the strength of the One, all-
knowing, all-pervading influence is within you.*

There are several variations of the charge but all signs point to it origi-
nating from *Aradia: The Gospel of the Witches* by Charles Leland. The beloved
foremother of modern witchcraft, Doreen Valiente, would later publish her
version, which was a collection gathered from various works. The charge is
used in many traditions as a ritual tool to empower ritual participants with
the female energies of the Goddess. Similarly, there is a *Charge of the God*,
which does the same with male energy.

I developed this version for use in Sacred Fires, which combines Valiente's version and some of my own channeled work. Here we have a version that removes the concept of gender and focuses more on the cosmic
frequency of oneness.

The charge can be used in ritual or meditation and can be used daily to
help you align with the frequency of the Star Goddess. There is a medicine
that is given to us when we work with the Star Goddess. She teaches us
about ecstasy and shows us how to connect to this source energy through
ecstatic practices.

For thousands of years people have known that the darkness holds
secrets, and many shamanic cultures turn to the darkness to cultivate
the inner mysteries. Creating a meditation and trance practice can bring
you deeper into yourself than you ever thought possible, and by doing

so closer to the Star Goddess. Take twenty minutes at least three times a week and devote it to the development of a meditation and trance practice. When you do so, even if you're listening to a guided meditation, invite God Herself to join you by leaving messages for you during that time. If you are someone who hates to meditate then devote that time to sitting in silence and thinking about any issues that might be blocking you in life and look for a way to resolve them.

Another way to add this energy into your life is through ecstatic practice.

Adding Ecstasy

Using forms of ecstatic practice places you in the center of the experience and helps us as witches connect fully to ritual, meditation, and even more so to life. In some ways ecstatic practice is a form of ritual possession; however, instead of a God or spirit form entering your body, the energy of the working enters your body. When we are channeling the energies of our magic through ourselves we become the work being done; magic is always a part of us, but when we are given the opportunity to be the magic, our souls fly, our words thunder through the heavens, and our feet pound with our will into the earth below.

There is something to be said about leaving a ritual or spell working and still feeling "buzzy" because you know beyond a doubt that it worked—you could feel it working. There's also something to be said about leaving a ritual or spell where you went through the motions of the work but hardly connected to it. In my experience the latter is due to a lack of ecstatic energy within the working. I have at this point become somewhat of a snob when it comes to ritual because after years of training and ecstatic ritual I cannot say that the normal garden-variety ritual moves me in the same way. Ecstatic ritual practices have become a staple for me as I have found great power, results, and success through them.

Spiritual ecstaticism is common amongst many Pagan traditions. Sacred Fires, the Anderson Faery Tradition of witchcraft, Voudoo, and the Wild Wood Tradition all practice ecstatic worship and ritual as a quintessential part of their priesthood (just to name a few). Ecstasy in many ways is surrender of the self. Ego is released, the senses are submerged in intense shamanic expression; in a way we lose our identity and become something else. Although, powerful ecstatic work should not merely be jumped into but should be naturally developed in us as witches. This form of magic requires one to test limits, yes, but to ease into an understanding of how we are affected by it as well.

There are a few easy ways to automatically add an ecstatic oomph to your practices, all of which require nothing but you. If you are able to work on these practices in a group setting, even better, but being a solitary witch the majority of my life I have found that some of the best forms of ecstatic practices are cultivated within the personal realms. Ecstatic practice is in many ways the practice of submersion into your magic that only results when you are aligned and all three souls are in tune with the work.

Ten Steps for Immediate Ecstasy

1. Before any work, align your three souls.

2. The cleaner your energy body is (as in, free of junk) the easier it will be for you to access ecstasy. Perform cleansing breaths, ground your energy, smudge, and take salt baths regularly.

3. Focus on allowing mana to rise from your primal soul, up through your ego soul, into your higher self, out through your crown, through your aura, and back through the primal soul. The more you "run" basic energies through your energy body the easier it will be to enter into an ecstatic space, and surely simply running this energy while in ritual or spell working will greatly influence your magic.

4. Do the third practice listed above, but instead of just running mana through your energy body, create a mental image of the desired outcome of your work and allow that to run through your energy body.

5. Everything starts with a proper and well-developed breathing technique. Using pranic breathing techniques, Ujjayi breathing techniques, and other breathing techniques such as the four-fold—breaths all described within this chapter—are excellent ways to increase and stimulate mana.

6. Movement. Adding movement to your work ensures that energy will move as well. This is a very simple technique; however, simply moving around your spell candle or tools clockwise or counterclockwise while casting will aid you greatly.

7. Dance, dance, dance. In advanced ecstatic practices one of the key components involves ritual dance. Turning on appropriate music for your magical stylings that you can move to helps you to raise energy, allow it to flow through you, and then absorb or channel it into your workings.

8. Drumming aids greatly in our ability to disconnect from the outside world and allows our natural vibration to sync with the overall working at hand. If you do not have a drum, clap your hands, stomp your feet, or purchase a drumming CD to play while doing magic or meditating.

9. Sing! Allow mana to course through you and instead of simply speaking your magic, sing it. If you can't sing (even though we all can sing!) then chant. Your voice has power, so use it to engage the experience of magic.

10. Darkness meditations before and after ritual will allow for you to leave your senses behind and enter ecstasy. I will go into detail about this later in the chapter; however, darkness meditations are done in several magical and spiritual traditions all over the world as a means of embracing the ecstatic via the dissolution of the ego and/or conscious self. The essential idea is that if we can quiet the mind and move beyond the conscious stream of thoughts then we can allow the subconscious to take over. In some ways I have seen darkness meditations as a way to allow the primal soul to take the conscious place of the ego soul.

Beginning Ecstatic Practices

The first thing to be aware of is always safety above all else. In the beginning of developing an ecstatic witchcraft practice there is little to fear, but some ecstatic practices can very well push your limits both physically and spiritually. As such there are a few rules to the practice:

1. Be aware of any limitation you may have. If you physically are unable to dance or stand for long periods of time, then don't risk it! Find a comfortable place to rest within the ceremony or ritual and focus on breath work.

2. Water, water, water. Be sure to remain hydrated as much as possible. I generally recommend that you drink lots of water before, during, and after ecstatic work but especially the day or two after as well. Your body will purge impurities during and after ecstatic work; if you drink water you can ensure these toxins leave the body.

3. Have a clear vision of what you are intending to do. Often we get into the ecstatic worship and very easily become

lost within it. If you are going into the work for a specific purpose, make sure that you are connecting to the purpose throughout the work.

4. If the work is light then make sure you ground afterwards; if the work is heavier, make sure to ground and have a designated driver to take you home! Operating heavy machinery is a big no-no.

Ecstatic Breath Work

These practices can very easily be done without the intention of them leading to ecstatic worship. The breathing techniques are designed to calm the inner world, build mana, and reestablish balance. When applying them to an ecstatic practice try building up a tolerance first. This means for the first several tries allow yourself to become comfortable with the techniques, then add longer breaths to the techniques, and lastly extend the overall duration of the practice slowly. I recommend that if you are looking to take full advantage of these practices you begin by dedicating fifteen minutes each day, three times a week, to breath exercises, and each consecutive week adding an additional five minutes to each practice period until you have reached one hour. Also, adding this work to a soul alignment, followed by a cleansing rite, will allow you to kill three birds with one stone.

Posture

Posture is incredibly important for achieving the optimal breath. If you are practicing the breath work in a seated position make sure you are not slouching and that your spine remains straight, which allows the lungs to open up naturally. Always keep your shoulders down as you breathe in and out. If you notice your shoulders rising as you inhale then you are actually denying the full breath from happening and are holding onto physical tension. It may help to roll your shoulders back before commencing with the first breath.

If you are seated in a chair be sure to also keep your feet firmly planted on the ground and never slouch or lean back too far. If you are practicing the work standing, make sure to bend your knees a bit to allow blood flow. If you lock your knees you could possibly pass out. While standing it is okay to rock back and forth as you breathe, as sometimes we naturally are inclined to rock back and forth; however, be sure not to become too distracted.

Taking Breath

Begin every breath exercise with three deep breaths of power and cleansing. As you do so announce to your body and mind that you are about to enter a meditative and deeply relaxed state.

Allow the air to enter your stomach first, then your diaphragm, and lastly your lungs. This allows for muscle control while breathing, but also ensures that you are taking deep breaths, which helps to involve parts of your lungs you often do not use in your day-to-day breathing.

If working with a count structure such as in pranic breathing or in the four-fold breath be sure to take full advantage of the counts. This means that if you have four counts to inhale and then are to hold for four counts, you begin to breathe in the second your brain perceives "one," and you do not stop the intake of air until your brain perceives "one" on the first count of the hold. As you exhale treat the release of the breath with the same reverence. I find it useful to use a metronome to ensure equal breaths (for a slow and full breath set at 35 bpm, and for a faster breath try 75 bpm).

The key with breathing for meditation or trance is to allow the air to enter and leave as fluidly as water. Try to avoid any harsh or abrupt starts and finishes with the breath work. As you inhale envision a cup of water being poured from one cup to another, and as you exhale the breath pours like the water from one cup to the next. Mana has fluidic properties, so if you are working on advanced breathing techniques with the hope of building mana, a liquid or fluid visualization in breath work is important!

Stillness and Silence

A key point to advanced breath work is not just the structure of the breath but also engaging your mind with the practice as well. Perceive points of stillness and silence at the beginnings and ends of each of your breaths. Although the transition from inhale to exhale should be fluid there is also a point of release where tension from the breath is let go, and within those points we find the stillness and silence. As you are meditating, focus on the breath count, but also perceive these moments of stillness and silence.

If you are working with a breath count structure that requires you to hold the breath in between inhale and exhale, allow yourself to feel the true depth of the hold by allowing your consciousness to fade into the points of stillness and silence. When done properly your body will become quite used to sinking into these points, which will allow you to easily slip into deeper levels of meditation on a more regular basis. These points of stillness and silence allow us to harmonize with other frequencies and the Star Goddess.

Intermediate-to-Advanced Breath Work

Pranic Breathing

Pranic breathing is designed to build prana (mana, life force) and can be done in easy, small three-count breaths or more complex ten-count breaths (or larger). The breath begins by breathing in for three counts, holding the breath for three counts, exhaling for three counts, and then holding before inhale for three counts. This series of breaths should be repeated no less than ten times.

First, practice this breath while breathing in and out through your mouth, and once you feel comfortable close your mouth and make it your practice to breathe in and out through your nose. As you grow in comfort with the breath add another count to the inhale and exhale, keeping the holds in between the same three counts as before. Continue to gradually add an additional number to the inhale and exhale all the way through ten, and then work your way back down to three counts on each end. A series of this form of advanced pranic breaths would be one round beginning at three counts, working your way up to ten, then back to three counts again.

Alternate Nostril Breathing (Nadi Shodana)

Alternate nostril breathing is another simple and effective breath practice. The advantages to this type of breath far outweigh most other breath forms as it is designed to allow both the left and right brains to receive equal amounts of oxygen at the same time and as such improves brain function, and is known to link the left and right brains together. Doing this both at morning and at night allows for stale air and toxins that rest in our lungs while breathing normally to be released, ultimately improving lung function.

Begin the breath by placing your right thumb over your right nostril; allow yourself to breathe solely through your left nostril and then pause for a moment. Release your thumb from holding the right nostril shut and place your index finger over your left nostril, then release the breath through your right nostril. Pause for a moment, and then alternate again. One series of this breath count would involve taking full breaths and exhaling fully for no less than five minutes.

Ujjayi Breath

Of all the breaths this is probably the strangest, but I assure you once you can get over the funny noise you will be quite impressed. The Ujjayi breath is designed to build life force, create wide channels of energy within the body, and to allow for the breathing process to be the focus of your work. I have found this breath to be extremely useful when preparing to do any form of magic, and it can easily be applied to almost any breath technique.

To understand this breath you first must begin it by breathing in and out of your mouth. Begin with a normal inhale, but as you exhale do so as if you were trying to fog up a pair of glasses. There is a tiny muscle called the glottis, which is responsible for helping us to pronounce H sounds, but also helps to warm oxygen as it enters our lungs. As you make the "HAAAA" sound like when you are fogging up glasses make sure to not involve any of your voice.

Now, from this point, breathe in with your mouth open with the intention that you are going to make a guttural-sounding inhale, the same type of "HAAA" sound you made when you exhaled, but this time you are breathing in. Try this a few times, making sure that you are actually feeling the glottis respond.

The actual breath technique requires the same glottis interaction, but instead of breathing with your mouth open you do so with your mouth shut and are breathing in and out through the nose.

The Four-Fold Breath

This breath is commonly taught to those who are studying ritualistic magic, as well as hermetic magic, and Kabala. Breathing in through your nose and out through your mouth, this breath places an important significance on a series of four repeating counts. Breathe in for four, hold for four, exhale for four, and hold for four. A complete series would involve ten repetitions.

Taking It to the Next Level

Once you feel comfortable with all of these breathing techniques and can do them easily, begin to add them into your ritual work as a means to raise energy.

Step one:

Align your three souls, perform a cleansing rite such as Kala or an uncrossing, and then allow yourself to ignite your holy fire. Begin first by combining the pranic breath style with the Ujjayi technique. As you run through the breath counts, moving from three to ten, see your holy fire rise and become bigger, eventually upon count ten completely filling the space you are in. As you decrease in count, absorb your holy fire back into your body.

Take three deep breaths to ground.

Step two:

When you have done step one successfully, replace the pranic breath with the alternating nostril breath, again adding the Ujjayi technique and holy fire visualization.

Take three deep breaths to ground.

Step three:

Combine both the four-fold and Ujjayi techniques and complete one series of breaths.

Take three deep breaths to ground.

Step four:

Combine both the pranic and Ujjayi techniques together as in step one, but once you have finished with the series of pranic breaths, complete a second round combining the pranic, alternate nasal breathing, and Ujjayi breath.

Take three deep breaths to ground.

Step five:

Combine both the pranic and Ujjayi techniques together as in step one; however, once you have finished with the series of pranic breaths, complete a second round, combining the pranic, alternate nasal breathing, and Ujjayi breath. After your second round of breaths complete a third round of breaths utilizing both the four-fold and Ujjayi breath techniques.

Take three deep breaths to ground.

I strongly encourage you to go at your own pace, and please, whatever you do, until you are ready do not try to complete all five steps at once if you feel strained by them. There is absolutely no use in pushing yourself past your natural limits. As with anything in magic, you can get hurt if you try to skip very important steps along the way. There is no sense in skipping through the breath work as the more advanced breath techniques require stamina, which can only be gained through fundamental practice.

Darkness Meditation

Some of the most powerful spiritual experiences I have ever had came through my work in Darkness Meditation. The theory behind this meditative technique is that after a period of time of being alone in the darkness our senses are forced to shift and the perceptive centers of the mind bloom like night flowers. We have all experienced this sensation, as it is responsible for giving us the "heebie-jeebies" on dark and silent nights. Our ancestors born without the benefits of electricity would have undoubtedly been familiar daily with this shifting of perception. This sensation is something that we would likely be able to trace far back in the human experience.

Several forms of initiatic traditions utilize the benefits of this technique to aid in the dissolution of the ego. In some African traditions such as that of the Yoruba, participants are wrapped in cloth and left in a dark hut for several days. In "Green Initiations," those being initiated are stripped nude, slathered in magical unguents and oils, wrapped in vines, and then left to be transformed overnight in a secret location. In the UK-based Path of Pollen, initiants are stung multiple times by bees and then placed in a small hexagonal wicker abode that mimics a hive and are left there for several days with honey and water as the only sustenance.

The common thread here is that during these rituals a sort of death and rebirth happens. The moments spent in darkness symbolize the time spent between the two and the journey one must undergo in order to ascend. This technique most benefits the primal and Holy souls as it connects our instincts and animal senses to our higher spiritual gifts. Darkness, in this sense, becomes the vehicle for spiritual transformation.

This technique isn't ecstatic just because it takes us to a place between the worlds, it's also ecstatic because it can easily be used to bring harmony between the universe and ourselves.

To do this, all you need to do is go somewhere that is as open and dark as possible. The best is to either go somewhere in nature at night, away from busy streets or traffic, or to find a Iso-tank (isolation tank.) Iso-tanks are wonderful because even though they are not open, by floating in high-selenic water, buoyancy produces a feeling of weightlessness.

Go to your home frequency, close your eyes, and allow yourself to breathe slowly and to gently settle the mind. During this time don't rush through any thoughts, just allow things to flow. Without the extra stimuli that light provides, your conscious mind will soon be forced to exhaust itself. You will know this is happening because you will likely become very aware of the tension in your physical body. At this time, begin a comfortable and steady breathing practice.

As you breathe in, focus on those points of stillness and silence at the beginning and end of each breath. Envision the darkness around you pouring into your lungs with each breath. As the air rests for that single moment in your chest, see it swell up in one pregnant pause. As you exhale, notice that tension and internal conflict ease as little by little with each breath they are cleared from your energy body. With each breath allow the space the darkness fills to grow larger and larger while maintaining consistency. Make sure this feels natural and do not push yourself to the point where you feel out of breath. Breathe like this until you feel the final bit of energy has broken away, leaving you feeling completely empty at the end of your exhales. At this point, I usually begin rocking back and forth or in a circular motion. Like many witches, my body naturally does this when I have entered a state of ecstasy.

Continue to breathe in this manner and envision now that as you inhale you become completely filled by the darkness around you. As you exhale envision that all of you is then poured into the darkness. Like tempering hot and cold liquids, allow yourself to be poured in and out of your body.

Spend as much time as you need here and visit this place often. In this ecstatic space can you ask anything of the Goddess and lift any worry to her. It is in this space that you will find answers to your innermost questions and are given VIP access to the divine.

Movement

The breaths will go a long way in helping you produce endurance; however, they are not necessarily combined with movement unless otherwise desired. Ecstatic movement is perhaps one of the hardest practices to describe as it involves a very personal and unique sense of body, space, and rhythm.

For those of you who say you can't dance, you are wrong! Dancing is one of the most natural things for us to do as humans and at one point was a very important part of our culture. Dancing in the style of the electric slide can be just as magical as doing the foxtrot, or grinding down on the dance floor. The truth is ecstatic dance is both the cause of ecstasy and also the byproduct.

Really letting go and surrendering to the energy, allowing it to move your limbs, hips, and thighs, is the primal soul's answer to ecstatic dance. Letting go of your inhibitions and simply giving way to the flow is just as important to the experience as breathing is. If you aren't sure where to begin, or even whether you have experienced this before, all you need to do is think back to the last time you heard your favorite tune on the radio and were tapping your feet.

It is in this experience of tapping your foot that the seed of ecstasy is planted. There is nothing like turning the radio full blast and throwing your arms up in the air and just dancing, but even when you are tapping your feet to the beat of a song you are allowing energy to sync and move through you. So, to begin the practice of ecstatic dance and movement, you need to connect to that feeling of jamming to your favorite song.

Exercise one:

Go somewhere free of distractions, sit down, and turn on your favorite song. First begin by picking out the beat of the song and start to tap your feet to that beat. Next, find the words or melody to the song and sing (or at least try to sing) along just like no one is watching.

Now you may need to put the song on repeat, but the next step involves standing up, and instead of tapping your foot to the beat you take a step forward, and then a step back, then forward, then back, all in accordance to the beat. Once you feel you can do that safely as you are stepping back and forth, start to clap your hands to the beat.

Space providing, move on to not just taking a step back and forth but now step and clap to the beat as you move in a circle. Continue to do this until the song ends.

Now that you know you are more than capable of dancing, it is time to move on, unless physically restricted, to the fundamentals of ecstatic dance.

There are essentially five different stages of the ecstatic dance experience. The first stage is visualization. When you embark upon the journey of ecstatic dance you need to first visualize what it is that you are working with. For instance, a popular ecstatic dance form among my classes is what we call "the summoning of the first witches," which essentially is our way to ritually invoke and summon the primal power of a witch. We begin with a guided trance into a deep and dark forest untouched by industrial human hands. We make our way to a grove in the heart of this forest, and in the center of the grove is a large fire. As we enter the sacred space others begin to join us, some of them ancient-looking witches; others seem to be faery beings, and some attendees may even be of the animal persuasion. As we visualize this gathering of witches we, too, are setting an intention to connect with their energy through dance.

The second stage of ecstatic dance is that of surrendering. We release our inhibitions, the worries, stress, and fears surrounding us, keeping us from connecting to our own wild nature. We seek to surrender our armor (often the ego-self) and to instead become the primal version of ourselves. Essentially we are surrendering to our wild and free nature. We do this by introducing drums or music, and as the beat begins to play we individually call upon our primal souls to come out and play. This stage takes some time but as long as you are focusing on just letting go of looking silly, letting go of the outside world, and embracing the experience fully, it will come. It may also help to envision yourself playing a part in a dramatic play: you become an actor, and then you surrender to the character's experience.

The third stage is to become the rhythm. At this point we are often well into the movement of the dance; however, the key point here is to all become in sync with the rhythm of the drums, music, or in some cases chanting. Within this stage we are focusing on allowing the rhythmic vibrations to move through us as if we ourselves were creating them. In this we are becoming the source, not just a participant.

The fourth stage in ecstatic dance is to embellish your imagery. In the first step we visualized and set our intention, and in the fourth step we are enhancing those visualizations. It is here that we awaken all of our senses: we are not just in the dark forest dancing with a bunch of wild ancient witches but are also smelling the burning fire, tasting the sweat in our mouths, hearing the pounding of the drum, and feeling the air grow thick. Essentially we are allowing ourselves to truly be within the experience. It is also within this step that if you were working magic to create an effect, not just to commune with divinity or spirits, that you would create the mental image of your magic's ultimate effect. In other words, now is the time to do your magic, cast your spells, send your will, etc.

The fifth and last stage to the ecstatic dance is to continue to lose yourself in the dance, focus on breathing full breaths, and simply tune in with your higher self. Allow the energy that is around you to flow through you.

Once all is done and the music has stopped I recommend sitting down and discussing with others, if they are available, about your experience. Drink lots of water, get your heart rate back down to a normal rhythm, and then ground.

You can easily do this on your own, but like I said before, do not push yourself. If you have a physical restriction, honor it. For those of you who do wish to be a part of this type of ritual energy-raising but cannot for health reasons, I recommend replacing the movement with focused breath work.

By adding ecstatic practices into your life you are better able to harmonize with the frequencies of the gods, not to mention how your personal power will be affected. Ecstasy allows us to become one with our gods and the greatest of all mysteries—those pertaining to our place in the universe. Ultimately ecstatic practices align us with the universe (God Herself) and allow us to experience different frequencies firsthand.

Chapter Ten

Diana, Dianus, and Aradia

*Our Gods and Goddesses, when those concepts are used, are alive
and not symbolic and, though they include us in their mystical ways,
are not human. In many traditions and witch-blood lines, they are
not seen as Gods or Goddesses at all. They are seen as the intelligence
behind the Gods and Goddesses. They are Primal and wild and
beyond the limits of humanity, though never beyond our touch.*
—Orion Foxwood—

The Nature of the Divine

Like the way in which the craft is practiced and the Witch Power manifests, culture has a lot to do with which deities one might work with.
Many witches find it comfortable and empowering to connect to their
Witch Power through their ancestry and study practices that developed
regionally in the places their ancestors come from. I found my own
studies into Scottish and German witchcraft to be quite influential and
would encourage anyone to reach into their roots similarly. This does,

however, tend to lock people into certain frequencies that might not be relevant or useful for them in their current life. For example, if you live in downtown Las Vegas, working solely with Irish magical forms might not allow you to use the energy around you to its fullest capability.

What I have learned on my travels is that different places have different energies. It is much easier (and nicer) to learn the ways of the native spirits and gods around you and to integrate them into your life, rather than try to impose your own upon the region. As I did this and studied different magical traditions I discovered that there was always a vein of energy present no matter where I was looking. This energy was touchable and always participating. What began to interest me the most was not what separated the various paths and traditions but rather what made them similar.

The deeper I looked the more the way I viewed the divine (especially as it is related to witches and psychics) would change. Of course it should be said that we can only truly speculate as to the nature of such beings, but I believe that gods and humanity have a lot more in common than we are usually taught. The earth-shattering question I always ask my students is, "If we didn't believe in them, would they exist?" For me, the answer is that I don't believe so, at least not in the way we know them to be. We can admit surely there must be a greater vein of mystery to it all, but it seems to me that our ancestors, regardless of where they come from, were tuning in to different frequencies on the same dial. How they tuned in created the many faces of the gods and might help to explain why today new gods are discovered for our modern time.

The Star Goddess contains all the frequencies that could possibly exist. She is the full spectrum of frequency and vibration and the dial we tune through in order to find the right channel. There are two frequency bands that we tend to focus on in many witchcraft traditions, which we refer to as Goddess and God. Depending on the tradition their names and faces change, but there is almost always some variant of these two forms. In some traditions they are siblings, in some lovers, in some they are enemies, but most often they are all of the above.

When I first came to the craft I fell in love with the frequency of the Goddess and had a very difficult time with the frequency of the God. This could be for many reasons and as I look back I can see where my personal bias would get in the way. The truth, at least my truth, is that these bands of frequency are so much bigger than a gender assignment. When you get to the deep heart of each of them you realize they are more than any one gender and represent a polarization of universal energy that is omnipresent. It wasn't until I saw the God as more than just a juvenile boy, a horny old man, or a sage mystic that I actually appreciated what this frequency could bring to me. I shared this with a friend of mine who had the same problem with the Goddess frequency, and he harvested similar results when he left the gender binary behind.

The true magic comes in understanding that our gods are shape-shifters and no shape-shifters like shackles that keep them in one form for too long. This isn't to say that the mysteries of the male and female are obsolete, just that this expression of those roles will not help you be a more appropriate vessel for one or the other.

The Gods of Witchcraft

As we grow and change as a culture so do our gods, and that is because it is we who create them, or at the very least the ways in which they present themselves. The deities that I am going to share with you are beings that I have worked with my entire life, who we work with in Sacred Fires, and to whom this book is dedicated: Aradia, Diana, and Dianus. Diana and Dianus are two polarized frequency bands of universal power found within the Star Goddess. Along with their daughter, Aradia, they spread the seeds of their magic long ago in human form.

Those I introduce to you here are modern interpretations of the mysteries as discovered by myself and my tradition. Though by name they are rooted in the Roman and Italian past, they no longer solely capture the craft of one culture or another. Diana, the Goddess of Witches; her concomitant Dianus, the God of Witches; and their offspring, Aradia, the teacher of the ways.

Originally I was introduced to most of these deities through the book *Aradia, Gospel of the Witches* by Charles Leland. Later I would be reintroduced to them through my studies in Wicca, the Cult of Diana, and once more through the works of Raven Grimassi.[4] These gods are derived from Italian folklore but have survived and spread to every continent as traditions like Gardnerian Wicca spread. As they entered other cultures they were assimilated and eventually blended in with other deity forms. The result from all this mixing in many ways has been modern witchcraft.

Diana, the Queen of the Witches

This was the first fascination, she hummed the song, it was as the buzzing of bees (or a top spinning round), a spinning-wheel spinning life. She spun the lives of all men; all things were spun from the wheel of Diana. Lucifer turned the wheel.
— Charles Leland, *Aradia, Gospel of the Witches*, 1899—

Diana

The three of us sat around the small campfire and meditated for hours. We called out to the Goddess, invoking her by many names. "Diana, Athena, Hecate…" We chanted over and over again until the fire eventually faded into embers and we had all but given up hope and opened our eyes. I remember thinking to myself that they looked disappointed and tired. It hadn't worked, nothing had happened, and I was the one who got them to try

---

4   Grimassi, Raven, *Italian Witchcraft: The Old Religion of Southern Europe.*

in the first place. The Goddess didn't exist and witchcraft wasn't real. "Let's just try one more time," I said.

I snuck a peek at the moon that rested above my friend's shoulder. It was big and full and beaming with silver light. "Diana, Goddess of Witches, hear my call … " I muttered to myself as I closed my eyes once more. "Give us a sign that you are real."

"Ugh!" said my other friend, "This isn't going to happen … "

Distraught, I opened my eyes and broke from attention. What happened next would change my life forever.

As if it had been choreographed, the three of us took a deep breath, sighed, and then simultaneously slapped our thighs in defeat.

Suddenly the fire burst back into life. The other two ran back home as fast their legs could take them while I stood in awe of what just happened. As the flames danced back into being I knew that Diana had made this happen. I knew that the Goddess of Witchcraft had heard me and that she was quite real.

That night under the largest full moon in my memory, I ran deep into the field of silver grass and pledged my life to her, the goddess of witches.

Diana, the goddess of witches, is a particularly powerful force of nature. She is classically seen in Roman myth[5]—as a virgin goddess who ruled over the wild places and helped women, especially during times of birth. In her Greek myth (where she appears as Artemis) she is born just seconds before her twin brother, Apollo, and actually helps her mother with his labor. A fierce protector and a remarkably skilled hunter, Diana is said to have dominion over the beasts of the world, known and unknown. She is ancient and she is powerful.

Diana was a common goddess figure with Latin tribes and as their civilization expanded she grew to assimilate regional goddesses and myths.

---

5   Hamilton, Edith, *Edith Hamilton's Mythology* (New York: Little, Brown, and Company, 1942).

She eventually would become the goddess of witches, among several other things.

Many of her attributions as a witch goddess in text come from Christian writings. In the tenth-century work *Canon Episcopi,* an early canonical writing of the Catholic church, Diana is described as a goddess who leads witches to their meeting places.

> *Have you believed or have you shared a superstition to which*
> *some wicked women claim to have given themselves, instruments*
> *of Satan, fooled by diabolical phantasms? During the night, with*
> *Diana, the pagan goddess, in the company of a crowd of other*
> *women, they ride the backs of animals, traversing great distances*
> *during the silence of the deep night, obeying Diana's orders as*
> *their mistress and putting themselves at her service during certain*
> *specified nights. If only these sorceresses could die in their impiety*
> *without dragging many others into their loss. Fooled into error,*
> *many people believe that these rides of Diana really exist.*
>
> —Canon Episcopi

This text would later be used in sixteenth-century witch trials to convict innocent people, still citing Diana as a goddess of witches. Inspired by this writing, other books were written and used during this time for the same purpose such as *Malleus Maleficarum* (The Hammer of the Witches).

> *... although these women imagine they are riding (as they think*
> *and say) with Diana or with Herodias, in truth they are riding*
> *with the devil, who calls himself by some such heathen name and*
> *throws a glamour before their eyes.*[6]

---

6 *Malleus Maleficarum* Question 1, Part 1.

It must not be omitted that certain wicked women, perverted by Satan and seduced by the illusions and phantasms of devils, believe and profess that they ride in the night hours on certain beasts with Diana, the heathen goddess, or with Herodias, and with a countless number of women, and that in the untimely silence of night they travel over great distances of land.[7]

These texts would be used all over the Christian world to condemn and falsely bring an estimated forty thousand people to their deaths.[8] Over the next several hundred years witchcraft would become synonymous with Diana and in the 1940s Gerald Gardner, the father of Wicca, would pull from Aradia and other sources to create the first Wiccan tradition,[9] which helped place Diana as the central goddess in modern witchcraft.

Diana as a Modern Witch Goddess

In the twenty-first century Diana sits upon an immense throne of folklore and occult connection. She has derived new mysteries and new worshippers and still finds a way to keep herself relevant in the human mind. Many witchcraft traditions, like Sacred Fires, work with Diana as a central goddess figure and we refer to ourselves as *Dianic Witches* or *Dianists*.

Diana is represented by the colors black, silver, and purple and has dominion over all of their attributes. Black is symbolic of the darkness of space and the occult. In the creation myth it is said that the Star Goddess divided herself into light and dark: the darkness was Diana, the light was Lucifer (Dianus). Darkness is symbolic of the void, the vastness of space, attraction, receptivity, and our own subconscious. Silver represents the

---

7   *Malleus Maleficarum* Part 1, QX.

8   Malcolm Gaskill *Witchcraft, a very short introduction* (Oxford University Press, 2010), 76.

9   Ronald Hutton *Triumph of the Moon* (Oxford University Press, 1999), 215.

arrow of will (arrows being classically associated with Diana), her divinity, and connection to the moon. Lastly, purple represents her sovereignty, mystical knowledge, and psychic clarity.

All animals are sacred to her; however, the deer, owl, lion, bear, and dog are particularly beloved by her. She rules over all magic including those beings who fall under this dominion, such as witches and the fae. Her symbols are the moon, the key, the broom, the sword, the chalice, and the heart. Pray to her on Monday.

Being ageless and ancient all at the same time, she assumes the ternion roles of maiden, mother, and crone simultaneously. She contains the secrets of the universe and is a master of the arts of manifestation and glamour. Her sacred sigil is in the design of a bow and arrow.

Invocation of Diana Triforma

I call forth Diana Triforma, She who wears three crowns!
The queen that quakes the heavens and whose feet dance upon the void!
Diana, Great Sorceress, I your child call to you! Hear me now!
Shape-shifter, wild-woman, queen of the unknown,
I summon you now as maiden, mother, and crone!
Queen of the Witches and Lady most true,
I invoke you now and am made anew!
Diana, Dee-anna, Dee-in-a, Hail Diana Triforma!

Tuning in to the Frequency of Diana

For me, developing a deep and lifelong bond with her was imperative. There have been times in my life when I felt so lost and helpless and, feeling so, have lifted my problems up to her in ritual or in a late-night sob session only to have them all fixed within a few days. I'm not talking miraculous letters that annulled the issues showing up in my inbox. I'm talking about how somehow I will find my entire schedule was booked the next week and that I really didn't need to worry about the money, I needed to worry about showing up and being present.

Once I was feeling particularly lost after my first time moving to a big city after living in rural Ohio my whole life. I had had some ridiculously life-changing and bruising things go down and I had to leave to go discover myself. When I moved I was still carrying the scars from battle and I felt disconnected from everything around me. All I had was Diana and my car. One night after a rough day I lit all my candles on my altar and prayed. I didn't pray to have everything fixed by divine intervention but I did pray that somehow I would find the tools to fix things myself. The next day I met other witches and quickly realized I was feeling lonely, not conquered.

She will scoop us up and receive all of our pain, then sit us back down and tell us to stand up on our own two feet again. Being a goddess of magic she is very direct about us taking action in our lives. Like the Empress in the Tarot, she is a reminder that we need to exceed our projected limitations and *carpe diem*. If there is one lesson I have learned since my relationship with Diana started, it's that she favors determination, independence, and an open mind.

Developing a relationship with her is life-changing and it can lead you to great personal power in life. To do this there are three essential practices you must bring into your day-to-day. The first is that you need to have a relationship with her other half, Dianus, and her daughter Aradia. Balance is everything and when these three are being accessed regularly, the relationship you have with others is deeper and richer for it.

The second is to align yourself with the frequency of Diana at least once a day. Every night before bed I say a few prayers to help tune in. This is one of them: "Holy Diana, mother of the craft, guide my soul each night. Bring me closer to my destiny and help me fulfill my dreams in the waking hours. Blessed be." As I say this prayer I draw a pentacle of silver over my head and visualize it sinking into my third eye.

The third is that of full-moon rituals or esbats. These rituals will align you with lunar energy and are part of the sacred contract we have with Diana. In the *Gospel of the Witches* Aradia is instructed to teach witches to hold rituals under the full moon.

Once in the month, and when the moon is full, Ye shall assemble in some desert place, Or in a forest all together join to adore the potent spirit of your queen.
—*Aradia: Gospel of the Witches*, Chapter 1

We may not all be able to go to a desert place to do our esbats but we can do our own versions of the ritual. Here is mine.

The Minor Esbat Ritual of Diana

What you need:

A bowl of spring water

Thirteen stones (preferably moonstone)

Small, dark-colored or black dish of salt

A piece of silver (jewelry, flatware, or specimens all work)

White cloth handkerchief or towel

Four white candles

This ritual can be done with a group or solitarily. The only requirements are that it be done on the full moon in a place that has access to a view of the moon and that you wear black. You can do this during cloudy nights, just check your local newspaper or your favorite app (visit my website, www.devinhunter.net, for an active list) to make sure the moon is full. The exact night of the full moon is preferred; however, the night prior to it and after it are both considered full in our lore.

Under the light of the full moon bless and sanctify the space around you by taking a deep breath at your altar, declaring your intention. As you do this announce to the space around you things like, "I/we intend to work magic in this space, let it be sacred in the name of Diana!" and "Let this space be claimed as holy in the name of the Diana, queen of the witches!"

Place the bowl of spring water in the center of the altar and lay the thirteen stones around it in a circle. Place the four white candles so that they are evenly spaced around the circle of stones. Place the bowl of salt and the silver to the left and the handkerchief to the right just outside the circle of candles.

Stand to face the altar and the moon and open your arms as if to welcome an old friend and invoke your personal allies and spirit guides by saying, "*Come now spirits who guide me, spirits who protect me, spirits who love me! Come now and let us worship in the secret ways!*" Take three deep breaths and ask for your magical spirit allies to appear,[10] then light all four candles in a clockwise motion.

Place your palms parallel to the ground and invoke the spirits of place and the fae by saying, "*Spirits in the dark, people in the shadows, come now if you are friend and let us worship in the secret ways. Be you enemy stay behind or bear the wrath of my allies and the great queen and be no more!*"

Take three deep breaths and as you exhale on the final breath place your right hand over the bowl of water and your left hand so that its palm is facing the moon. In your mind's-eye see the light of the moon touch your hand and pour through your arms, through your chest, and down to your right hand. When the light reaches your right hand draw the sigil of Diana over the water and say, "In the name of Diana I summon the door!"

Pick up the small bowl of salt and shine moonlight on it. Draw a pentacle with your right hand over it and say, "By the power of my will I conjure its lock!" Take a generous portion of the salt and sprinkle it into the water and then stir it clockwise.

---

10 We will discuss allies in the next chapter, but know that you have a magical support team that is always willing to help when asked.

Pick up the piece of silver so that it catches a glimpse of the moon and then draw a pentacle in the air over it. As you do this say, "By the goddess Diana may this be cleansed. By the power of silver I conjure the key!" Gently place the silver into the bowl.

Lift both hands up, palms facing the moon, and invoke the queen by saying, "Crescent queen, I unlock the door, by magic and allies and sacred lore. By light of moon and sacred vow, come Diana and be with us now!" Slowly bring your hands down so that your palms are once again parallel to the surface of the water.

At this time take up the handkerchief in your right hand and plunge it into the water. Wring it out and then gently wash your third eye and forehead. As you do this say, "In the name of Diana may my psyche be clear." Plunge the handkerchief into the water and wring it out once again. Gently wash your hands with the handkerchief and say, "In the name of Diana may all that I touch be blessed." Plunge the handkerchief into the water a third time and once again wring it out. This time, wash your feet and say, "In the name of Diana may my path be clear of obstruction."

When finished, stand facing the altar and say three times, "Queen of Heaven, Queen of Hell, Hail the Queen of book and spell!"

At this time it would be customary to meditate and/or proceed to do any other magic you might want to do during the full moon to take advantage of the space and energy. When you are finished with any other business you have to "release" Diana and thank the spirits.

Stand facing the altar and place your hands up towards the moon once more. Say, "Hail Diana! Hail Diana! Hail Diana! You have blessed us, goddess, with your magic, stay if you will, go if you must, but if you depart I/we bid you, Hail and farewell!"

Place your palms to the ground and thank the spirits of place and the fae by saying, "Bless you, shadows, for gathering around the flame, may we celebrate again. Hail and farewell!"

Open your arms equally in front of your chest and thank your spirit guides and allies by saying, "Bless you, spirits, for coming to my aid, may we bathe in moonlight again! Hail and farewell!"

Dianus, The King of Witches

Deep within the woods in a hidden cave lives a magician. He is cloaked in moss and autumn leaves and from his head grow a pair of antlers. He shines in brilliant light as he stands to reveal his sturdy legs and cloven feet. Butterflies and dragonflies dance around him as he walks towards you. With every step he changes form. First, he has the head of a man, then that of a stag, with the next step the head of a wolf, and then two heads—one pointing to the east and the other the west. As he embraces you he settles into the figure of a tall man draped in the colors of autumn and his touch is as warm as the summer's day.

Dianus

Lucifer, who is spoken of as Diana's consort in *Aradia, Gospel of the Witches* would take on a very cerebral form much like the Christian God, and was eventually pushed out to make way for the horned god. Perhaps it was an attempt to distance ourselves from the overbearing weight the name Lucifer carries in pop culture, or perhaps it was a way to prove we weren't evil, but Lucifer, the god of logic and expression, light and illumination, was assimilated into another god form. The god of witchcraft has gone through a makeover but he still exists within witchcraft.

Dianus is the other half of the Star Goddess, that of light and action. According to Grimassi the name Dianus comes from Italian witch clans.[11] He is Janus, god of transitions and doorways, who is the escort at the crossroads and seer of past and future. He is Jupiter, Roman king of gods and ruler of the skies. He is Apollo, the god of the sun, god of the oracles of ancient Greece, musician, poet, and muse. He is Lucifer, the logical morning star who brings fire, clarity, insight, and free will to the world. He is Cernunnos, god of the woods, hunter of the forests, and reaper of souls. He is Pan, god of the untamed places and bringer of mischief and sexual potency. Dianus is the king of all magic and those who dwell in its domain.

He is bursting with sexual energy, just like Diana, but doesn't display it aggressively or through deception. In our pantheon the sexually aggressive one is Diana. Diana tricked him once by trading places with his cat and curling up in his bed. That night Diana deceived him into having sex with her. When he woke up to find that she had tricked him he was incredibly angry and it is said that she enchanted him with a song to soothe his anger. From this he gained the power to heal through sexual intimacy.

He is the torch that illuminates the darkness, the energy of manifestation, and the light that reflects off the moon.

His sacred colors are white, gold, and teal. White represents the light, knowledge, his connection to awakenings, and clarity. Gold represents sovereignty, his relationship to the sun, and his powers of manifestation. Gold is a common color associated with male god forms in modern witchcraft. Finally, teal represents his mystical influence, psychic mastery, and connection to the animal world.

His sacred symbols are the sun, the torch, the blade, the shield, and the diamond. Like Diana, all animals are sacred to him; however, deer, wolves, butterflies, hummingbirds, turtles, cats, goats, and bulls are particularly sacred to him. Pray to him on Sunday.

---

11 Grimassi, *Italian Witchcraft*, 4.

A shapeshifter, magician, and oracle who contains the entire knowledge of the cosmos inside him, he can be quite the formidable ally. He is ageless and as such contains the ternion roles of son, father, and sage.

Invocation of Dianus Triformis

I call forth Dianus Triformis, He who wears three crowns!
The king that lights the heavens and whose feet dance upon the void!
Dianus, Great Magician, I your child call to you! Hear me now!
Shape-shifter, cunning-man, king of pen and page
I summon you now as son, father, and sage!
King of Witches and Lord most true,
I invoke you and am made anew!
Dianus, Dee-awn-us, Dee-in-us, Hail Dianus Triformis!

Tuning in to the Frequency of Dianus

Developing a relationship with him has been quite helpful for me on multiple levels. There are not many male deity forms in the craft. Though Dianus is different from many of them in that he is pretty fluid with his form, working with him has helped me to understand a lot about myself as a man. We take on the energy of the spiritual forms that are presented, and in the craft there has always been plenty of female energy to emulate, but there hasn't been a lot for men. Generally the male gods in the craft tend to be driven by sex and intoxication. Dianus is more interested in going on a journey or helping you push yourself to the next level.

He wants us to thrive and become as successful as we possibly can and teaches us to use our passion to better our world. Dedicate part of each triumph to him and bring any issue to him that you feel is keeping you down. As a ruler of manifestation and oracles he will be able to guide you in your times of need. Just be sure to thank him.

Learn a divination system and dedicate it to him. As a master of divination and the god of past, present, and future sight, he will aid you as you learn any divination or oracular system. Dedicate a Tarot deck or rune set to him and only use it to commune with him.

He promotes Tantra and sexual self-care. He teaches us that the healing powers of intimacy are a gift that first must be cultivated within and then shared only when we are moved by the urge for union. When we work with him through meditation and trance he can teach us to heal wounds left from negative sexual experiences. A great way to honor him I have found is through sexual victim advocacy.

He is a lover of the arts, architecture, and nature. Spending time expressing yourself through any of these is a fantastic act of devotion. He is also an excellent being to work with for any health concerns like disease, addiction, or affliction.

There are regular practices that when adopted can bring the frequency of Dianus closer to your life.

Cleanliness is next to godliness and he takes regular hygiene maintenance and physical care very serious. He in general wants us to be as healthy as possible both mentally and physically and considers these things to be directly tied to the aforementioned. Keeping yourself and your environment clean will help keep you working like a well-oiled machine. For those who suffer from chronic illness or at any time when you are recovering, a shrine should be built to him to encourage the propagation of healing and cleansing energies within the environment. He comes with an entourage of spirits who help in these matters.

On the first of each month and the last day of each year you should perform an Energy Dedication Ritual in which you invoke him for guidance. This ritual is intended to align you with his frequency but also align his frequency with your goals.

Monthly Energy Dedication Ritual

What you need:

White candle

Black candle

Paper and pen

Fire-safe container

Oracle system (Tarot, runes, bones, stones, etc.)

Cleanse and consecrate the space as you did in the minor esbat ritual for Diana. Go to your home frequency. Practice ecstatic breath work (any one of the previously mentioned methods from the last chapter); once you feel you have raised enough energy, lift your arms upward. Resonate and sing his name, DIAN-NUS (Dian-oos), three times. Light the black candle first, and then the white candle.

Stick your hands, palms together, between the two candles and say "Dianus, King of witches, I summon you between the past and future. Aid me as I dedicate my will!"

Shuffle your divination system and choose one card or piece for the black candle. As you place it down in front of the black candle say, "This is my past, my lesson, that which I did not see." Choose another card or piece for the white candle and as you place it down in front of it say, "This is my future, my path, that which I foresee!"

Take a moment to divine the meaning of the selection for both the past and the future. Look to see what you missed about last month and what is coming your way in the month to come.

On the piece a piece of paper write down everything you feel you accomplished in the previous month. (In the future write them down as they come so you won't miss a thing!) These should be things that were goals you had that actually came to fruition. Below that write down anything that you wish to let go of from the previous month. On a separate piece of paper write down your goals for the current month. You may want to adjust them based off of what you pulled from your divination system.

Pick up the piece of paper that has the list of accomplishments and blocks and say, "This is my past, my lesson, that which I did not see." Put the tip of the paper in the flame of the black candle to catch on fire and then immediately place it in the fire-safe container. Pick up the piece of paper that lists your current goals and say, "This is my future, my path, that which I foresee!" Put the tip of the paper in the white candle's flame to catch on fire and then immediately place in the fire-safe container.

Draw a third and final piece from your divination system and place it in the center of the two candles. As you do, so say, "The bridge between the past and the future is today." This piece is specifically pulled to tell you what you need to do right now to get yourself started on the right foot to achieving those goals.

Collect your divination system and place it to the side. Stand before the black candle and say, "By Dianus I release failed attempts and self-sabotage! By Dianus I forgive all and release the ties that bind me!" Then blow out the candle. Stand facing the white candle and say, "By Dianus I clear the path ahead and manifest my destiny! By Dianus I claim my right to thrive!" Preferably you should let this candle burn totally down.

Do ecstatic breath work once again to raise energy and resonate/sing his name three times like before. When you are done say, "I am the heir and he is the throne, I am the crown and he the pentacle! Hail the King of Night! Hail the King of Day! Hail Dianus the King of Witches!"

Take three breaths to ground and center the energy. When you feel that the energy is settled and you have returned to your home frequency, seal this working by saying, "I've aligned my soul and speak this whole, let nothing stand in my way. Within my heart I master this art and declare that magic is made. By the light of Dianus and the focus of will all obstacles ahead shall fade!"

Again, if you can, let the white candle burn out completely; that would be preferred. If you can't then snuff the candle out and burn it each day until it has been completely consumed. Keep the black candle and use it only for this purpose.

Aradia, The Teacher of Ways

Aradia

In a grove of trees deep within the forest there rages a campfire at midnight. On the other side of the fire, just across from you, you notice a woman dancing. As your gaze shifts focus to her you start to hear the beating of drums and the shaking of rattles. She is clad in blood-red robes with black sigils drawn on the chest and back. Lit only by this sacred flame you notice that she seems to be slightly levitating while she dances and is casting a shadow under her feet, but she never shows her face. As you listen to the drumming deeper you hear the hooting of owls and then, as if in response, you hear the howling of wolves. Her black hair pours from the hood of her robe like fog rolling from a marsh. As she raises her arms you notice tattoos mark her skin. She stops dancing and you instinctively know to approach her. You reach out to her with your right hand and as you do she turns to greet you. Just before you see her face the drumming stops and as your eyes fix on what's beneath the robe you suddenly realize there is nothing there, no person, just a hollow form. You look closer and see that the empty form contains balls of swirling light and you soon make out nebulas and galaxies. She laughs and as she does she takes the form of a vibrant woman. She reaches out and takes your hands in hers with a big smile on her face. "Have you come to learn the ways of the witch?" she asks…

In many witchcraft traditions Aradia is a most beloved goddess. In Leland's *Aradia* we are given a set of accounts that describe her life from conception to adulthood, and later the work Raven Grimassi provides an account of her early life,[12] political motivations, and magic. She is in many ways a Christ-like figure for those who practice the craft.

According to Grimassi, who claims to have been trained by direct magical descendants from Aradia, she was very much a real woman. In his account she is said to have been born in the year 1313 and would lead a revolution of the "old ways" in the later part of the fourteenth century. He goes on to say that she had twelve disciples who, after her death, spread the teachings of Aradia orally, keeping the mysteries alive for hundreds of years. These mysteries eventually were discovered by Leland in the nineteenth century and the rest is history.

There is much debate and speculation as to the authenticity of Aradia and the claims of her followers that there is an unbroken line of magic that has been passed on in secret for hundreds of years. What we do know is that there was a surge of witch trials in that area of Europe during the time that Aradia was supposedly traveling and teaching. In my opinion, none of that really matters. Most myths start out as a true story and over time they grow to become something more. Whether she was a living, breathing person or not doesn't matter to me because so many of us have had experiences with her. Her story, as best as I can piece together from my research and what I was taught, is this:

Aradia was born in the year 1313 and her mother died during the birth. She was sent to live with her mother's sister, who raised her and who also happened to be a witch. Her aunt taught her the arts of magic

---

12 Grimassi, *Hereditary Witchcraft*, 223–224.

and eventually brought Aradia to her coven where she then took on a more formal training. She was reserved and quiet and spent most of her time in the forest near Lake Nemi, where she would meet many poor people, escaped slaves, and outcasts. She is said to have possessed an otherworldly connection to the faeries and spirits that lived in the forests and had just as strong of a connection to the moon. She would be told one day during a trance experience while on an excursion that she was the daughter of Diana and Dianus and that she had been chosen to teach the ways of the craft to the poor and hungry so they might rise up against their oppressors and reclaim their sovereign rights.

After her initiation she traveled up and down the countryside, stopping at villages where there were many poor, and taught the people of their old ways. They were reminded of the connection they once had to nature and to each other and over time she sparked a magical revolution amongst the people of Tuscany. She taught for many years, always avoiding the church, which was constantly hunting her down. She was in many ways a magical resistance fighter.

After this her story gets blurry. There are two accounts about what happened to her. The first claims that she was eventually caught and sentenced to death for witchcraft. It is said that on the morning of her execution when the guards went to remove her from her holding cell they found that she had somehow vanished. Rumors of a woman fitting the description of Aradia teaching witchcraft to peasants were heard for years after. The other story suggests that she made an exodus from Italy to Serbia where later accounts claim a witch cult there worshiped a "mistress of faeries" called Arada.

Aradia in my tradition plays a major role in the development of a witch and their Witch Power, and she is seen as a spirit guide for any of those who would study the craft. She is a symbol to us of gnosis, wisdom, power, and freedom. She comes to us at our dedication and continues to work with us throughout our life as a witch. She helps us to learn and assimilate new magic into our life and keeps us on a never-ending quest for magical/spiritual knowledge and self-mastery. It is she we summon before we embark on a new practice, she we call to when we desire discipline, and she we pray to when we have lost the ability to understand the lessons presented to us.

Her colors are blood red and black. The red represents the witch blood and your connection and your Witch Power. These two things are natural and inherent inside of you. Black represents the mysteries, those magical ways that we must study in order to use. There is often a third color that presents itself after working with her for some time. Usually it will show up in the way of a thread, chord, or ray of light. This color is unique to your relationship with her.

She has mastery over all magical arts and psychic abilities. Owls, wolves, snakes, and spiders are associated with her, as well as the domesticated dog and cat. She often comes to us through animal relationships and encourages us to build these bonds. When I inquired as to why, she informed me that animal-human relationships remind us that we are members of the animal kingdom and that these bonds groom us for relationships in the spirit world. Pray to her on Wednesday.

In addition to her mastery of the craft she is a warrior priestess and the leader of the rebel forces who fight against any kind of oppression. She has appeared to me as every race, gender, and creed and has been very specific in that she works with all those who fight against unjust oppression, her primary method, of course, being the use of magic and enchantment to take down her foes.

Invocation of Aradia

I call forth Aradia, She who teaches the art!
Lady of spirits and of the fae, weaving magic both night and day!
Aradia, Great Teacher, I your student call to you! Hear me now!
I conjure to you, come forth with the power, and guide me in this
sacred hour!

Tuning in to the Frequency of Aradia

Aradia is perhaps the most eager of the deities to work with us. She genuinely loves to guide seekers of magic and, regardless of the length of dedication, she treasures all whom she encounters in this manner. The best way to build a relationship with Aradia is to study the craft and cultivate your Witch Power. When you embark on any new magical study ask Aradia to join you by placing her sigil on a candle and burning it over a series of three days. You can make a special bookmark with her sigil to help you tune in to her frequency during times of study.

Reading passages from *Aradia: The Gospel of the Witches* is also an excellent way to connect to her. On full moons I read the following passage, known as the charge of Diana:

> *In those days there were on earth many rich and many poor.*
> *The rich made slaves of all the poor.*
> *In those days were many slaves who were cruelly treated;*
> *in every palace tortures, in every castle prisoners.*

Many slaves escaped. They fled to the country; thus they became thieves and evil folk. Instead of sleeping by night, they plotted escape and robbed their masters and then slew them. So they dwelt in the mountains and forests as robbers and assassins, all to avoid slavery.

Diana said one day to her daughter Aradia:

> *'Tis true indeed that thou a spirit art,*
> *But thou wert born but to become again*
> *A mortal; thou must go to earth below*
> *To be a teacher unto women and men*
> *Who fain would study witchcraft in thy school*
> *Yet like Cain's daughter thou shalt never be,*
> *Nor like the race who have become at last*

Wicked and infamous from suffering,
As are the Jews and wandering Zingari,
Who are all thieves and knaves; like unto them
Ye shall not be…
And thou shalt be the first of witches known;
And thou shalt be the first of all i' the world;
And thou shalt teach the art of poisoning,
Of poisoning those who are great lords of all;
Yea, thou shalt make them die in their palaces;
And thou shalt bind the oppressor's soul (with power);
And when ye find a peasant who is rich,
Then ye shall teach the witch, your pupil, how
To ruin all his crops with tempests dire,
With lightning and with thunder (terrible),
And the hall and wind…

And when a priest shall do you injury
By his benedictions, ye shall do to him
Double the harm, and do it in the name
Of me, Diana, Queen of witches all!
And when the priests or the nobility
Shall say to you that you should put your faith
In the Father, Son, and Mary, then reply:
"Your God, the Father, and Maria are
Three devils…
"For the true God the Father is not yours;
For I have come to sweep away the bad,
The men of evil, all will I destroy!
"Ye who are poor suffer with hunger keen,
And toll in wretchedness, and suffer too
Full oft imprisonment; yet with it all

Ye have a soul, and for your sufferings
Ye shall be happy in the other world,
But ill the fate of all who do ye wrong!"

Now when Aradia had been taught, taught to work all witchcraft, how to destroy the evil race (of oppressors), she (imparted it to her pupils) and said unto them:

When I shall have departed from this world,
Whenever ye have need of anything,
Once in the month, and when the moon is full,
Ye shall assemble in some desert place,
Or in a forest all together join
To adore the potent spirit of your queen,
My mother, great Diana. She who fain
Would learn all sorcery yet has not won
Its deepest secrets, them my mother will
Teach her, in truth all things as yet unknown.
And ye shall all be freed from slavery,
And so ye shall be free in everything;
And as the sign that ye are truly free,
Ye shall be naked in your rites, both men
And women also: this shall last until
The last of your oppressors shall be dead;
And ye shall make the game of Benevento,
Extinguishing the lights, and after that
Shall hold your supper thus.[13]

---

13 Leland, *Aradia, Gospel of the Witches.*

Spending time with animals and connecting to the energies of your environment are also great ways to tune in to the frequency of Aradia. Spending time outdoors, even if you live in an urban area, allows you to get the energetic lay of the land. If possible go to a park or wooded area and ask Aradia to introduce you to the local spirits and faeries that live there and might want to work with you. These connections will give you an influential edge in your local surroundings, so be sure to follow up any positive meetings by making an offering. Spirits prefer milk or alcohol; faeries enjoy nectars, alcohol, and milk. Continue to visit these energies from time to time, but never invite them back home with you.

In the text cited above there is a term, "game of Benevento," which is very important to understand when working with Aradia. It refers to the Italian city of Benevento, which was known for hosting orgies and parties. Modern witches today regard this as an instruction to enjoy sex and sexual liberation. Strong sexual energy produces powerful magic so we must cultivate it as often as possible. This is to say that we should have sex responsibly, frequently, and as a tool to activate primal energies, all of which Aradia is known for being a fan of.

Activism of any kind is also a great way to work with Aradia. You can even join a social club that promotes change and reform to oppressive laws, that stands up for or aid the poor and minorities, or even better, an environment like park cleanups. She likes active and proactive people who are willing to help their fellow humans.

Final Thoughts on the Gods

Tuning in to the frequencies of these emanations of the source of all things is important for us as witches as we grow in power. In the case of Diana and Dianus, these forces exist in tandem with one another, always possessing their own current of energy, which is the opposite of the other. They teach us how to hone our own ability to be powerful while living in balance with the opposing forces around us. They teach us to give and to take, and each possesses a piece of the other. Aradia is one of their children, just like you and I are, who became a deific spirit guide for those with the Witch Power.

They are shape-shifters who call upon us to move between the worlds and become the authentic person they know us to be. They permeate our lives, and after working with them for just a short time you will see them in your own relationships to people and environment. As mentors they give us magical lessons and access to unseen realms. As guides they help us navigate the murky waters of the soul. As lovers they show us to be passionate and responsive. As friends they show us how to forgive ourselves and find the humor in an otherwise uncomfortable situation. As parents they show us to be consistent and steadfast, always willing to lend us their shoulder and always there to help us get back up.

Perhaps most importantly, and I say this from a purely selfish place, they teach us to heal and empower ourselves. They aren't concerned about a war for your soul, they just want your soul to shine and to become the god it is meant to be. My relationship to them has taught me that with a lot of hard work I can be anything I want to be, but it has also shown me what I am capable of becoming. There are no better partnerships than the ones we make with the divine.

I have always said that Diana and Dianus were the Queen and King of the Island of Misfit Toys. They will take you with a missing button or a broken zipper. Even if you don't wind up all the way anymore. Those who follow them have always been the ones who never felt quite like they belonged or those who were pushed out from where they feel they do belong. They teach us that we do belong and we have a lot to offer.

Chapter Eleven

The Allies of the Witch

In the spirit world, it's all about who you know.
—Malach, My Familiar Spirit—

Working with allies on a consistent basis can really amp up your game. My magical effectiveness doubled when I started to devote meditation, trance, and ritual time on a regular basis to "walking between the worlds." One theory behind magic is that it works by causing change within a specific plane of being, which ultimately will manifest within our own. In other words, some witches believe that if we create change in one world, that change manifests in others as well. By befriending spirits and building bonds with them we are able to build connections within other realms, providing much-needed influence when the time comes.

Another reason to work with allies is that they have a totally different perspective than we do on existence and what's important. Having such perspective allows for them to relay information to us that can help us better handle situations. For example, if you befriend a spirit who resides within your place of school or work you can petition them to help you find a speedy resolution to issues that arise. You can also work with these spirits to help provide you information regarding any future changes that might be coming down the pipeline or to give you a heads-up when you might be getting called into a meeting unexpectedly.

Allies of a high frequency like *spirit guides* will relay information from your higher self, the divine, and surrounding areas on a regular basis. This alone is reason enough to work with them on a daily basis. You can also ask your spirit guide to relay information or requests to the spirit guides of others.

Working with allies will inadvertently develop your psychic abilities and Witch Power as well. Because you will be using those psychic muscles when you tune in to your allies, you will be giving yourself a workout each time. Like any workout routine, this is best done no less than three times a week, five times a week for optimal growth. Doing this effectively will entail a change in lifestyle that will get easier as time goes on. I view tuning in to the frequencies of my allies as a great opportunity to blend the mundane and the magical and have found several ways to do this as I go about my normal day, which I will mention later in this chapter.

Allies can be invoked during magical workings to act as primary or secondary sources of energy. If you have larger magical projects that require a lot of energy or would like to feel the energy of multiple beings within a magical space, this is a practice I highly recommend. For those witches who work solely as a solitary practitioner but would like to have the magical potency of a coven, befriending spirits that you can bring into your work can replace the need for a coven altogether.

Tuning in to the Frequencies of Your Allies

Each ally is different and they all will require something unique of you. Some might ask that you donate time to a shelter in exchange for their support, others might want you to leave alcohol as libation. Allies like household spirits tend to enjoy a bit of honey and milk, whereas spirits of the dead prefer flowers and plain milk. Each time you meet a new ally you should be prepared to ask it what you can do in return for its favor. By doing this you are essentially drawing the ally into the physical world and creating a bridge to connect you to them. In my experience these things are easy, totally doable, and often negotiable. I have never been asked to do something that was not in my best interest or something that wasn't for my highest good. If you don't like what you feel you are being asked to do in return, then you can always negotiate a more reasonable request.

There are four different types of connections that we can have with an ally. Depending on the type of ally you are working with, you might find that one type of connection is more desirable over another and, in theory, you could build any one of these connections with any ally.

Casual Connection: A casual connection is when you work with an ally for limited magical or psychic purposes only. These connections are brief and to the point, usually requiring very little but a traditional offering. This type of connection is what we see during cultural observances such as memorials, feast days, and rites of passage. They are allies that we only connect to during special occasions. Once annually, this connection is reinforced.

Working Connection: A connection that is established between the witch and the ally that primarily involves the employment of that ally for magical purposes. These connections require steady offerings for services rendered and professional attachment only. Often seen in the world of professional witchcraft and *rootworking*, these connections are based on rewarding allies for assisting in magical intervention. These connections require steady and responsive reinforcement.

Personal Connection: Personal connections run deeper energetically than the others and tend to have the greatest impact on us overall. We have these connections with our personal allies, the ones we work with on the intimate matters of love, destiny, and karma. These connections are greatly impactful because they shape us daily regardless of if we are consciously connected to them or not. Personal allies are those whom we allow to enter our energy field directly and, because of this, they have the greatest influence over us internally. These connections require lots of TLC and demand little from us but attention and follow-through.

Divine Connection: A connection to chief god-forms that involve ecstatic union. These connections are required for possessory work, drawing-down work, aspecting work, and work involving the channeling of "higher powers." Divine connections are built through regular exposure, ritual work, initiation, and ecstatic practice. These require traditional offerings, dedicated time, and devotional practice.

Though each ally is different, there are always three things I do before approaching a potential ally. First, I do a little research and read up on their histories and myths, and see if there is one story in particular that appeals to me. I also look for clues to any offerings that might be appropriate. For example, pomegranates are an acceptable offering to Persephone because in her myth she ate six pomegranate seeds, making them sacred to her. Another example is that in Hoodoo you offer pound cake to St. Expedite for his help.

Next I look for an image of the ally or I make one. This will allow for you to harmonize with their frequency over time. This image can become the centerpiece for an altar or a hidden reminder that you are connected to something else. If you are a witch who keeps your magic secretive, putting images around you that symbolize your magical allies is a great way to blend the magical with the everyday.

Third, I determine how much time I am willing to put into the connection and how much energy I am willing to devote to it. Once I know what I am willing to do I break out my calendar and figure out which times in the next few weeks I can donate to actually making that happen. When I do this I am always pleased with how willing those allies are to actually work with me seriously.

My best advice when embarking on developing a relationship with an ally is to remember that your Witch Power is going to guide you to meet who you need to meet. Trust your gut, follow your heart, and let your conscience and your standards be your guide. Have lots of fun with the process and learn something new about yourself. Always remember that if you ever get the creeps or feel uneasy about working with an ally, that ally probably isn't for you. There is nothing wrong with you, there is something wrong with the ally. Never force yourself or allow yourself to be coerced into working with an ally that doesn't instinctually feel harmonic with your own frequency.

The following allies are known for their connection to magic and the occult. With each description I will tell you a little about them and how to connect to them. I will always suggest that you do your own research independent from this book so that you can learn even more about them. The more you educate yourself about each ally you work with, the stronger your connection to them will be.

How Allies Will Communicate

Allies will communicate to us in varying ways depending on what type of energy they possess. With the majority of allies, like those listed here, communication can often be negotiated. The only ally with whom I want to establish the type of connection that can be physical is my Familiar spirit. This is because they are the only type of spirit that is tethered to the higher self, which, as you will see later, places certain rules on the relationship between witch and ally. All other spirits and allies that don't possess this type of connection could inadvertently cause harm to us. It is best to only allow spirits that can manifest positively in your life to come through with such gusto.

It is important to understand the need for discernment in matters of spirit communication. It is easy to fill in missing psychic data with improvised information by accident. Gaining this ability is not done overnight and can only be obtained through experience. Test your skills regularly, test the information you receive from your spirits regularly, and document when you receive accurate and inaccurate information. Through a conscious study of this information you will be able to develop a sense of the feelings that come along with spirit communication. Over time this will blossom into an instinctual response to psychic data and you will build confidence in your receptive abilities.

You should never hear literal voices in your head when communicating with spirits. Mediums like myself will be the first to tell you to seek professional help if this happens. The voice that you hear, if any, will be that of your own internal voice. There will, however, be noticeable difference in inflection and pacing.

In most cases these messages will present themselves as an inner knowing or strange instinct. In my experience these messages come through in very practical ways. I will be in my office thinking about all the work that is piling up and then get the instinctive urge to look at my phone just moments before I get called into a surprise meeting. Another example is when I get a mental flash of an image that is related to the spirit while simultaneously getting a knock on the door from an employee telling me I have a walk-in client. When this happens I have learned that Malach, my Familiar spirit, is letting me know to expect a heavy session.

I like to think that spirits speak to us in every way but actual speech. Be diligent and observant once you start the process of spirit communication as you never know how they will choose to speak to you directly.

The Allies

In no way can this be a complete list of allies. Those I have listed here are known for working with witches and have made themselves known in various traditions.

Angels

Angels aren't the fluffy-winged, baby-faced creatures of love and warmth that you may have been led to believe and they certainly don't belong to any one religion. They are actually irrepressible forces of nature that are more often like computer programs than friends. Angels are responsible for keeping the universe working. They are the forces that create the revolution of the planets and are the keepers of order and universal law.

Angels have a long-standing connection to the occult and in some circles they are thought to be the beings who originally mixed with humankind to create the magical creatures of the world, witches included. In contemporary new-age culture angels have been repackaged to have a softer look and often human features. Belief in angels goes back to include systems of worship based in Egypt, Sumer, Babylonia, and Persia, to name a few, and their imagery has changed depending on which culture was writing about them.

In general, there are a few distinctions that are often associated with angels. Angels are said to have lightning-like features and their skin is metallic. Their eyes burn with fire and their voices sound like many people speaking at once. They can take human form but can also look like a combination of several animals or just a simple ball of energy. It is believed that if you were to look upon an angel's true form you would go blind.

Angels are not bound by the laws of good or evil, as they simply have work to do. Those angels we work with are within the lowest caste of angels, known as the Ishim; however, they are bound to work in our best interest.

In my experience, the most vital piece of information regarding angels is that they are completely celestial energies. This means that they are not spiritual allies from our planet but come from somewhere else that is cosmic in origin. It is my belief that angels are allies to all of creation, but are more concerned with the overall movement and maintenance of the cosmos rather than who slighted whom. Petitioning an angel can be done on any level.

In Western religions angels are classified into three hierarchies (or spheres), each sphere containing three orders making for nine separate classifications. Most of these are only accessible to us through deep trance journeying.

The First Sphere

Seraphim: These angels are the highest-ranking and most powerful of all the angels. They are the pillars of the universe and are the oldest of spirits. The Seraphim rule over the raw energies of space and time and are the foundation for all creation. We cannot petition them but we can visit them through trance.

Cherubim: The angels that guard the tree of life and maintain its three layers are known as the Cherubim. We can come across them guarding sacred places of energy and knowledge. These angels are the guardians of the crossroads of life and death and rule over all such passings. We can see them when we visit the world-tree in the top of the branches.

Ophanim: The Ophanim are the angels that carry out the will of the divine. Closely related to the Cherubim, these angels are said to look the strangest of the angels, with often mechanical-like features. We will almost never encounter them and we should never hope to, as seeing them is almost a sure sign of trouble and destruction to come. They cannot be petitioned but can be accessed through trance.

The Second Sphere

Hashmallim: The Hashmallim govern over the responsibilities of all other angels, as well as over all dominions and nations. Each country has its own Hashmallim. In only the rarest and most extreme cases do these angels make themselves known to mankind. We can petition them, especially when political changes are needed. Burn a new red candle at high noon for forty days to get the attention of the Hashmallim. Each day, chant your request as you light the candle.

Virtues: These angels are specifically responsible for the motion of heavenly bodies like planets, comets, asteroids, and black holes. Each planet has its own Virtue and we can only petition the Virtue of Earth. The others we only encounter through trance.

Powers: The Powers are responsible for the distribution of power through humanity and are the bringers of conscience and the keepers of history. When you say "the Powers that be" you are referring to them. These angels are very important to work with when expanding your influence. Petition them by lighting white, gold, or red candles at dawn or dusk.

The Third Sphere

Principalities: Principalities carry out the orders of the Hashmallim, and govern over the creatures of the Earth. They inspire us in the ways of the arts and in the scientific studies. Petition them for help when you feel stuck or when you feel like the weight of the world is on your shoulders by lighting a blue or purple candle at dawn and dusk.

Archangels: These angels are the messengers of cosmic divine will and can manifest as forces of nature like volcanic eruption, typhoon, and earthquakes. These angels are who we are said to be invoking by another name when we invoke the Watchers. We can petition them through traditional prayers and offerings, invocations, and toning.

In some mythologies there are only four archangels, in others there are seven, and it is speculated that there are many more than that. The archangels that we tend to work with the most are Michael, Gabriel, Uriel, Raphael, and Metatron.

Michael *(pronounced MEE-KAY-EL)* is the sword of the Star Goddess and is the leader of the Angels who deal with humankind. He can act as a mediator between you and God Herself when needed and is said to take the souls of the ascended to the other side. He rules over fire and wears a golden crown. Petition him when you need protection, seek asylum, wish to banish unwelcome energy, or when you need to remove negative energy patterns or astral threads. His color is red and his spice is cinnamon.

Gabriel *(pronounced GAB-REE-EL)* is the represented strength of the Star Goddess and is the second-highest-ranking angel below Michael. Gabriel is the angel of the Moon and is responsible for lunar energies such as those of inspiration, intuition, and mysteries of resurrection. Gabriel is said to have a face as white as virgin snow and has a trumpet that when played calls a soul to its new destiny. Petition Gabriel when you have need for vengeance, when you need help redirecting energy, or when you need help changing the course of your life. His color is blue and his spice is jasmine.

Raphael *(pronounced RA-PHAE-EL)* is the healer of the Star Goddess and is said to rule over the kingdom of air. He is most known as a healer, as well as for his powers of exorcism. In addition to being able to extract negative and low-frequency entities he also has the ability to heal any damage done to the soul caused by the entity. Raphael is also responsible for the maintenance of planet Earth and is entrusted to keep it a suitable home for mankind. Petition Raphael when you have need of healing of any kind, especially if it involves healing the soul. His color is yellow and his spice is mint.

Uriel *(pronounced UR-EE-EL)* is the fire of the Star Goddess and has rulership over earth. He is responsible for the movement of heavenly bodies and of time, possessing the ability to see anything at any place in time. Uriel is responsible for modern invention and is attributed to lightning. He is said to protect the creatures of earth. Petition Uriel when you are in need of stability, need access to past, present, or future events, or are in need of technological help. His color is green and his spice is cumin.

Metatron *(pronounced MET-A-TRON)* is the wisdom of the Star Goddess and has rulership over consciousness, over the akashic records, and is said to be the most powerful of all angels. Metatron also has dominion over spiritual planes and has the ability to aid one in traveling through them as well as to connect us to our spirit guides. He is the scribe of God Herself and is said to guard all heavenly secrets. Petition him when you need help breaking through mental blocks, connecting to others (especially on other planes), when you wish to advance to the next level of something, or when you need access to the akashic records. His color is purple and his spice is saffron.

Ishim: These angels are concerned with the affairs of humans and are the most recognized throughout history. There are many different types of Ishim and if we were to look at angels through the Jewish system, this group would also be the group associated with what we call spirit guides. We can petition them by lighting a white candle and observing silence for thirty minutes after inviting them to come.

Offerings for Angels

Angels enjoy the burning of sacred herbs and resins. Burning separately or combining a mixture of sage, lavender, tobacco, sweetgrass, cedar, frankincense, myrrh, dragon's blood, and/or copal, and chanting their name ninety-nine times makes for a great offering.

Demons

Demons have a long and fascinating history with witchcraft. Like the craft itself, what a demon is depends on who you ask; however, there is a basic history to demons that is often overlooked. Many demons are the remnants of ancient mystery cults and village gods who were demonized by the church as they canonized belief. As Christianity spread, so did the practice of turning the people against their gods, and any belief that was not in agreement with canon was considered heresy, making one an enemy of the church. Because this was a life-or-death decision for people, many would agree to give up their old gods in favor of a new one. What we have left are the shells of land spirits and local gods who were forced to change by the tip of a sword.

The word *demon* actually comes from a Greek word, *daemon,* which means "force like god."[14] To the Greeks, daemons were benevolent nature-like spirits who were responsible for the fate of mankind. In Plato's *Symposium,* Diotima teaches Socrates the mysteries of love in telling him that love is not a god but a great daemon. She also teaches him that "everything daemonic is between divine and mortal"[15] and that daemons are "inter-

---

14 Liddell, Scott, Jones, and McKenzie, *A Greek-English Lexicon.*
15 Plato, *Symposium,* 385–370 BCE.

preting and transporting human things to the gods and divine things to men: entreaties and sacrifices from below, and ordinances and requitals from above…"

In some traditions demons are associated with lower-frequency beings and are rejected as fallen angels, or angels who have denied their divine purpose. In other traditions demons are responsible for the darker side of humanity and are supposed to be responsible for addiction, abuse, war, neglect, and just about anything that we do to cause harm to ourselves or someone else. Demons are in general considered to be malevolent.

Though most witches I know don't typically tend to work with demons, those who do take it nice and slow. The issue is that demons develop from the negative emotions, habits, acts of violence, disease, and suffering that typically come with the devastation of one's life and potential. These problems are so big and full of dissonance that they create the entities known to most of us as demons. Demons are made from human tragedy and because of this there is always a chance that they can bring that frequency into your life if you work with them.

My preferred way to work with them is through a type of ceremonial magic known as *Goetia* or *Goetic magic*. Goetic magic involves the summoning and invocation of both angels and demons for the purposes of doing one's bidding. Modern Goetic magic is a derivative of *The Lesser Key of Solomon*, which is a seventeenth-century grimoire that details the magic supposedly used by King Solomon to build his sacred temple. This art demands a very sharp sense of purpose and command over the influences summoned.

There is one other popular way to work with demons, which involves, summoning them not to be an agent of your will, but rather as an agent for personal growth. A witch can work with these forces to banish the lower frequencies represented by the demonic energy. This process takes place over a period of usually six months. During this time the Holy Guardian Angel, or the Higher Self, is channeled ritually while energetic cleansings are done.

Derived from *The Book of Abramelin* this system of demonic medicine exchange is believed to have been around since the fourteenth century.

Offerings to Demons

Demons will let you know what they want in return for services rendered. In general, coaxing them with dark liquors like brandy, port, or rum does quite nicely.

The Dead

The dead are an invaluable resource for witches. They contain power and knowledge beyond our comprehension and, if worked with properly, can become allies along our path. I have been a professional medium for over a decade and in that time I have learned that the dead are just people who are having a human experience even after physical death. Sometimes these people are our ancestors, relatives, and chosen family who have passed on, whom we call the *Beloved Dead*. Sometimes these people achieve greatness and rise to the ranks of what we call the *Mighty Dead*. Those dead who are not mighty or beloved but are spirits who still roam the Earth without station are known as *Disincarnate*.

The Beloved Dead

Beloved dead have a vested interest in us. These dead usually made direct sacrifices in order to bring us into existence and maintain life. They are our ancestors by blood or lineage and without them we wouldn't be here today. They're so interested in us because we are the latest model to come off the showroom floor. We are their descendants and inside of us we contain a piece of their potential. Our beloved dead generally want nothing but for us to thrive and continue to live, to pass the genes or wisdom to the next generation, and to invest our potential into things that will better our lives. The beloved dead are the ancestors of our blood.

Mighty Dead

The mighty dead are those who have achieved greatness and are believed to have ascended into a divine role. Every culture has their mighty dead, be they saints, martyrs, or masters. The belief is that these beings were capable of finishing any karmic lessons they had to and in their final life achieved enlightenment. These dead are therefore no longer obligated to return to Earth in the physical, but instead are invited to remain on the other side to act as guides, teachers, or anchors for spiritual truth. These dead are believed to be holy. The mighty dead are the ancestors of our soul.

Disincarnate

Disincarnate dead are those who are not connected to us through blood or heart but still make their presence known in our lives and want to work with us from the other side. This connection is not something we see too often but has been reported on multiple occasions. Sometimes these beings were friends of relatives, sometimes they are ghosts who haunt your local forest or place of work, and sometimes they are spirits who follow you home after a long day of shopping. Unlike the mighty and beloved dead who want us only to succeed and grow, these dead tend to have their own agendas and therefore should be approached with caution.

Offerings to the Dead

The dead like candles, white foods like rice and milk, sugar, and alcohol. When making these offerings be sure to replace regularly especially if offerings are perishable. They also like incense and candles and it is customary to burn both on holy days and their birth/death days.

Fae

The fae aren't the tiny-winged little people we see in children's movies. They are actually large and powerful beings with a knack for mischief. The fae appear all over the world, ranging in appearance from long, skinny white-light beings in parts of North America to entities made from blue, smokeless fire in the Middle East. We are perhaps most familiar in contemporary witchcraft with the Celtic fae, Tuatha De Danann, who ruled over modern-day Ireland before the coming of mankind. In Italian folklore the fae are ruled by Diana and are seen as magical beings who, with a few exceptions, teach and protect us.

In the Faery Tradition it is believed that the ancestors of the witch blood are the members of the faery race. It is thought that through interspecies relations the faery and human bloodlines mixed and that some of us have a genetic inheritance to the faery world. This story is eerily similar to the stories put forth by other traditions depicting angelic beings.

Faeries are known for being quick-witted and cunning, usually looking out for their own interests. Some enjoy the company of humans but generally do not enjoy human environments, requiring you to leave the comfort of home to venture off into the wilds in search of them. They are known for their ability to exist in multiple worlds and do not have a linear connection to time, effectively making them time-traveling inter-dimensional beings. In our world they are most often seen as "nature beings" who commune with us through the trees and the land. In their world, known simply as *Faery,* they can take on any shape or size that they see fit and are notorious for trying to make contracts with us.

It is a common practice to never take food or drink or make any contracts with a faery without long consideration. These offers are most often extended to us during states of trance or meditation. We may perceive the offer of a simple apple as a blessing or even as a well-intended gift, but to them it is an agreement. Before making any agreement with a faery being you should seek consultation from two sources. The first is from your higher self. This can be done with a simple divination, or during meditation after you have gone to your home frequency. Ask if this being is trustworthy and comes for your highest good. If the answer is inconclusive or no, then cease all contact immediately. If, however, the feedback is positive then you should seek a consultation with Diana or Dianus. Ask for their blessing and protection regarding this matter and then ask to receive a sign within the next three days. If you receive a sign in the following days, then their response is yes and you will know that your union with this faery has been blessed by the king and queen of faeries and witches. This will provide you protections so that if the contract ever goes sour you can petition them to use their authority in the matter. If, however, you do not get the sign, then your union with this faery is not blessed and you will not receive their protection. To be sure you didn't miss the sign, do a reading with your preferred divination system on the third day before the time is up.

Offerings to the Fae

The beings of faery have an insatiable appetite ranging from sweets to alcohol. A safe bet is to give them sweet alcohols like mead or dessert wine, or for a non-alcoholic offering, nectar, juice, and milk (especially the milk from a lamb or goat). They also enjoy copious amounts of these things, so don't be too stingy. Each year at Beltane I offer at least one entire bottle of wine or mead to the local faery.

Familiars

A *Familiar or Familiar Spirit* is an entity that a witch can summon to act as a mediator between them and the spirit worlds, and in some cases do their bidding. Working with Familiar spirits is almost synonymous with witchcraft. In Christian mythos the infamous Witch of Endor used her familiar spirit to summon the ghost of Samuel in order to consult the king Saul about invading Philistine forces. Scottish witch Isobel Gowdie, during her confession for the crime of witchcraft, is reported to have said, "Each one of us has a spirit to wait upon us, when we please to call upon him." Even if she wasn't practicing witchcraft herself she certainly was under the impression that that's what witches did. In Anne Rice's Witching Hour series, a family of witches passes along a Familiar spirit from generation to generation.

In pop culture the Familiar spirit has taken the form of a cat, toad, or a dog, no doubt influenced by the testimonies of the witch trials. These images are derived from the concept of imps, which were malevolent spirits supposedly given to witches by the devil himself. The witch was suppose to feed the imp blood from something called a witch's teat and in return gain access to demonic powers. After someone was accused of witchcraft an investigation would take place in which the accused witch would be searched for this witch's teat. It could look like anything: a bug bite, a mole, or a birthmark. If any of these were found it was submitted to the court as proof of witchcraft.

To summon a Familiar you need to go on a quest to find one. To do this, go to your home frequency and proceed to perform pranic breathing for the course of ten minutes. Continue to perform pranic breathing while you envision yourself standing at a train station. Before you a train stops and you see a stream of people exit from it onto the platform. As you stand there, look at every face regardless of what it may look like or the form it may take and wait for one of them to make eye contact. As your eyes meet, see that they have a big smile on their face like they have been waiting to see you. Ask them first if they come for your highest good. If the answer is no or it is inconclusive, wave them on. If the answer is yes, then ask them what their name is and to show you a symbol in this vision that you can use to bring them into our world. Once they give you this symbol return to your home frequency and ground your energy.

Take time and ask your higher self if this partnership is in your best interest. If you get the go-ahead from your higher self, proceed with the binding. For this you need an object like an amulet, talisman, or a jar that has been constructed and consecrated specifically for the purpose of containing the energy of the familiar. An easy way to do this is to use a glass jar with a metal lid that has been cleansed by empowering it with your holy fire and then adding a few special ingredients like rue, cedar tips, and mugwort. Once you have added the herbs, draw your planetary power sigil on a piece of paper. On the other side of the paper draw the symbol the spirit gave you in your meeting on the platform. Kiss the piece of paper three times. After the first kiss, say, "Three times I kiss this and bring it life." After the second, say, "Three times I kiss this and give it power." Finally, after the third time, say, "Three times I kiss this and give it purpose."

Place the paper in the jar with the herbs and trace a pentacle of holy fire above the mouth. As you draw the pentacle, say, "By sacred star and sovereign right, I summon this spirit and give it flight, come to me (name of spirit) and take your seat, in this vessel you are complete. Bound by will and sealed by fate, your presence here I now instate." Send the pentacle of holy fire into the jar and seal it. Dress a candle with dragon's blood oil and place it onto the jar. Light the candle and let it burn completely down. During this time your spell is slowly manifesting and shouldn't be tampered with. Whenever you need to summon this spirit all you need to do is light a candle on top of the jar.

Offerings for Familiar Spirits

These allies are partial to clear alcohols like vodka, gin, and white wines. They also enjoy candles and incense and a well-maintained vessel. Keep fresh offerings available and change out the old once a week. Add crystals and shiny objects to the space around the vessel to help project vibration and influence.

Spirits of Place or Land Spirits

These allies are representative of the community of spirits that naturally exists within your environment. These spirits are everywhere and as terrain changes so do the type of spirits. Area spirits vary from location and are closely tied to the fae. The majority of these spirits are caretakers and otherworldly protectors; however, some possess a high degree of intelligence. Not all of these spirits come from the natural environment; some are local demons and others could be local mighty dead. These spirits are tied to that area for specific reasons and can be petitioned when you need help with local life.

You can petition the spirits of place for protection and abundance or for a shift in weather. Generally these spirits are not the kind who grant wishes or should ever be bound to a spell. These beings are not for us to control but rather to make friendships with. Ideally, working with these spirits will increase your sensitivity to the psychic and atmospheric shifts that happen around you. By having allies in your area you can widen your own ability to channel environmental frequencies and gain an extra set of eyes as to local energetic happenings.

For the most part these spirits are benevolent and make friends with humans who are willing to help them by being a mediator. These relationships tend to require that you act as a steward for the land under the spirit's dominion. By helping to beautify, keep clean, and restore these areas you further your connection to the spirit, which may even require you to do so before it agrees to work with you.

On occasion there are lower-frequency malevolent beings that are bound to an area for one reason or another. These spirits aren't always easy to get along with and should be avoided. If you feel there might be a low-frequency land spirit around you or your home, you need to do a deep, energetic cleansing of your space and place protection talismans at the entrances of the home. You can also petition high-vibrational local spirits for protection.

Offerings to Spirits of Place

These spirits most appreciate our time, so spend time volunteering with your local clean-up group. Each time before your work, say a prayer to the spirits and invite them to come along with you. When you are done for the day, tell the spirit three things you learned while being of service and then thank it for joining you.

Spirit Guides

Spirit guides are a witch's best friend and in my opinion are critical to successful witchcraft. My work in psychism has taught me of the usefulness of these partnerships but my relationship with my own spirit guide, Malach, has taught me so much more about my capabilities as a witch.

I began working with Malach a few years ago after petitioning the Goddess for a little help. I was having a difficult time in life at that time and was totally lost with no direction. I was living with some friends who were generous enough to let me live rent-free while I picked up the pieces of my life after a big personal blow. I felt like the gods had forgotten about me and that my connection to spirit was gone. Without the ability to connect I couldn't do my work, and if I couldn't do my work then I couldn't pay the bills. One night, after a few drinks, I shouted out to the Goddess for help. I had for years been working with a spirit named Paul who seemed to have vanished right about the same time my life had exploded.

A few days after petitioning the Goddess for a little help, Malach showed up during meditation. At first he showed himself to be an owl sitting atop a tree branch and over the course of a few weeks he would eventually show himself to be my spirit guide. He is unlike anything I had expected or had experienced before and has been with me every day since. We go everywhere together and do just about everything together. Over the years friends have reported seeing or feeling him and he has developed a habit of turning on and off lights and making noises during my spirit guide workshops.

Spirit guides exist in a unique partnership with us. They are connected to our divinity and act as a mediator between our higher selves and our ego, conveying messages and guiding us when we are unable to commune directly with the higher self. Because they are so closely connected to our higher selves, our spirit guides cannot lie to us or misdirect us. This distinguishes them from other spirits who can mislead us. The relationship between the witch and their spirit guide is built on trust and gnosis and can take many years to establish.

Spirit guides can take any form and can come from anywhere. As a medium I have seen these guides look like everything from a snake that wraps itself around the leg of their charge to multiple beings that stand like a forest of birch trees behind a client, even entities made of light that claim to come from the Pleiades. The common factor with all of them appears to be that they are connected to the cosmic underground and have access to your karmic information.

To meet your spirit guide you should make frequent visits while meditating to a space on the astral plane that only you know about. Let your higher self fill in the images of this place. Tell your higher self that you want to be taken to the place where your spirit guides are. Once you are there, wait for your spirit guides to make themselves known. This can be a tricky process for some, so if you don't succeed the first time, keep going back. After you have met your spirit guide you should ask it what its name is, if it comes for your highest good, and for some sort of symbol that you can use to tune in to its frequency. After your meditation is complete draw that sigil on a white candle and light it every day for thirty minutes until the candle goes out. During this time sit near the candle and allow yourself to be open, free yourself of distraction, and sit in silence. Pay attention to the thoughts and ideas you perceive during this time.

Regularly light a white candle that has the spirit guide's sigil drawn on it. This will bring their frequency into your life in a more reliable way. I do this weekly on Sundays just to be sure I haven't missed anything important and to realign my spirit guide and myself to our spiritual work.

For free meditations and tips on spirit guide communication, check out my website, www.DevinHunter.net.

Offerings to Spirit Guides

Spirit guides don't often require much in the way of feeding. The majority of the offerins that you will make to them will be those of time and discipline. They are fed through our successes, so the more you strive for excellence in whatever you do, the more they will make themselves known. Malach is partial to champagne and gets a glass on special days.

CONCLUSION

There are many different kinds of power. True power comes from
serving and helping others. Such behavior makes people respect you.
They are willing to listen to your views and advice, and they support
you. The energy of many people is thus channeled through one
person. This kind of power is positive and authentic.

—HH the Dalai Lama—

A few years ago I started instructing a class focused on the teachings of Aradia called "The People's Witchcraft." Inspired by the stories of a pilgrim who traveled, spreading the message that every human was sacred and that the old ways still thrived, I developed a curriculum that focused on personal accountability and self-respect. The class started out large and over the following months it slowly dwindled in size. Though we lost a few members along the way we continued to keep our eye on the prize and our hearts close to our sleeves, and soon a new tradition would arise. The remaining members of the class decided to form a coven and from there Sacred Fires was born.

I remember looking back on the early days of the formation of our first formal coven and wondering why over half of the class dropped out in the first three months. Perhaps it was my teaching skills, but I think a closer investigation of the matter would produce a different culprit. The work was hard and not everyone was able to do it. The techniques in witchcraft that focus on personal development and empowerment are amongst the hardest to perform. They require a brutally honest look at oneself and sincere personal dedication.

There also tends to come a point in our spiritual development when the newness of introductory witchcraft wears off and we are left with the realization that we are in charge of keeping ourselves going along the path. In my experience these plateaus tend to make us feel stuck and isolated as well as spiritually overwhelmed and unsure as to our true place. It is at this point that many witches abandon ship and move on, having obtained what they needed in the moment and moving on to the next challenge where they aren't required to make their own decisions.

Most people equate spirituality with enlightenment and only search for the aspects that bring them comfort at the end of the day. These people prefer to be led to their enlightenment rather than forging their own. Witchcraft is like soul-smithing. We take the raw materials of experience and heat them in the flames of discipline in order to forge ourselves. We take whatever it is that comes our way and see it as an opportunity to grow in power. Like the Star Goddess, we create ourselves, choosing to master the tools presented to us and to find comfort in our capacity to manifest our own path. I believe that witchcraft teaches us to be the engineers of our own power and that it can show us how to master the skills needed in order to do so.

As you search for power and find the hidden veins of it all around you, never forget that if used properly it can lead you to even more. You are a child of the Goddess and the heir to the throne of magic and power; wear your crown and always keep your head held high. Regardless of what it takes, put your needs ahead of everything else and never stop fighting for your sovereignty. It may get rough and it may get scary but the rewards will always outweigh the sacrifices.

BIBLIOGRAPHY &
RECOMMENDED READING

Anaar. *The White Wand: Towards a Feri Aesthetic.* Self Published, 2005.

Anderson, Victor. *Etheric Anatomy.* OR: Acorn Guild Press, 2004.

Berney, Charlotte. *Fundamentals of Hawaiian Mysticism.* CA: Crossing Press, 2000.

Buckland, Raymond. *The Spirit Book: The Encyclopedia of Clairvoyance, Channeling, and Spirit Communication.* MI: Visible Ink Press, 2005.

Casey, Caroline W. *Making the Gods Work for You.* NY: Harmony Books, 1998.

Cheung, Theresa. *The Element Encyclopedia of the Psychic World.* NY: Barnes & Noble, 2006.

Coyle, T. Thorn. *Evolutionary Witchcraft.* NY: Tarcher/Penguin, 2004.

Grimassi, Raven. *Hereditary Witchcraft: Secrets of the Old Religion*. MN: Llewellyn Worldwide, 1999.

———. *Italian Witchcraft: The Old Religion of Southern Europe*. MN: Llewellyn Worldwide, 1995.

Harner, Michael. *The Way of the Shaman*. CA: Harper San Francisco, 1980.

Hawkes, Joyce Whiteley. *Resonance: Nine Practices for Harmonious Health and Vitality*. CA: Hay House, 2012.

Heaven, Ross, and Simon Buxton. *Darkness Visible: Awakening the Spiritual Light through Darkness Meditation*. VT: Inner Traditions, 2005.

Illes, Judika. *Encyclopedia of Spirits: The Ultimate Guide to the Magic of Fairies, Genies, Demons, Ghosts, Gods & Goddesses*. NY: Harper Collins, 2009.

Leland, Charles G. *Aradia or the Gospel of the Witches, with Additional Material from Chas S Clifton, Robert Mathiesen, and Robert E Chartowich, with foreword by Stewart Farrar*. Translated by Mario Pazzaglini and Dina Pazzaglini. Blaine, WA: Phoenix Publishing, 1998.

———. *Etruscan Roman Remains*. WA: Phoenix Publishing, 1999 (reprint of original 1892 edition).

———. *Gypsy Sorcery and Fortune Telling*. NY: Citadel Press, 1962.

Liddell, Henry George, Robert Scott, Henry Stuart Jones, and Roderick McKenzie. *A Greek-English Lexicon*. Oxford, UK: Oxford University Press, 1819.

Madden, Kristin. *Magic, Mystery and Medicine*. MO: WillowTree Press, 2008.

Miller, Jason. *Sex, Sorcery, and Spirit: The Secrets of Erotic Magic*. NJ: The Career Press, 2015.

Parker, Julia and Derek. *Parker's Astrology*. NY: DK Publishing, 1991.

Parma, Gede. *Ecstatic Witchcraft: Magic, Philosophy & Trance in the Shamanic Craft*. MN: Llewellyn Publications, 2012.

Penczak, Christopher. *The Mighty Dead: Communing with the Ancestors of Witchcraft*. NH: Copper Cauldron Publishing, 2013.

———. *The Plant Spirit Familiar: Green Totems, Teachers & Healers on the Path of the Witch*. NH: Copper Cauldron Publishing, 2011.

Starhawk. *The Spiral Dance*. NY: Harper One, 1989.

Stephen, Drake Bear. *Soul Sex: The Alchemy of Gender & Sexuality*. CA: Wisdom Weaver Press, 2015.

Yukie, Chiri. *The Song the Owl God Sang: The Collected Ainu Legends of Chiri Yukie*. Translated by Benjamin Peterson. BJS Books, 2013. http://www.okikirmui.com/the-complete-yukar/1-the-song-the -owl-god-sang/.

INDEX

C

D

E

F

Q

R

S